# Bringing Fantasy Alive for Children and Young Adults

By Tim Wadham and
Rachel L. Wadham

*PROFESSIONAL GROWTH SERIES*®

A Publication of THE BOOK REPORT & LIBRARY TALK
Professional Growth Series

Linworth Publishing, Inc.
Worthington, Ohio

**Library of Congress Cataloging-in-Publication Data**

Wadham, Tim
    Bringing fantasy alive for children and young adults/by Tim & Rachel Wadham
       p. cm.–(Professional growth series)
    Includes bibliographical references.
    ISBN 0-938865-80-3
    1. Fantasy literature–Study and teaching Handbooks, manuals, etc.
    2. Young adult literature–Study and teaching Handbooks, manuals, etc.
    3. Young adults–Books and reading Handbooks, manuals, etc.  I. Wadham, Rachel, 1973-
    II. Title.  III. Series.
    PN56.F34W33  1999
    809' .915–dc21                                              99-31435
                                                                                   CIP

Published by Linworth Publishing, Inc.
480 East Wilson Bridge Road, Suite L
Worthington, Ohio  43085

Copyright©1999 by Linworth Publishing, Inc.

Series Information:
    From The Professional Growth Series

All rights reserved. Reproduction of this book in whole or in part, without permission of the publisher, is prohibited except for not-for-profit educational use in the classroom, in the school library, in professional workshops sponsored by elementary and secondary schools, or other similar not-for-profit activities.

ISBN  0-938865-80-3

5  4  3  2  1

# Table of Contents

Preface .......................................................................... v
Acknowledgements................................................................ vii
About the Authors............................................................... viii

**SECTION ONE: AN OVERVIEW OF FANTASY**
**CHAPTER ONE:** Introducing Fantasy ............................................. 3
                Definitions.................................................... 4
                Types of Fantasy............................................... 5
                Traditional Fantasy............................................ 5
                      Folktales................................................. 6
                      Fables.................................................... 7
                      Myths..................................................... 8
                      Epics and Legends......................................... 8
                Contemporary Fantasy.......................................... 8
                      Contemporary Fantasy with Traditional Elements............ 9
                      Categorizing Contemporary Fantasy......................... 9
                      High Fantasy.............................................. 9
                      Enchanted Realism........................................ 10
                Scope......................................................... 12
                Conclusion.................................................... 12
                List of Works Cited........................................... 13
**CHAPTER TWO:** Appreciating Fantasy ............................................ 15
                Children's Response to Fantasy................................ 16
                      Belief That Inanimate Objects Have Life................... 16
                      Belief in Magic........................................... 16
                Barriers to Appreciating Fantasy.............................. 17
                      Internal Barriers......................................... 17
                            Effort................................................ 17
                            Sexism................................................ 18
                      External Barriers......................................... 18
                            Violence.............................................. 18
                            Escapism.............................................. 19
                            Fear.................................................. 20
                Conclusion.................................................... 20
                Works Cited and Further Reading............................... 21
**CHAPTER THREE:** Discovering Fantasy ........................................... 23
                Setting....................................................... 23
                Point of View................................................. 25
                Characters.................................................... 26
                Plot.......................................................... 27

# Table of Contents continued

        The Hero Journey........................................... 28
            Outward Journey ....................................... 28
            Inward Journey......................................... 30
            The Child and the Hero Journey ............................ 30
    Theme .................................................... 31
    Style...................................................... 32
    Conclusion................................................. 33
    List of Works Cited.......................................... 34
    Further Reading ............................................ 35

**SECTION TWO: PRACTICAL WAYS TO SHARE FANTASY WITH CHILDREN**
**CHAPTER FOUR:** Connecting Fantasy
    Suggestions for Integrating Fantasy into the Curriculum ........... 37
    Science ................................................... 39
        Plants ................................................ 39
        Animals and Animal Habitats ............................ 39
        Human Body ......................................... 40
        Technology ........................................... 41
        Ecology .............................................. 41
    Social Studies .............................................. 42
        Geography and Geology................................. 42
        Culture .............................................. 43
        History .............................................. 43
        Psychology and Sociology ............................... 46
    Humanities ................................................ 47
        Art................................................... 47
        Books, Libraries, and Language .......................... 47
        Music ............................................... 48
    Mathematics ............................................... 49
    Language Arts.............................................. 50
    Sample Lesson Outlines...................................... 52
        Outline 1: Discovering Dinosaurs and Fossils ............... 52
        Outline 2: Discovering Nouns ........................... 55
        Outline 3: Discovering Polygons ......................... 57
        Outline 4: Discovering Stereotypes........................ 59

**CHAPTER FIVE:** Programming Fantasy ................................. 63
    Some Notes on Programming ................................ 63
    Booktalking Fantasy......................................... 64
        Booktalk 1: White, E. B., *Charlotte's Web*................. 65
        Booktalk 2: Cooper, Susan, *The Dark Is Rising*.............. 66
        Booktalk 3: L'Engle, Madeleine, *A Wrinkle in Time* .......... 68
        Booktalk 4: Levine, Gail Carson, *Ella Enchanted*............ 69
        Booktalk 5: McKinley, Robyn, *Beauty* ..................... 70
        Booktalk 6: Banks, Lynne Reid, *The Indian in the Cupboard*.... 71

# Table of Contents continued

    Booktalk 7: Cassedy, Sylvia, *Behind the Attic Wall* . . . . . . . . . . . . 72
    Booktalk 8: Wrede, Patricia C., Searching for Dragons . . . . . . . . . 74
  Programming with Fantasy: "Oh, the Places You'll Go!" . . . . . . . . . . . . . . . 74
    Program 1: "We're Off To See the Wizard". . . . . . . . . . . . . . . . . . 75
    Program 2: Camelot: Stories of King Arthur . . . . . . . . . . . . . . . . 83
    Program 3: The Enchanted Forest—Fairy Tales. . . . . . . . . . . . . . 84
    Program 4: The Imagination of Chris VanAllsburg . . . . . . . . . . 85
    Program 5: A Birthday Party for Pooh . . . . . . . . . . . . . . . . . . . . . 85
    Program 6: Scotland and Canada . . . . . . . . . . . . . . . . . . . . . . . . 86
    Program 7: London . . . . . . . . . . . . . . . . . . . . . . . . . . . . . . . . . . . 86
    Program 8: Narnia . . . . . . . . . . . . . . . . . . . . . . . . . . . . . . . . . . . . 87
    Program 9: Outer Space . . . . . . . . . . . . . . . . . . . . . . . . . . . . . . . 87
    Program 10: The Internet . . . . . . . . . . . . . . . . . . . . . . . . . . . . . . 88
    Program 11: Earth . . . . . . . . . . . . . . . . . . . . . . . . . . . . . . . . . . . . 88
    Program 12: Hogwarts . . . . . . . . . . . . . . . . . . . . . . . . . . . . . . . . 89
    Program 13: Redwall. . . . . . . . . . . . . . . . . . . . . . . . . . . . . . . . . . 89
  Fantasy Storytimes for Younger Children
    Sharing Traditional Fantasy . . . . . . . . . . . . . . . . . . . . . . . . . . . . 90
    Storytime 1: Animal Fables: All the Miles of a Hard Road
      Are Worth One Moment of True Happiness. . . . . . . . . . . . . . . 90
    Storytime 2: Trip Trap, Meow, Huff Puff . . . . . . . . . . . . . . . . . . . 91
    Storytime 3: The Sky Is Falling! The Sky Is Falling! . . . . . . . . . . 93
    Storytime 4: She Ate It All!. . . . . . . . . . . . . . . . . . . . . . . . . . . . . . 94
    Storytime 5: We Mice Are the Greatest of All . . . . . . . . . . . . . . . 95
  Toddler Time (18 months-2 years)
    Storytime 6: "May We Come Too?" Animals All Crowd In . . . . . 106
  Storytime (3-8 years) . . . . . . . . . . . . . . . . . . . . . . . . . . . . . . . . . . . . . . 107
    Storytime 7: Royalty: The King Said "Hello"
      And the Queen Said "Wheee!". . . . . . . . . . . . . . . . . . . . . . . . . 107
    Storytime 8: Witches and Ghosts: "Let's Frighten Somebody" . . . . . 110
    Storytime 9: A Monster Is Coming! A Monster Is Coming! . . . . . . . 113
    Storytime 10: Stuffed Animals: I've Always Wanted a Friend. . . . . . 115
  Upper Elementary Programs (9-12 years) . . . . . . . . . . . . . . . . . . . . . . 118
    Storytime 11: Giants: Fe Fi Fo Fum, I Smell the Blood
      of an Englishman! . . . . . . . . . . . . . . . . . . . . . . . . . . . . . . . . . . 118
    Storytime 12: Toy Stories: "We Should Fix Ourselves
      up as New Toys, the Kind Kids Like." . . . . . . . . . . . . . . . . . . . 119

Appendix: Celebrating Fantasy . . . . . . . . . . . . . . . . . . . . . . . . . . . . . . . . . 121
  Online Resources to Celebrate Fantasy . . . . . . . . . . . . . . . . . . . . . . . 121
  General Children's Literature Sites. . . . . . . . . . . . . . . . . . . . . . . . . . . 121
  Author Sites . . . . . . . . . . . . . . . . . . . . . . . . . . . . . . . . . . . . . . . . . . . . 121
  Other Fantasy Resources on the Web . . . . . . . . . . . . . . . . . . . . . . . . 121

# Table of Contents continued

- Listserv Discussion Groups .................................................. 122
  - Kidlit-L ............................................................... 122
  - ChildLit .............................................................. 122
  - Pubyac ............................................................... 122
  - Folklore ............................................................. 122
- Selected Author Biographies ................................................ 123
  - Alexander, Lloyd ..................................................... 123
  - Babbitt, Natalie ..................................................... 123
  - Baum, L. Frank ....................................................... 124
  - Cooper, Susan ........................................................ 125
  - Dahl, Roald .......................................................... 125
  - Duane, Diane ......................................................... 126
  - Garner, Alan ......................................................... 127
  - Jacques, Brian ....................................................... 127
  - Jones, Diana Wynne ................................................... 127
  - L'Engle, Madeleine ................................................... 128
  - LeGuin, Ursula K. .................................................... 128
  - Lewis, C. S. ......................................................... 129
  - Tolkien, J. R. R. .................................................... 129
  - White, E. B. ......................................................... 130
  - White, T. H. ......................................................... 131
  - Wrede, Patricia C. ................................................... 131
- Annotated Book List ....................................................... 133
  - Picture Books ........................................................ 133
  - Chapter Books ........................................................ 137
- Titles Listed by Grade Level .............................................. 172
- General Index ............................................................. 190
- Names Index ............................................................... 192
- Titles Index .............................................................. 194

# Preface

As siblings who have both pursued professional careers in librarianship, we have noted that many of our colleagues seem to have a prejudice against fantasy. For example, while participating in her local children's literature discussion group, Rachel noticed that frequently when participants present a fantasy book, they preface their remarks by saying "I usually don't read fantasy but…" Another often-heard comment is "That sounds interesting, but I don't read fantasy." Tim recently gave a presentation on fantasy to a graduate class. Near the end, a student made the point "I never thought I liked fantasy, but I am very interested in reading some of the books you talked about. I think the reason I didn't like fantasy was because no one ever presented it to me." She realized that her lack of interest owed simply to the fact that fantasy books had never been offered to her in such a way that they were appealing. We believe that the general bias against fantasy literature can be overcome. The purpose of this manual is to inspire readers to seek out fantasy books that intrigue them and give them the tools to share those books with children. It is only through reading fantasy that teachers and librarians can, in turn, bring it alive for children.

We have written this manual in hopes of conveying the magic we have found in fantasy literature to children through their teachers and librarians. We will begin by providing some basic definitions of fantasy. We add some commentary on issues that have caused some to find fantasy objectionable, and our responses to them. A discussion of ways fantasy uses the basic elements of literature gives teachers and librarians the information to teach fantasy as a genre. Practical applications on using fantasy in the classroom are found in Chapter 4, which shows how fantasy literature can be connected in all areas of the school curriculum. Chapter 5 includes ready-to-use booktalks and program and display ideas to be used in sharing fantasy with kids. The programs in both these chapters were developed in the field.

Rachel developed the curriculum ideas while working with at-risk children in a public school and in talking with teachers. Tim developed and tested all the library programs. We provide information about the most important authors, without whose imaginations our reading lives would be considerably poorer. We also include an extensive annotated list of works cited as an aid in selecting fantasy literature for use with children.

# Acknowledgements

Tim acknowledges Dr. Barbara Stein for facilitating the idea of this manual, and Rachel for her work and effort. He is especially grateful to his daughter, Hannah, who pulled herself up on his legs while he was working at the computer to see what he was doing, and for the support of his wife, Penny, who used her experience in the classroom to help develop programs and who spent countless hours editing.

Rachel wishes to acknowledge Dr. Barbara Stein for listening to an offhand remark; her co-author and brother for his advice, guidance, and love; her mother and sisters for asking, "Is it done yet?"; her father, Rex Alvon Wadham, for his passion, beliefs, and the legacy he left behind; and finally, the authors of fantasy novels for children who believe in their craft and share their talents with the world.

# About the Authors

**TIM WADHAM** has worked professionally as a children's librarian for over thirteen years. Currently he is the Children's Services Coordinator for the Maricopa County Library District in Phoenix, Arizona. He served on the 1998 Newbery Award selection committee. He is the author of "Programming with Latino Children's Materials" published by Neal-Schuman and is co-author of the 1993 Texas State Reading Club Manual focusing on fantasy.

**RACHEL L. WADHAM** received her BS in Sociology and Music from Brigham Young University and MLS from the University of North Texas. She is currently on the faculty of the Harold B. Lee Library at Brigham Young University. Rachel has worked with children in various capacities in schools and the community and is an accomplished puppeteer.

# Section 1

# An Overview of Fantasy

# CHAPTER 1

# Introducing Fantasy

Fantasy has always been an integral part of the human experience. Oral forms of fantasy, such as myth, folktales, and fairy tales, can be found among all cultures. Ancient tribes gathered around the glowing embers of dying fires to spin tales of fantasy that explained their world and gave life meaning. Bards and troubadours traveled from village to village entertaining nobles and peasants alike with their fanciful tales of heroes and their deeds. Immigrants and pioneers used tales of fancy to ease hardships and to hasten the passing of cold, hostile nights. As much as fantasy has been an indispensable part of our oral history, it has long been part of our literary history as well. Scholars like Perrault and the Grimm brothers gave oral tales new life as they collected stories from the common people and committed them to paper. Authors from Chaucer to Swift, Orwell, and Verne have, for centuries, used fantasy to comment on social ills, to predict the future, and to express the most basic human emotions.

From its inception, literature that is produced expressly for children has also shown a strong link to fantasy. From the fairy tales of Hans Christian Andersen to today's modern fantasy by notable authors such as Lloyd Alexander and Susan Cooper, a chronology of the milestones of children's literature will demonstrate that the books listed are in large part fantasy. For example, over half the books listed in a recent *New York Times Book Review* 50th Anniversary retrospective of 59 classic children's books from the last 50 years can be classified as fantasy.

> ... Over half the books listed in a recent *New York Times Book Review* 50th Anniversary retrospective of 59 classic children's books from the last 50 years can be classified as fantasy.

# ▸ DEFINITIONS

Many fantasy novels include maps that help the reader visualize where the characters are within the imaginary territory that the author has created. In the case of realistic fiction, such maps are not necessary, as it is fairly easy to imagine the characters in a setting such as Texas or New York. But imagine reading *The Wizard of Oz* without Baum's map showing the yellow brick road leading from the blue Munchkin country to the Emerald City. Similarly, students of fantasy need maps to understand where the books they are reading fit within the universe of literature.

In this chapter, we attempt to provide that map. To begin, we need to know what map we are looking at, just as it would not be helpful to be looking at a European road atlas if one wanted to locate a street in Des Moines. It is important to know that a number of critics have attempted to map out this same territory in slightly different ways. For those who want to see the categories others have developed to make sense of fantasy, we strongly recommend three books: Sheila Egoff's book *Worlds Within*, Ruth Nadelman Lynn's *Fantasy Literature for Children and Young Adults*, and Zena Sutherland's standard text, *Children and Books*. Beyond the categories they provide, each of these books provides an excellent discussion of these categories which expands greatly on the brief overview we provide here.

We prefer to define fantasy as any fiction in which plot elements occur that cannot be explained rationally or by current scientific facts. In saying this, we understand that it is difficult to represent fantasy with one simple overreaching definition, since fantasy includes both the magical as well as the supernatural. However, we like this broad definition because it demonstrates for those who may not find fantasy their preferred genre, that fantasy really encompasses many books one might not at first think of as fantasy. Fantasy is like a mythical creature able to take on many shapes and forms. There are stories, for example, in which seemingly unexplainable events occur, but in the end are explained as being a dream or part of a character's mental disturbance—the "fantasy" takes place in the protagonist's mind. Realistic explanations for fantasy experiences create an easy way out, and it is tempting to reject them as members of the genre. However, it is legitimately possible for fantasy to take place in the mind, and certain dream-based fantasies such as *Alice's Adventures in Wonderland* and *Where the Wild Things Are* are too important to dismiss. A more recent example is *The Kingdom of Kevin Malone* by Suzy McKee Charnas. In this book, Kevin creates a fantasy world in his imagination as an escape from a violent father. A girl named Amy finds her way into Kevin's world through a gateway in New York's Central Park. This book functions as fantasy because no rational explanation is given for Amy's ability to inhabit Kevin's fantasy world alongside him. While these sorts of books reside on the boundaries of what can be called fantasy, it is ultimately the magic of events that cannot be explained rationally that becomes the essence of fantasy and is what sets it apart from other types or genres of fiction.

Special mention needs to be made of science fiction, often considered a separate genre. Science fiction can be defined as any fiction that takes place in the future and that describes technology extrapolated from cur-

> Fantasy is like a mythical creature able to take on many shapes and forms.

rent scientific facts. In light of this definition, we believe that science fiction should be considered fantasy. Sheila Egoff recognizes "Science Fiction Fantasy" as a specific category, and Zena Sutherland includes science fiction as a subset of modern fantasy. Even though the magic of science fiction is rooted in the realm of possibility, it is very much a literature of the imagination and makes a fine companion to fantasy. In fact, many works of science fiction blur the borders with fantasy. Madeleine L'Engle's classic work, *A Wrinkle in Time*, is classified by some as science fiction because the plot involves children who follow their scientist father to another planet, where he has been taken prisoner. While the story does involve space travel, it offers no scientific or technical background. Thus it crosses the line into fantasy—one more case that makes it difficult to apply hard and fast rules when dealing with fantasy.

## ▶ TYPES OF FANTASY

The two primary categories into which fantasy has most often been placed are traditional fantasy and contemporary fantasy. The easiest way to understand the difference is that traditional fantasy comes from the oral tradition; the author is unknown. In contemporary fantasy, on the other hand, the author is known. Any retelling of a tale that comes from the oral tradition would be considered traditional fantasy, even if an author were credited. Authors of contemporary fantasy may use elements of traditional tales, but since they are creating something entirely new, their work would still be considered contemporary fantasy. With this framework in mind, it is important to understand that several different types of books fall under the general umbrellas of these two basic categories. Fantasy literature for children can be everything from a story like *Charlotte's Web* with talking animals, to supernatural tales of horror, such as the "Goosebumps" series.

Categories often overlap, and the boundaries between them blur. Frequently, it is possible to classify the same book or story in more than one category. Because of this, we offer a strong word of caution: The tendency to focus on categorizing as a way of understanding fantasy can lead away from enjoyment of the books into what can become pointless pigeonholing. There is certainly room for disagreement with the way we've attempted to map out the territory of fantasy. The important thing is not to get so caught up in categorization that the only thing that matters is placing a book within the "right" category. This is the difference between looking at a place on a map and actually going there. The important thing is the experience of reading the book itself. But, as with travel, you still need a map in order to arrive at an unfamiliar place, so in order to make things less confusing, we are trying to offer the clearest explanation we can without oversimplification.

> ...The tendency to focus on categorizing as a way of understanding fantasy can lead away from enjoyment of the books into what can become pointless pigeonholing.

The purpose of discussing these different divisions is not to make ironclad rules as to the specific categories of fantasy, or determine whether any certain book should be classified in a particular way. Instead, we hope to provide a more general guide for students and young library patrons through the territory of fantasy. Think of this as a map of the interstate highways, rather than a detailed street map.

### *Traditional Fantasy*

Traditional fantasy is defined as a tale that originated in a spoken form and has been handed down orally. A key element to traditional fantasy is that the original author is unknown. Almost all traditional literature falls into the realm of fantasy. Traditional fantasy includes folktales, fables, myths, and epics.

## FOLKTALES

Folktales are stories created by the people, or "folk." These tales are not considered historical. They may or may not have happened, and they usually are not taken seriously. One of the most important characteristics of these stories is their universal appeal. These tales come from all geographic regions and all cultures, yet they are remarkably similar. They all contain common narrative motifs, such as witches, giants, and wizards. They also contain common themes, such as quests and struggles of good against evil.

There are many types of folktales. Cumulative tales such as "Henny Penny" and "The House That Jack Built" are distinguished by rhythmic language and repetition and are closely related to Mother Goose rhymes. Pourquoi tales specifically explain why or how something came about, such as "Why the Sun and the Moon Live in the Sky" and "How the Elephant Got its Trunk." Animal or beast tales such as "The Three Bears" and "The Three Little Pigs" have animals as the main characters. Tales of animal tricksters, like Coyote, Brer Rabbit, and Anansi the Spider, celebrate the idea of a smaller but more intelligent creature outsmarting a larger one, and show that mental prowess can be more valued than physical. On the other hand, noodleheads such as "Lazy Jack" have been immortalized in stories about characters that are not very smart. Realistic tales might even be based on real persons or events, but over the years, the characters became so embellished that they take their place in folklore, such as the boy who stuck his finger in the dike, or the exploits of Davy Crockett.

> These tales come from all geographic regions and all cultures, yet they are remarkably similar.

In general, folktales that are stories of magic and wonder have come to be called fairy tales. "Cinderella," "Jack and the Beanstalk," and "The Elves and the Shoemaker" are just a few of these stories that have some roots in the real world, but are shot through with magic—a pumpkin that turns into a coach, magic beanstalks, and elves who happen to know a thing or two about leather. The works of Hans Christian Andersen are commonly regarded as fairy tales, but because they originated in written instead of oral form and the author is known, they are contemporary fantasy rather than traditional fantasy. This distinction is easily forgotten. The reader who opens almost any collection of traditional fantasy will find Andersen's stories, such as "The Princess and the Pea," "Thumbelina," and "The Snow Queen," interspersed with traditional tales.

In Europe and Scandinavia, the fairy tales of each country or region are primarily known through standard collections. It is important to remember that these stories were not originally told as "children's" stories. If children heard them, it was because they were with a larger group. Children's literature, as such, did not exist. The Grimms were Germanic philologists who collected stories. Their intent was to preserve culture, not to amuse children. The most important and influential collections are summarized on the next page by the country, the reteller, and representative tales from the collection. It is through these collections that the stories mentioned truly entered the popular consciousness.

There are collections of tales from many other countries, but none of the other collections is so clearly associated with a particular reteller.

American folktales can be placed in three broad categories: first, stories from original

> **FRANCE:** Charles Perrault.
> Collection: **Contes de ma Mére l'Oye**
> (Tales of My Mother Goose) (1697)
> Published in English in 1729
> Representative tales: "Little Red Riding Hood," "Puss in Boots," "Sleeping Beauty," "Beauty and the Beast"
>
> **GERMANY:** Grimm Brothers
> Collection: **Kinder und Hausmärchen**
> (Children's and Household Tales) (1812)
> Representative tales: "The Elves and the Shoemaker," "Hansel and Gretel," "Rapunzel," "Snow White and the Seven Dwarfs"
>
> **SCANDINAVIA:** Peter Asbjørnsen and Jörgen E. Moe
> Collection: **Norwegian Fairy Tales** (1845)
> Representative tales: "East of the Sun, West of the Moon," "The Three Billy Goats Gruff," "The Lad Who Went to the North Wind," "The Princess on the Glass Hill"
>
> **BRITAIN:** Joseph Jacobs
> Collections: **English Fairy Tales** (1890)
> **More English Fairy Tales** (1894)
> Representative tales: "The Three Little Pigs," "The Little Red Hen," "The Three Bears," "Jack and the Beanstalk"

cultures, namely Native American Indian, Eskimo, and Hawaiian; second, folklore that developed out of the American experience ; and third, the variants of African and European stories that came from other countries and were changed in the process. Virginia Hamilton's beautiful collections of African American folklore have become the standard versions and put her name alongside the collectors of European folklore.

The most familiar of the American folktales are the Uncle Remus stories, "Rip Van Winkle," "Johnny Appleseed," "Pecos Bill," "Paul Bunyan," "John Henry," and "The Little Old Lady Who Swallowed a Fly." Note that the primary type of American tale is the tall tale—an exaggerated story about a larger-than-life hero who often tames the wilderness. This reflects the pioneering spirit that is so much a part of the history and culture of this country.

Folktales continue to gain new life year after year through endless adaptations. Newly retold and illustrated picture book versions of the classic tales appear with frequency. We have stated before that a story is defined as "traditional" because the author is not known, and that the story was passed down through the generations, often orally. However, anyone who retells a traditional story is drawing on the cultural heritage of the place where the story originated, as well as the different versions that have appeared previously. In a landmark two-part article in *School Library Journal,* professor Betsy Hearne proposed that authors who produce picture books that retell traditional tales "provide source notes that set these stories in their cultural context." For Hearne, the ideal source note "cites the specific source(s), adds a description for cultural context *and* describes what the author has done to change the tale, with some explanation of why."

Some authors choose to flesh out familiar tales to novel length; in so doing, they add enough original material that these stories are generally classified as contemporary fantasy. Examples of this type of book are Robin McKinley's *Beauty* and *Rose Daughter,* two novels that retell the story of "Beauty and the Beast."

## FABLES

Fables are brief didactic tales distinguished by a moral lesson given at the end. Fables are generally associated with the Greek slave Aesop. Popular examples of his stories are "The Boy Who Called Wolf" and "The Ant and the Grasshopper." Many of the moral lessons learned from these fables have become part of our everyday language, such as "Don't count your chickens before they hatch."

This simple format has also inspired authors of contemporary fantasy. Arnold Lobel's

Caldecott award-winning book *Fables* is a good example of fables for our age. His stories are not so much didactic as sly commentaries on human foibles. His uncomplicated tales with their honest maxims demonstrate how fantasy can arrive at simple but profound truths. Jon Scieszka and Lane Smith present twisted modern fables in *Squids Will Be Squids*.

## MYTHS

The people of ancient civilizations relied on supernatural explanations for natural events, which gave rise to a rich body of stories that we know as myth. Mythology evolved as a way of explaining the world and most often told of the exploits of immortal heroes and gods and their relationship with ancient man. Among the common myths found around the world are creation stories that attempt to explain how the world and the beings that populate it came to be. Greek and Roman mythology are certainly the best known bodies of myth. While these mythologies were created in ancient times to serve a particular human need, mythology continues to be relevant to children. Children respond to mythology because the myths are first and foremost good stories. The twelve labors of Hercules are a myth that can still enthrall because of the basic appeal of overcoming obstacles with strength. Its popularity is evidenced by the appearance of this character in animated films and a television series. Norse mythology is also familiar to children today in part through the works of Ingri and Parin D'Aulaire, who collected both Greek and Norse myths in separate volumes published in the 1960s that are still standard today.

## EPICS AND LEGENDS

Epics are stories that cluster around the actions of a single hero. Epics are often told in verse. The hero generally has all the ideal characteristics of greatness for his time. Because of their complexity, epics are most suitable for older readers. However, many adaptations are available that retell epics in a way that younger children can enjoy. Among the most famous epics are *The Odyssey* and *Beowulf*. Legends are based on events or on the exploits of heroes such as Robin Hood or King Arthur, who were probably real people. The deeds attributed to them may have been enhanced over the years as the tales were passed down orally from one generation to the next. The fact that legends involve characters and events for which there may be some basis in historical fact distinguishes them from myths, which have no historical origins.

> Children respond to mythology because the myths are first and foremost good stories.

## Contemporary Fantasy

As we stated before, contemporary fantasy is distinguished from traditional fantasy because there is a known author. Beyond this, one could say that contemporary fantasy is primarily a literature of the imagination. Common imaginary elements found in modern fantasy for children are talking animals, toys that come to life, worlds apart from the one we know, time shifts, eccentric characters, and unrealistic situations. Traditionally, contemporary fantasy has been classified according to these motifs—the elements incapable of rational explanation that make fantasy, fantasy. Sometimes, the inclusion of one of these elements may be the only thing that makes a book fantasy. For example, everything else in a story may be totally realistic, but the animals talk. In fact, some of the more common story types such as talking animals are sometimes considered subsets of contemporary fantasy.

## CONTEMPORARY FANTASY WITH TRADITIONAL ELEMENTS

Contemporary fantasy often makes use of elements from traditional tales. While some authors, such as Susan Cooper, weave traditional tales into modern stories, their works are clearly contemporary fantasy. Other authors retell and expand folktale material with an eye to casting it in a new light or twisting it with a warped modern sensibility. This can be one of those gray areas of classification. Donna Jo Napoli is a notable author who has rewritten traditional tales from a different perspective. In her book *The Magic Circle,* she retells "Hansel and Gretel" from the witch's point of view. Vivian Vande Velde has written *Tales from the Brothers Grimm and the Sisters Weird,* which wickedly skewers such tales as "Rapunzel," recasting it as an advertisement for shampoo. For younger children, Jon Scieszka and Lane Smith's *The Stinky Cheese Man and Other Fairly Stupid Tales* is a true classic. Even though these books have their roots in traditional fantasy, the thing that differentiates them and makes them contemporary is the manipulation of the story. They require a familiarity with the original story in order to have any real impact.

No such familiarity is required with folk or fairy tales in order to appreciate them. These stories may be told over and over again, but no matter how many variations there are to the way a traditional tale is retold, if the story remains true to the "tradition" of the original, we consider it traditional fantasy. When the Little Red Hen is eaten by Jack's giant, and Little Red Riding Hood dons running shorts instead of the traditional cape and walks out of the story, the tales become contemporary fantasy.

> When the Little Red Hen is eaten by Jack's giant, and Little Red Riding Hood dons running shorts instead of the traditional cape and walks out of the story, the tales become contemporary fantasy.

## CATEGORIZING CONTEMPORARY FANTASY

As we have already noted, the problem with fantasy is that books are often difficult to categorize because the line between categories is not clear. Rather than focusing on the magical elements, which makes for a number of categories, we prefer to more simply categorize contemporary fantasy by setting. Fantasy takes readers on a journey out of the rational world. Whether the fantasy is based on the world we know, takes place entirely in an invented world, or goes back and forth between the two, the readers need to know where they are. This is why one of the distinguishing features of fantasy is a strong sense of place. When considered this way, all types of fantasy fall loosely under two general headings that we choose to call *high fantasy* and *enchanted realism,* understanding that others have chosen to use these terms in slightly different ways.

### HIGH FANTASY

High fantasy is generally defined as fantasy taking place completely within an invented world, with no reference to the world we know. In its contemporary incarnation, high fantasy is more easily found on the young adult and adult shelves than in children's books (books written for children up to age 12). In fact, children who are drawn to this genre seem to migrate directly to adult titles after a certain age, partly because very little high fantasy is currently being published for middle grade readers. One characteristic of this genre is an epic scope to the plot and settings, leading Sheila Egoff to call this genre "epic fantasy."

Some of the worlds created by authors writing in this genre are well known and we think of them in terms of the universe the authors have created. For example, it is difficult to discuss Tolkien's books without thinking of Middle Earth. Lloyd Alexander's classic five-volume work of high fantasy is known by the name of the world he creates: Prydain. We refer to Brian Jacques' continuing series collectively as the "Redwall" books. Since novels of high fantasy take place within a wholly imaginary realm, they give a wide scope to the imagination. High fantasy is also often filled with elements of myth and folktale as it deals on a grand scale with large issues such as the conflict between good and evil. High fantasy is particularly equipped to be a vehicle for the exploration of moral issues.

Along with novels that take place entirely within an invented world, we also class as high fantasy those that open in the primary world we know, but where most of the story takes place in another world. The most recognizable examples of this type of fantasy are Lewis Carroll's *Alice's Adventures in Wonderland* and *Through the Looking-Glass*, C. S. Lewis' "Chronicles of Narnia," and L. Frank Baum's "Oz" books. In these stories, the world we know exists only as a set of bookends for the journey into the fantasy realm. In the case of the Oz books, Baum eventually tired of creating mechanisms for transporting Dorothy back and forth between Kansas and Oz, so finally took her to Oz permanently and installed her as a princess.

The most commonly recognized stories of high fantasy take place in a vaguely familiar setting that has its roots in the medieval world, the setting of most of the European fairy tales. Castles, kings, queens, and princesses are common elements. Some authors "play it straight" within this setting, creating tales of battles and heroic quests. Others, such as Patricia Wrede in her hilarious "Enchanted Forest Chronicles, take these elements and infuse them with a more hip, modern sensibility.

## ENCHANTED REALISM

The term "enchanted realism" was coined, as near as we can tell, by the critic Sheila Egoff in her highly recommended book *Worlds Within*. This is a variation on the literary term "magical realism," which is primarily associated with Latin-American fiction and refers to a literature in which magic is a part of everyday life and is treated matter-of-factly. Egoff's notion of enchanted realism is probably a more accurate term to identify the most common type of fantasies written for children. We will use the term more broadly than Egoff does to apply to any fantasy in which magic is combined with realistic elements. Books of this type take place, at least in part, in the world we know, but fantastic events occur. Fantasy can be interpolated with realistic elements in a story in a number of different ways. In these books you can journey between our world and another, elements from another world can impinge upon reality, or the magic can occur in an entirely realistic setting.

In a book where characters journey between worlds, the dominant setting determines whether the work is high fantasy or enchanted realism. An example is *The Lives of Christopher Chant* by Diane Wynne Jones, a novel that takes place in a realistic setting similar to Edwardian England and in "The Place Between," which is a crossroads that links multiple exotic worlds. Throughout the book, Christopher travels back and forth between the two settings, and since both play equally crucial roles in the novel, it is considered fantasy

> High fantasy is also often filled with elements of myth and folktale as it deals on a grand scale with large issues such as the conflict between good and evil.

combined with realism. Another common device used in this type of fantasy is time travel. *Tom's Midnight Garden* by Phillippa Pearce is a fine example of this type of book. When Tom hears the clock in his aunt and uncle's apartment strike 13, it creates a time slip that allows him to enter an enchanted garden, where he plays with Hatty, a girl from the past.

A second type of fantasy combining fantastic elements with realism is stories in which things from another world affect the world we know. Novels that fall into this category often have realistic settings, but unusual or magical things happen. Susan Cooper's "The Dark Is Rising" sequence is a good example of this type of fantasy. In this five-book sequence, the world apart is parallel to the world we know. The Old Ones, a group of people set apart to battle the forces of the Dark, are able to shuttle back and forth between these worlds. Incidents occurring in the other world affect the real world, such as when, at the end of *The Grey King*, the Sleepers ride out from a mountain into our world and herald the return of King Arthur. It should be noted that because of its incorporation of Arthurian myth, other critics have classified this sequence as high fantasy.

Another wonderful example of this type of enchanted realism that falls more into the realm of science fiction is John Christopher's "White Mountains" trilogy. Fantasy intrudes on the world we know when an alien race called the Tripods descend to earth and build massive cities. It is up to the free people of the earth to destroy the Tripods before the world is annihilated.

A gentler type of fantasy blended with realism occurs when magic simply happens in a realistic setting. *Charlotte's Web* is a well-known example. Firmly grounded in the realistic Maine farm setting, animals just happen to talk, and spiders can write words in their webs. Talking animal stories are representative of this type of fantasy. George Selden's *The Cricket in Times Square* and its sequels come quickly to mind. Beverly Cleary also does a delightful job of injecting a talking animal into familiar settings in her three books about Ralph S. Mouse. A type of tale similar to this personifies toys or other objects. In Russell Hoban's *The Mouse and His Child,* a wind-up tin mouse father and son try to find a home. *Winnie the Pooh* and *The House at Pooh Corner* are all about a child's stuffed toys that come to life through the stories told about them.

> In a book where characters journey between worlds, the dominant setting determines whether the work is high fantasy or enchanted realism.

Supernatural fantasies, in which ghosts, vampires, witches or werewolves are a natural part of a realistic setting, also fall into this category. Margaret Mahy's *The Changeover: A Supernatural Romance* takes place in a normal small town in New Zealand. Magic encroaches on real life when Laura's little brother, Jacko, becomes possessed by an evil spirit and Laura must turn to the neighborhood witches for help.

The most important current trend in fantasy that incorporates realistic elements is stories that use the possibilities suggested by the new computer culture. In these books, computers are seen as something almost magical, or magic can be accessed through them. While the new technology works in entirely rational and explainable ways, this is not readily apparent to the lay person. So the mystery of how the computer chip allows words and pictures to appear on the screen makes computers a perfect vehicle for fantasy. Computers are now tools that can transport children to different realities, or bring a different reality to life within the context of the real world, as in Richard Peck's books *Lost in Cyberspace* and *The Great Interactive Dream Machine*. In *The Boggart* by Susan Cooper, the mischievous poltergeist realizes he can transport himself back to his Scottish castle home through cyberspace. A computer becomes a wizard's tool in Diane Duane's *High Wizardry*.

## ▶ SCOPE OF THIS BOOK

Given our broad definition of what constitutes fantasy, the question of what to include in a book of this sort is problematic. One particular problem is the question of the picture-book format. Under our definition, we could include a very large percentage of picture books. Any story that includes talking animals, such as Marc Brown's "Arthur" books, could be considered fantasy under this definition, even if the story line features animals standing in for humans in recognizable domestic situations. However, we prefer to focus on picture books that show animals interacting with humans in a nonrealistic fashion, such as the animals who crowd into *Mr. Gumpy's Motor Car*. Picture books can also show human characters entering into fantastic situations, such as Max sailing to the island *Where the Wild Things Are* in Maurice Sendak's classic book, or the brother who follows his sister into a fairy tale realm through *The Tunnel* in Anthony Browne's book. In the bibliography, we include a sampling of picture books that we feel most clearly exemplify fantasy in this format.

Similar questions regarding what actually constitutes fantasy can be raised when considering longer, chapter-length fiction. Our definition of fantasy allows a wide berth for anything that cannot be said to be of this world. This means that works of science fiction that include such elements as alien creatures would be considered fantasy. Books that are primarily realistic but include elements of the supernatural would also be included. The currently popular horror genre can be seen as fantasy because no rational explanations exist for the scary supernatural events or apparitions.

Given the wide range of literature that can, in one way or another, be considered fantasy, it seems that to give this manual maximum usefulness, we should include representative examples of most of the possible types of fantasy. In making this decision, we realize that we cannot be all-inclusive in the titles we cite. What we do hope, however, is to provide activity, program, and lesson ideas using outstanding examples of each of the types of books mentioned above. The scope of this manual, then, will be to provide librarians and teachers with programming and lesson plan ideas using books that are representative of all types of fantasy literature. We hope that this approach will give this manual the widest possible application for teachers and librarians working with children at all age levels.

> The most important current trend in fantasy that incorporates realistic elements is stories that use the possibilities suggested by the new computer culture.

## ▶ CONCLUSION

The remainder of this manual offers the reader the tools to bring fantasy alive for children. More than one student has noted that she would have liked fantasy if she had been given the opportunity to experience it. Chapter 2, "Appreciating Fantasy," addresses the issues of barriers to understanding and enjoying fantasy and how they can be overcome. In Chapter 3, we discuss the basic components of fiction and how they relate to fantasy. Chapter 4 is devoted to ideas for teachers to integrate fantasy into the classroom and curriculum. Chapter 5 presents ideas for fantasy-related programs, primarily for use in public and school library settings. Although these chapters are aimed primarily at teachers and librarians respectively, we encourage both teachers and librarians to look into all of them. You will discover ways you can use teaching ideas in the library and programming ideas in the classroom. Last, we will present some biographical information on notable fantasy authors, and an annotated book list.

## WORKS CITED IN CHAPTER 1

Charnas, Suzy McKee. **The Kingdom of Kevin Malone.** New York: Harcourt, 1983.

Egoff, Sheila A. **Worlds Within: Children's Fantasy from the Middle Ages to Today.** Chicago: American Library Association, 1988.

Hearne, Betsy. "Citing the Source: Reducing Cultural Chaos in Picture Books, Part One." **School Library Journal.** July 1993: 22-27.

"50 Years of Children's Books." **The New York Times Book Review.** November 16, 1997: 25-26.

Lynn, Ruth Nadelman. **Fantasy Literature for Children and Young Adults: An Annotated Bibliography.** Fourth Edition. New Providence, New Jersey: R. R. Bowker, 1995.

Paul, Lissa. "The Politics of Dirt: Or Mucking About With **Piggybook, Harry the Dirty Dog** and 'Cinderella.'" **Horn Book.** September/October 1997: 534-542.

Sutherland, Zena. **Children and Books.** Ninth Edition. New York: Longman (Addison Wesley), 1997.

# CHAPTER 2

# Appreciating Fantasy

There is a curious dichotomy in our culture regarding the popularity of fantasy. On one hand, professors who teach children's literature on the college level report that their college students, in general, dislike fantasy. In general, society seems to expect entertainment to be totally realistic. To assume, however, that fantasy is somehow a dying genre is erroneous. In fact, fantasy seems to be gaining in popularity, especially in media other than books. Movies, television shows, computer and video games, and other pop culture artifacts whose content fits within our definition of fantasy are tremendously popular. In movies particularly, computer graphics technology allows anything the mind can imagine to be portrayed completely realistically on the screen. The film *Jurassic Park* is a prime example of this new phenomenon. Completely realistic dinosaurs terrorize people in an island amusement park. This movie points out one reason why fantasy portrayed in media other than books is more popular: It can be portrayed realistically enough to be believed; no use of the imagination is required. With *Jurassic Park* and similar films, we understand why interest in fantasy can dwindle and increase at the same time. It is because the line between fantasy and reality has been blurred.

How does this relate to literature? The advent of computer-generated visual fantasy in movies and in media such as computer and video games makes it harder for children to take the leaps of imagination that fantasy in literature requires. Even so, among the world's best-selling children's titles are books such as R. L. Stine's supernatural horror series "Goosebumps" and

> **The advent of computer-generated visual fantasy in movies and in media such as computer and video games makes it harder for children to take the leaps of imagination that fantasy in literature requires.**

K. A. Applegate's "Animorphs" series, in which a group of children are given the power to morph into animal forms and fight to protect the earth from being taken over by evil. Brian Jaques' "Redwall" books are also high on the children's bestseller list. These are stories about talking animals who battle to save their peaceful abbey. They appeal to children because of the breathless adventure and nonstop action.

The challenge now becomes finding the aspects of fantasy that children respond to naturally and focusing on ways to highlight those aspects when sharing fantasy with children. Children have a definite interest in the fantastic, which more often than not finds its outlet in media other than books. Teachers and librarians have the opportunity to use fantasy literature, which has more depth than video games, to tap this natural interest and help children develop their creativity and imagination.

## ▶ CHILDREN'S RESPONSE TO FANTASY

Children respond naturally to certain aspects of fantasy. In essence, the world of fantasy is the world of a child. This worldview lasts generally up to age 10, at which time children have outgrown fantasy and become part of a more adult world. This point was underscored in a recent conversation with a school librarian who said that in his school children lose interest in imaginative literature (both realistic and fantasy), and are reading almost entirely nonfiction by the time they are in fourth grade (about age 10). Many of the plots of children's fantasy can be seen as metaphors of a child's passage from innocence, where magic is possible, to adolescence and adulthood where, sadly, the ability to believe has been lost. A poignant example of what we mean is the ending of Chris VanAllsburg's book *The Polar Express.* In this story, the magical bell the boy has retrieved from Santa's sleigh quits ringing for his sister as she grows older, but never stops ringing for him.

It has been suggested that children have two ways of thinking that allow them to look at the world as an enchanted place. The first is an innate belief in the idea of intelligence or life existing in inanimate objects and animals. The second is a belief that magic is real. A number of articles in the bibliography at the end of this chapter greatly expand on the ideas briefly summarized here.

> Many of the plots of children's fantasy can be seen as metaphors of a child's passage from innocence, where magic is possible, to adolescence and adulthood where, sadly, the ability to believe has been lost.

## Belief that inanimate objects have life

The first worldview held by children that relates to fantasy is a belief that inanimate objects have life (Favat 30). Children assume that objects have life and spirit, so they are not surprised when inanimate things do something unusual, because they would if they were alive, which they are in the child's mind. Children see only a very faint line between living and nonliving things. With such a mindset, children see animals as thinking entities and stones as living objects (Bettleheim 46). Fantasy literature shares this ability to animate and personify animals, objects, and other elements. In fact, stories of this type form entire subgenres of fantasy. All talking-animal fantasies would certainly fall into this category.

## Belief in magic

The second paradigm of a child's mind that correlates to fantasy is a belief in magic. Children can believe in the magical connection between an action and an object or event. Children can believe that if an action is performed it will directly influence an object or event. The old skipping rhyme, "step on a crack, break your mother's back," is one example of this sort of superstition that permeates children's folklore (Favat 26). Children can also believe in magical causality between one's thoughts and any resulting events. In this view, thinking is all that is needed to make an event happen. In *The Secret Garden* by Frances Hodgson Burnett (New York: HarperCollins, 1987), Colin believes that the magic from the garden has made him well. The same expression of a belief in magic can be seen in many older fantasies such as the works of Edith Nesbit. This notion can extend to inanimate objects as well. The mindset of a child allows him to believe that an object can exert its will on the will of others. After running into a wall, for example, a child may insist that it was the wall that attacked and not the other way around.

Fantasy literature exists because of these magical paradigms. They are what allows the author to go beyond the normal, the expected, the real. A child's magical worldview accepts as real, events such as a kiss that wakes a princess, a magical sword that eliminates evil, or a fairy godmother who has the power to grant a wish to go to the ball. There is a correspondence between a child's view of reality and fantasy.

## ▶ BARRIERS TO APPRECIATING FANTASY

Even though a child's views blend reality and fantasy, we have to understand that there are barriers to appreciating fantasy and learn to get beyond them. We divide such barriers into two categories: internal and external. Internal barriers are innate personal prejudices and preferences. External barriers are those that come from without, such as objections raised by child development experts, parents, or other adults to what they see as offensive aspects of fantasy. Internal barriers to enjoying fantasy can be found in both child and adult readers. External barriers are those that lead adults, primarily, to dismiss fantasy. However, external barriers are raised for children when adults keep them from reading fantasy because of their own prejudices.

## *Internal Barriers*
### EFFORT

Many of our colleagues tell us that fantasy is not their favorite genre, or that they don't "relate" to fantasy. One of the main reasons we hear for this is that reading fantasy, especially high fantasy, takes a lot of effort. There are a few identifiable reasons for this. Fantasy requires readers to exercise more imagination than do realistic novels, in which the setting and characters correlate to things the reader can easily picture in the mind's eye. With fantasy, the reader must put forth some effort to imagine the setting and the unusual creatures that might inhabit a fantasy world. There are certainly authors who are adept at creating visual images through words. Cover or interior illustrations in which an artist has visualized the fantasy world can help. Still, fantasy requires readers to go beyond that which is familiar to them.

We have also heard people say that they especially dislike high fantasy because they cannot keep track of all of the strange names. Granted, characters in fantasy novels are more likely to have strange or unpronounceable names. Nevertheless, a desire and just a little effort are all that is needed to enjoy a book of this sort. Practical ways to engender such a desire within children will be presented in the next two chapters. In general, all

> Even though a child's views blend reality and fantasy, we have to understand that there are barriers to appreciating fantasy and learn to get beyond them.

reading requires some effort, so this is not a charge that can be laid solely at fantasy's feet. If it is presented enthusiastically, in a way that captures a child's imagination, fantasy will be devoured just as readily as any other type of book.

Since fantasy, and especially high fantasy can be an acquired taste, give children the option of the "50-page rule." Tell them that they are not required to read the entire book, but they should give it a trial run. If after 50 pages they find they are still not interested, they can go on to something else. Because fantasy is such a broad genre, almost anyone is bound to find a fantasy book he will like. Forcing children to read a book they dislike of any genre is always counterproductive. You can use the same "50-page rule" for yourself, with all types of books.

### SEXISM

Some people seem to be prejudiced against fantasy for gender reasons. One interesting comment we have heard is that men seem to like fantasy more than women do. The suggested reason is that fantasy seems to be a male-oriented genre; there are few female heroines in fantasy. The truth of the matter is that many fantasy novels feature female protagonists who are not meek and subservient. The novels by Patricia C. Wrede, Diane Duane, Sherwood Smith, and Robin McKinley all contain dynamic women characters. The claim that fantasy is solely the domain of men is also false. In addition to the women mentioned above, we find that the authors of some of fantasy's most classic works are women: Jane Yolen, Susan Cooper, Vivian Vande Velde, Ursula K. LeGuin, Patricia McKillip, and others. Even when some of these, such as Cooper and LeGuin, write about male protagonists, they write from a female sensibility. Deborah Stevenson even makes the claim that fantasy is actually *more* popular with girls "due to the prevalence of active female protagonists..." She cites Robyn McKinley's work as an example.

## External Barriers

Among the concerns that can be classified as external barriers is the tendency of fantasy toward violence. Since fantasy concerns itself with themes such as the battle between good and evil, violence certainly takes place. There is also sometimes the impression that because fantasy is not "real," it somehow does not carry the same weight as realistic fiction. Fantasy as a genre is often viewed as "escapism," and marginalized as something less than real "literature." There are also those who conclude that children will find fantasy frightening and somehow traumatizing. We would like to address these issues in order to help those who might be skeptical about fantasy to appreciate it better, so that they may pass that appreciation on to children.

> Since fantasy, and especially high fantasy can be an acquired taste, give children the option of the "50-page rule."

### VIOLENCE

Because of its possible effects on children's behavior, violence is rightly a concern. While it may not precipitate the performance of violent acts, constant exposure to media violence may lead a child to become desensitized to it. The concern about the portrayal of violence is reflected even in children's literature for the very young, such as in the selections made for the book *My Very First Mother Goose,* edited by Iona Opie and illustrated by Rosemary Wells. No nursery rhymes dealing with violent acts were included in the book. You won't find any babies in cradles falling out of trees, or blind mice getting their tails cut off.

It seems to us that the objection to violence is more validly raised with media in which the bloodshed is graphic, such as in movies, computers, and video games. Since much of this type of programming has fantasy scenarios, the objection is carried over to fantasy literature as well. However, violence in fantasy can perform a cathartic function. Researchers have observed that children who experienced fantasy situations are able to lower their feelings of aggression and anger significantly. It was also observed that children who were exposed to fantasy had active imaginations and played in more creative ways. As children are exposed to fantasy, they become better able to find non-violent solutions to frustrating situations (Biblow).

In fantasy literature, much of the violence takes place as evil battles good. In most fantasy, good is permitted to win and evil is vanquished. Children, in fact, seem to be bothered if the evil is not dispatched in some permanent fashion. Ann Trousdale tells a story in her article "Who's Afraid of the Big, Bad Wolf?" that dramatically demonstrates this point. She was reading the Walt Disney version of "The Three Little Pigs" to a young girl. In this version, instead of being boiled in the pot, the wolf shoots back up the chimney and runs away. Every time the story was read, the child told Trousdale, "He's gonna come back." The child's mother told Trousdale that she chose the Disney version because she wished to "shield" her child from the death of the wolf, but the child became more disturbed by the possibility that the wolf could return, even dreaming of the Big Bad Wolf coming to her house. It was the lack of violence that provoked this reaction.

> Researchers have observed that children who experienced fantasy situations are able to lower their feelings of aggression and anger significantly.

## ESCAPISM

The renowned fantasy author Ursula K. LeGuin tells a terrific story at the beginning of her essay "Why Americans are Afraid of Dragons." LeGuin says a friend reported, "Ten years ago, I went to the children's room of the library of such-and-such a city, and asked for *The Hobbit*; and the librarian told me 'Oh, we keep that only in the adult collection; we don't feel that escapism is good for children.'" In a similar vein, Tim overheard a customer in a bookstore tell the bookseller that she was trying to discourage a child from reading any more "Star Wars" books. "I want him to get more down to earth," she said.

These incidents clearly demonstrate that reading non-realistic fiction is seen by many to be a waste of time or symptomatic of a loss of touch with reality. The objection that fantasy is merely "escapism" denies the benefits of reading. Whether it is a nutrition label or a fantasy novel, reading increases our awareness of the world and our ability to communicate. Even if we disregard the fact that reading *anything* is inherently beneficial, this criticism still has little validity. At its most basic level, reading fantasy helps a child develop his or her imagination, which is not a waste of time. Beyond that, fantasy is not a retreat from reality, but a way to see reality from a different point of view. Fantasy may be untrue, but it is certainly not unreal. Fantasy presents strong plots and moral themes, and provides examples of fine writing. Fantasy gives the child's intellect opportunities to go beyond a literal level of thinking to being able to ask, "What if?" Fantasy is an important part of cultural literacy.

## FEAR

Another concern is that elements of fantasy may traumatize children in some way. The presence of witches or dragons or evil forces of any kind may be seen as frightening. This concern is immediately belied by the fact, mentioned earlier, that horror is currently the most popular type of fantasy. Kids love to get scared. There is legitimate concern about needlessly frightening very young children, but after a certain age, children begin to look for books or other entertainment that will elicit an emotional response. They are often looking to be scared. Children approach Tim regularly asking for directions to the "scary" books.

## ▶ CONCLUSION

We have discussed the reasons why people may object to fantasy, but we have not discussed the basis of its appeal for those who let it work its magic. At its core, fantasy has a completely visceral appeal that speaks to the wonder of the unknown, of what lies on the other side of the hill, of the mystery contained in ancient volumes of lore, and of the magic of prophecies fulfilled. The earlier children are exposed to fantasy, the easier it will be for them to accept it as they grow older. Ursula K. LeGuin has said, "I believe that all the best faculties of a mature human being exist in the child, and that if these faculties are encouraged in youth they will act well and wisely in the adult, but if they are repressed and denied in the child they will stunt and cripple the adult personality. And finally, I believe that one of the most deeply human, and humane, of these faculties is the power of the imagination: so that it is our pleasant duty as librarians, or teachers, or parents, or writers, or simply as grownups, to encourage that faculty of imagination in our children, to encourage it to grow freely, to flourish like the green bay tree, by giving it the best, absolutely the best and purest, nourishment it can absorb. And never, under any circumstances, to squelch it, or sneer at it, or imply that it is childish, or unmanly, or untrue." If children's imaginations are developed at a young age, they will not dismiss fantasy later just because it requires them to use their imaginations.

It is important to focus on the positive effects fantasy can have on children. Fantasy has the ability to encourage children to develop their imaginative and creative abilities. Creativity gives them the ability to take known quantities and rearrange them into new combinations, the ability to see beyond reality and connect ideas in new ways. Fantasy gives a child's intellect the chance to visualize and try out new possibilities. It also tells children that whatever they can dream or imagine can become real. Much of the technology taken for granted today was nothing more than fantasy at the beginning of the twentieth century. Leaving fantasy out of a child's experience means that we could be raising practical, sober individuals who will likely never aspire to become mathematicians, scientists, or inventors (Chukovsky 117, 124). Raising children with the sense of wonder that fantasy can provide is what this book is all about.

> **Fantasy gives a child's intellect the chance to visualize and try out new possibilities. It also tells children that whatever they can dream or imagine can become real.**

## WORKS CITED IN CHAPTER 2; FURTHER READING

Arthur, Anthony. "The Uses of Bettelheim's The Uses of Enchantment." *Language Arts* 55 (1978): 455-9, 533.

Bettelheim, Bruno. *The Uses of Enchantment: The Meaning and Importance of Fairy Tales.* New York: Vintage Books, 1989.

Biblow, Ephraim. "Imaginative Play and the Control of Aggressive Behavior." *Child's World of Make-Believe: Experimental Studies of Imaginative Play.* Edited by Jerome L. Singe, (et. al.). New York: Academic Press, 1973.

Boden, Marguerite M. "The Role of Fantasy in Children's Reading." *Elementary English* 52 (1975): 470-71, 538.

Chang, Margaret. "Fantasy Literature: Encounters in the Globe of Time." *School Library Journal.* 36 (1990): 163-64.

Chukovsky, Kornei. *From Two to Five.* Translated and edited by Miriam Morton. Berkeley, CA: University of California Press, 1966.

Cullinan, Bernice E. and Lee Galda. *Literature and the Child.* Third edition. Fort Worth, TX: Harcourt Brace, 1994.

Degh, Linda. "Grimm's Household Tales and Its Place in the Household: The Social Relevance of a Controversial Classic." *Western Folklore.* 38 (1979): 83-103.

Favat, F. Andre. *Child and Tale: The Origins of Interest.* Urbana, IL: National Council of Teachers of English, 1977.

Gauch, Patricia Lee. "A Quest for the Heart of Fantasy." *The New Advocate* 7 (1994): 159-167

Harms, Jeanne McLain. "Children's Responses to Fantasy in Literature." *Language Arts.* 52 (1975): 942-46.

Hepperman, Christine. "Invasion of the Animorphs." *Horn Book.* Jan/Feb 1998: 53-56.

Jacobs, James S. and Michael O. Tunnell. *Children's Literature, Briefly.* Englewood Cliffs, NJ: Merrill, 1996.

Kranowitz, Carol Stock. Living With the Three Little Pigs: The Enduring Value of Fairy Tales. *Child Care Information Exchange.* 86 (1992): 26.

LeGuin, Ursula K. *The Languages of the Night: Essays on Fantasy and Science Fiction.* Ed. Susan Wood. New York: G. P. Putnam's Sons, 1979.

Lewis, Claudia. "A Sudden Love of Reading." *Elementary English.* 50 (1973): 767-69.

McCracken, Glenn. "Violence and Deception in Children's Literature." *Elementary English.* 68 (1972): 422-24.

Neugebauer, Bonnie. "Little Red Riding Hood Meets the Wolf—Again and Again and Again." *Child Care Information Exchange.* 86 (1992): 27-30.

Nilsen, Alleen Pace and Kenneth L. Donelson. *Literature for Today's Young Adults.* Fourth edition. New York: Harper Collins, 1993.

Norton, Donna E. *Through the Eyes of a Child: An Introduction to Children's Literature.* Fourth edition. Englewood Cliffs, NJ: Merrill, 1995.

Orbach, Israel, Edith Vinkler and Dor Har-Even. "The Emotional Impact of Frightening Stories on Children." *Journal of Child Psychology and Psychiatry and Allied Disciplines.* 34 (1993): 379-89.

Poskanzer, Susan Cornell. "A Case for Fantasy." *Elementary English.* 52 (1975): 472-475.

Purcell-Gates, Victoria. "Fairy Tales in the Clinic: Children Seek Their Own Meanings." *Children's Literature in Education.* 20 (1989): 249-54.

Richardson, Carmen C. "The Reality of Fantasy." Language Arts. 53 (1976): 549-51, 563.

Rochelle, Larry. "Quest: The Search for Meaning Through Fantasy." *The English Journal.* 66 (1977): 54-55.

Smith, Charles A. ***From Wonder to Wisdom: Using Stories to Help Children Grow.*** New York: New American Library, 1989.

Stevenson, Deborah. "Rewriting the Rules: Girls and Books." ***Horn Book.*** November/December 1997: 654-659.

Stone, Kay. "Marchen to Fairy Tale: An Unmagical Transformation." ***Western Folklore.*** 40 (1981): 232-244.

Tomlinson, Carl M. and Carol Lynch-Brown. ***Essentials of Children's Literature.*** Second edition. Boston, Allyn and Bacon, 1996.

Trousdale, Ann. "Who's Afraid of the Big Bad Wolf?" ***Children's Literature in Education. 20*** (1989): 69-79.

Tunnell, Michael O. "The Double Edged Sword: Fantasy and Censorship." ***Language Arts. 71*** (1994): 606-12.

Vallasekova, Maria. "The Child and the Fairy Tale." ***Educational Media International.*** 4 (1974): 27-34.

# CHAPTER 3

# Discovering Fantasy

We have discussed the benefits of fantasy to children and the fact that fantasy novels can provide children with unique adventures and a world of possibilities. The question that logically arises from this is: How can we best share fantasy with children? As librarians, teachers, and parents, we can be instrumental in arousing children's interest. This is the first of three chapters that will present practical ways to do this. This chapter will focus on teaching fantasy as a genre.

A prerequisite to teaching fantasy, or any literature, for that matter, is the ability to evaluate and make critical judgments. To do this requires an understanding of how authors do what they do. This, in turn, requires an understanding of the basic literary elements that authors use to create a work of fiction and that we use to evaluate all literature: setting, point of view, character, plot, theme, and style. In this chapter we will discuss each element and how it uniquely relates to fantasy.

> A prerequisite to teaching fantasy, or any literature, for that matter, is the ability to evaluate and make critical judgments.

## ▷ SETTING

Where and when does the story take place? In fantasy, setting is of special importance, since stories frequently take place in a world other than that in which we live. We have already discussed how fantasy novels may begin in a realistic setting and move to a fantasy realm or be set in a completely imaginary one. In order to capture and sustain our interest, the author of fantasy must describe these extraordinary settings in concrete detail. Without a clear depiction of our location, it is impossible to suspend disbelief and accept the fantasy world as if it truly exists. One device writers of fantasy use to make their settings clear is imagery, which they create through words that appeal to the senses: sight, smell, sound, taste, and touch. Using descriptive words, the author is able to create a vivid sensory picture that makes unusual fantasy worlds tangible. Through imagery, the reader is able to connect real world sensory experiences to a fantasy environment, mentally "seeing" the setting so he feels comfortable there and wants to stay through the end of the book. Setting can also establish the mood of a fantasy story. Settings such as dank dungeons or mysterious underground passages, for example, create a disconcerting and claustrophobic mood.

Susan Cooper, author of numerous award-winning fantasy novels, is one of the great masters of imagery to convey setting. One reason her images are so powerful is that they often come from dreams. She places a great deal of importance on the idea of the single visual image and its power to excite the imagination. "It seems always to be an image of one kind or another that sparks off this reaction of fierce delight" ("Nahum Tarune's Book" 83). Cooper speaks of a dream she had while working on the final book in her "The Dark Is Rising" sequence, *Silver on the Tree*, that led to the imagery she used in a scene in that book. Here is an example of Cooper's use of imagery. This is the view her protagonists see from a balustrade overlooking the city in the Lost Land, a mythical place drowned by the sea:

> They saw the roofs of the city end, giving way to a green-gold patchwork of fields stretching into the haze of heat. Far, far away in the distance through the haze, Will thought he could see dark trees, with behind them the purple sweep of mountains and the long glimmer of the sea, but he could not be sure. Only one thing out there seemed distinct: A glowing pencil of light rising out of the hazy green blue where the lost land seemed to meet the sea" (158-59).

The quality of Cooper's prose approaches poetry. One can feel a flow of her prose, especially if it is read out loud, in much the same way as she describes the flow of landscape itself. By infusing the settings of her novels with dream imagery, Cooper excites the imagination and draws the reader into her created fantasy world.

*The Subtle Knife,* the second book in Phillip Pullman's "His Dark Materials" trilogy, is especially notable for its use of setting to create a mood. Pullman rises ably to the challenge of creating three different settings in this volume. First there is the world of his protagonist, Lyra, an alternative universe with some similarities to our own (an Oxford College, for example). Lyra's friend Will comes from our contemporary world, which also has an Oxford, but one quite different from the one Lyra knows. Finally, there is a "strange and haunted place" (jacket copy) known as Cittágazze, which lies in a neverland between these two worlds. Cittágazze has been haunted by Spectres that suck the souls from adults, but leave children untouched. The city is empty, because everyone has fled to escape the Specters. Pullman effectively describes the setting in which Lyra and Will arrive in such a way that it is clear that something is horribly wrong.

As they explore the deserted city, Pullman says "Will could see how ancient the buildings in the heart of the city were, and how near to ruin some of them had come. Holes in the road had not been repaired; windows were broken; plaster was peeling. And yet there had once been a

> **Through imagery, the reader is able to connect real world sensory experiences to a fantasy environment, mentally "seeing" the setting so he feels comfortable there and wants to stay through the end of the book.**

beauty and grandeur about this place." Through this concrete description of the setting, Pullman establishes a mood of uneasy uncertainty, with neither the reader nor Will and Lyra knowing why this once grand place is now in decay.

These examples make clear why setting is such a crucial element of fantasy. The reader must be able to visualize an unusual or unfamiliar setting, and this can happen only through the author's description. But the author can go further and effectively use the language through which a setting is described as a tool to assist in setting the tone or mood of a story.

## ▶ POINT OF VIEW

Point of view addresses the question of who is telling the story. There are three main points of view. In the first, one of the characters tells the story. We are told how that person thinks and feels; our perspective is limited to his. First person is most effective when the author creates a genuine voice for the character who is telling the story. Use of first person can make readers sense that someone they know and can visualize is relating the story to them. Gail Carson Levine achieves this feeling in the opening sentences of her novel *Ella Enchanted*: "That fool of a fairy Lucinda did not intend to lay a gift on me. She meant to bestow a gift. When I cried inconsolably through my first hour of life, my tears were her inspiration." The reader senses that Ella is a willful character. Thus the fairy's curse, one of obedience so that Ella must obey any command given her, becomes deliciously ironic.

Second person is the least regularly used because the subject becomes the person spoken to, that is, the reader. This is awkward in most cases. However, the second person has been used effectively in books such as the "Choose Your Own Adventure" series conceived by Edward Packard, in which the reader is in fact the hero. These books are written in the second person so that the reader controls the events of the story, and are full of sentences like "You might be their only chance to return to their own time zone" (Foley 19).

The third person offers two points of view: omniscient third person and limited third person. In third person, the author uses the pronouns *he* and *she* to refer to a character, and usually enters into the mind and thoughts of characters. In omniscient third person, the story is told from an all-knowing narrator's point of view. We are told the thoughts and feelings of everyone in the story. Eloise McGraw's Newbery Honor Book *The Moorchild* provides an excellent example of a switch in perspective from the mind of one character, the changeling child, Saaski, to her father, Yanno. A fisherman named Fergil has come to ask a favor of Yanno, who is a blacksmith. He overhears Saaski playing bagpipes, and is for some reason disturbed by it. After he leaves, Saaski gets the feeling that her mother doesn't want to answer her questions about Fergil. The passage begins with the author inside Saaski's head:

> "Doesn't want to talk about that man, Saaski thought, looking after her—and grew more curious than before. Yanno had already gone back to his anvil and the spade rim, on which he was venting some of his baffled spleen with ringing hammer blows. It was now plain to him: The child [Saaski] and her piping had to be got out of the village and as far out of earshot as he could manage."

Notice how easily the author moves from the thoughts of one character to another within the space of a few short sentences. The ability to explore the motivations of many characters is a

> **The reader must be able to visualize an unusual or unfamiliar setting, and this can happen only through the author's description.**

major strength of the third person omniscient point of view.

In limited third person, the story is still told from a narrator's point of view, but the narrator knows only the thoughts and feelings of one of the characters. Diane Duane's novel *So You Want to Be a Wizard* provides an excellent example of this point of view. In this book, the only person whose thoughts and feelings we get to see completely is Nita, the protagonist. Even though the novel is told by a third person, by focusing only on Nita, the reader is able to create a close bond with this spunky character. Even though she does not tell the story, the reader knows her, as is evidenced in this brief passage: "Life can be really rotten sometimes, Nita thought. She wasn't really so irritated about that at the moment, however. Running away from a beating was taking up most of her attention."

While realistic fiction is often written in first person, from the point of view of one of the characters, it seems that the most frequently used view in fantasy is third person, usually omniscient. This may have its roots in traditional fantasy, where almost all stories begin with "Once upon a time."

## ▶ CHARACTERS

Who are the characters? Do they grow and change? Characters serve as a crucial link between the reader and the story, a link established when the reader identifies with the actions, motives, and feelings of the character. We respond to fictional characters that we see as similar to ourselves. They need not be exactly like us, but for a connection to occur, they must possess at least a few traits and responses that we are able to recognize. Authors of fantasy are not limited to human characters. Before them is a palette of personality traits and physical characteristics that they are free to combine in any way they see fit to create hobbits or hags, monsters or magicians. This act of original creation peoples fantasy worlds with a wide range of memorable characters.

Authors can create characters through physical description as well as through dialogue. Sometimes it is possible to identify a particular character through his or her manner of speech. Lloyd Alexander is particularly adept at this method of characterization. In his novel *The Iron Ring*, he introduces the character of Garuda, an eagle. Alexander tells us a little about this character through the title of the chapter in which Garuda is introduced: "A Miserable Bird." Garuda doesn't disappoint. He appears on the scene with cries of *"Shmaa! Shmaa!"* as Tamar, the novel's protagonist, and his companions are burning a pathway through some vines. Garuda flops on the ground. Tamar questions the nature of this creature. Hashkat the monkey pokes him and says, answering Tamar's question, "It looks like a cross between a buzzard and a trash heap...whatever it's called." Garuda immediately, indignantly responds: "Garuda is what it's called. Not that it matters. Who cares? It's just poor, helpless Garuda. Call him a buzzard, call him trash, whatever you please. Go ahead, you grinning idiot, aren't you going to kick me when I'm down? You might as well. You've done your worst already."

With a few broad strokes, using speech patterns as well as the delightful comparisons of Garuda to a buzzard and a trash heap, Alexander lets us know that we are dealing with a whiny, miserable, not altogether good-looking bird. Throughout the rest of the novel, Garuda's

> **Authors of fantasy are not limited to human characters. Before them is a palette of personality traits and physical characteristics that they are free to combine in any way they see fit to create hobbits or hags, monsters or magicians.**

rants can be easily spotted as he continues to utter his cries of *"Shmaa!,"* refer to himself in the third person and, in general, complain.

Characters can also be created through tone of voice, if the story is told in first person. The author is able to get inside a character's head and let the character's personality show through the way that character tells the story. If the story is told in third person, the author can give insight into the character's personality by describing his or her thoughts and motivations.

A novel needs well-delineated characters because the reader needs someone in the story to identify with. Writing fantasy is a special challenge in this regard, because in some cases the characters may not be human. When a skilled author is able to create characters a reader can empathize with, they become memorable. It doesn't matter whether they are human, animal, or any other species. In the fantasy world Middle Earth, created by J. R. R. Tolkien, one can find some of fantasy's most unforgettable characters. Bilbo Baggins, the timid hero of *The Hobbit,* is one character that children easily identify with. He is an ordinary hobbit whose small stature and simple nature mark him as an unlikely hero. Despite his apparent weaknesses, Bilbo finds the strength to become a true hero. Young people who feel small and weak themselves have great compassion for Bilbo as he is forced from his home. As they defeat dragons, recover treasure, enter battle, and confront death with him, children are able to find the encouragement they need to face their own fears. Middle Earth also accommodates human beings, of whom the wizard, Gandalf the Gray, is the most impressive. By his very nature, Gandalf is too commanding for children to identify with as they do with Bilbo. Even though children may not establish a bond with the wizard, it is through him that they learn many valuable lessons. Basic to Gandalf's personality is his belief that power should not be used to dominate others. Gandalf's actions subtly teach children about the responsible uses of power. They learn, through him, that if you resort to force to solve a problem, even the best intentions become corrupted.

## ▶ PLOT

The plot is the chain of events that come together to form a story. The ultimate test of a plot's success is how well the story sustains interest and gives pleasure, keeping the reader asking the classic question: What happens next? Especially with today's competing influences of television and computers, it is important that novels present interesting plots. Few readers will be compelled to finish a dull story. The number of elements an author can combine to create engaging plots are as limitless as the imagination. Fantasy novels are among the best examples of the possible plot lines that authors can create. From dragon-slaying quests to travels in other worlds, fantasy probes the boundless possibilities of the human mind. As authors create stories that explore these possibilities, however, it is important that they have consistent laws that govern their worlds. They are free to create whatever rules they want, but the magic must always be consistent or it is impossible to find credence in a story that describes things already outside of our normal experience. For example, if hearing the clock strike 13 times allows you to travel in time, as in *Tom's Midnight Garden* by Phillipa Pearce,

> The ultimate test of a plot's success is how well the story sustains interest and gives pleasure, keeping the reader asking the classic question: What happens next?

then it must always happen. Special thought must be given to the powers and attributes of the characters and how they interact within their world. With respect to the nature of plots found in fantasy literature, we have noted that regardless of the trappings of magic, unusual characters, and otherworldly settings, at their core, most traditional and contemporary fantasy stories subconsciously follow a pattern that is older than recorded history, which we will call the "hero journey."

## *The hero journey*

At its core, the hero journey pattern is about growth and the risks involved in growing. Two basic types of journeys are found in children's fantasy. First is the outward journey that happens within the plot and action of the story. Second is the inward journey that allows the protagonist to move from innocence to greater understanding.

### THE OUTWARD JOURNEY

Joseph Campbell provided a model which can, with some modifications, provide a way of understanding the nature of the outward journey as it appears in fantasy. The purpose of Campbell's book *The Hero With a Thousand Faces* is to demonstrate the universal truths that lie beneath the surface of mythology and folklore. Campbell found many parallels in the numerous myths and folktales he studied from around the world. From this study he was able to generalize a pattern he termed "the hero-journey." Within the journey, Campbell identified three phases: "Departure," "Initiation," and "Return."

The starting point of a journey is the everyday surroundings of the hero. There he or she receives a call to adventure from a herald. For Dorothy Gale in *The Wizard of Oz*, the tornado heralds the beginning of her journey. Taran's call comes unintentionally when he plunges into the woods following the escaping pig, Hen Wen, in *The Book of Three* by Lloyd Alexander. With that one act, Taran accidentally rushes into five books' worth of adventure, even though he believed that it was not in his destiny to go anywhere or do anything interesting. Symbolic imagery may be used to create a dividing line between the known and the unknown, as the character passes from one world into another. Even in a work of high fantasy such as *The Book of Three*, where the action takes place in the entirely invented world of Prydain, Taran still leaves familiar surroundings and ventures into unfamiliar ones.

The image of a door seems obvious, but is still a perfect metaphor for a departure. It is often used to facilitate the passage from one realm to another. The doorway that stands between Kansas, Dorothy Gale, and the land of Oz is particularly memorable. After being deposited in Oz by the cyclone, Dorothy springs from her bed and runs to the door. She opens it to see the land of Oz in front of her, a sight "very grateful to a little girl who had lived so long on the dry, grey prairies." This initial image of Oz through a doorway is intriguing. Baum uses the word "amazement" to describe Dorothy's reaction to her first sight of Oz. Her eyes get big, she begins to look eagerly at the sights, yet she does not step beyond the doorway. She stays, even when approached by the Munchkins and the Good Witch of the West. Dorothy has practical sense; she won't leave the house for good until she realizes that it is necessary for her to do so in order to be able to see the Wizard, and thus find a way back to Kansas. When she is finally ready, Baum

> At its core, the hero journey pattern is about growth and the risks involved in growing.

reports her actions very curtly: "She closed the door, locked it, and put the key very carefully in the pocket of her dress." There is a nice sense of finality about the act of locking the door, especially since Dorothy knows that the house may never be lived in again.

Another doorway that provides a memorable image is Will Stanton's in *The Dark Is Rising* by Susan Cooper. In one haunting moment, Will comes to an understanding that he is one of the "Old Ones," called and set apart to fight the Dark. It is a midwinter morning, and time stands still. Will ventures out of his house and later finds himself on a snow-covered hill. He looks up to see two giant carved wooden doors standing on the slope. They have no handles and on their surface are carved symbols "in endless variation." The doors swing open as Will hears a phrase of music. He moves dreamily forward and sees Merriman, the wizened, white-haired old sage who will become his mentor. Will stares at his face and experiences his point of departure: "The world he [Will] had inhabited since he was born seemed to whirl and break and come down again in a pattern that was not the same as before." Susan Cooper perfectly orchestrates this moment, which follows a series of events that Will finds increasingly inexplicable. Coupled with the splendid image of the doors, the feeling of leaving the boundaries of the everyday world is all the more vivid.

Doors are only one of the many devices that can separate the familiar from the unfamiliar. Julia Sauer uses fog in her book *Fog Magic*. The fog in this case is also a dividing line between present and past. It functions "like a magic wall. You stepped through and walked until your own familiar house was gone. And then, sometimes, something strange and wonderful would happen."

Having been removed from his or her ordinary life, our hero next crosses into what Campbell terms a "zone of magnified power," an unfamiliar place. It can be a place in the real world with which the hero was previously unfamiliar, such as the world beyond the castle for Gaylen in Natalie Babbitt's *The Search for Delicious*. Or it can be a fantasy world, or even the world of the imagination, as in Maurice Sendak's *Where the Wild Things Are*.

Leaving home can be difficult, but if growth is to occur, it is imperative that the hero leave comfort and security behind. Once in an unfamiliar setting, the hero has begun the adventure and now must face obstacles that test his or her abilities and determination. During this phase of the journey, our hero may receive supernatural aid through magic objects, such as the six signs in Susan Cooper's *The Dark Is Rising*, or through a wise helper such as Gandalf, the wizard, in Tolkien's *The Hobbit*.

> ...The initiation phase of the journey seems to divide itself quite naturally into two main types. The first is the journey of instruction, the second the journey of initiation.

We have noticed in our reading of children's literature that the initiation phase of the journey seems to divide itself quite naturally into two main types. The first is the journey of instruction, the second the journey of initiation. In the journey of instruction, the hero learns something about himself, about others, or about life that will have lasting impact. Very often, driving forces behind the scenes cause the hero to have his adventure precisely because he has a lesson to learn. One of the classic examples of this is Norton Juster's *The Phantom Tollbooth*. Milo is transported by means of the tollbooth into "the lands beyond" where he learns that there is much about life that is exciting and that there was no excuse to sit around the house and be bored. At the end, it becomes apparent that the tollbooth appeared because Milo needed to learn that lesson, and many other children need to learn it as well.

More common is the journey of initiation. In this journey, a child passes from the innocence of childhood to become an experienced adult. This passage is a test, for certain things must be left behind forever. There is much sadness, but there is always a sense of inevitability. Lloyd Alexander's characterization of Taran provides us with a good example. At the beginning of *The Book of Three,* Taran is portrayed as an impetuous youth, with not much experience beyond that of tending pigs. At the end of his adventures, Taran has discovered the meaning of friendship, honor, and responsibility. Campbell's pattern calls this wisdom the hero gains from the adventure the "boon."

After acquiring the boon, the hero is required to take it back to the people who were left behind at the start of the quest and use it to bless their lives. It is often difficult for the hero to leave the realm he has visited, but the journey is not complete unless he returns. Throughout his adventures, Bilbo Baggins of J. R. R. Tolkien's *The Hobbit* wishes only that he was once again home in his cozy hobbit hole. Throughout his journey, he aches for regular meals, a clean handkerchief, a soft bed, and a good pipe. Just as he wishes, Bilbo's adventures conclude, and like all heroes, he finally gets to return home. But at the end of the trip, as the wizard Gandalf observes, the hobbit that left is not the same hobbit that returns. This fact is the key to the purpose of all hero journeys. If the hero did not return changed, there would have been no reason for the journey in the first place.

## THE INWARD JOURNEY

The issue of growth, of being different at the end of the adventure, is a key to the hero experience in fantasy. If the hero is going to have some new level of understanding about the world, then there has to be contrast. Home does not provide contrast, which is why the hero is forced to leave. It is seeing the contrast between the new place and home that allows the hero to end the journey a changed person. The process of change the hero undergoes by having adventures and gaining insights into himself, his world, and the other people in it is the inward journey. Unlike the outward journey, the inward journey has no specific stages, parts, or procedures, and the process of change on the inward journey is not universal. Each journey will be slightly different, since growth depends on many different factors. Change depends on the character's personality and disposition, as well as his or her capacity to overcome adversity. It also depends upon the adventures the hero has and the outcomes of those adventures. It really does not matter how the change occurs, only that it does. For after all, the entire purpose for the journey in the first place was to allow the hero to make new discoveries and to change because of them.

> ...The entire purpose for the journey in the first place was to allow the hero to make new discoveries and to change because of them.

## THE CHILD AND THE HERO JOURNEY

Perhaps one reason the hero journey is so pervasive as the basis for plots in fantasy literature for children is that the pattern can be seen in the everyday life of a child. Like the heroes of fantasy, young people are heralded into journeys every day. Leaving home to go to school is a departure point in the lives of most children—perhaps one of the most common departure points. Leaving home or some safe, secure place is used as well in a symbolic context, a context in which home is not an expensive brick structure, but a comfortable state of being, a feeling of fitting in, a feeling of having a place in the universe. Children's adventures consist of the first day of school, learning to read and write, moving to a new neighborhood, or standing up to a bully. The only difference between the journey in the novel and the journey of the child is the outward trappings. Young people, knowing this, respond to the hero journey because their journeys follow the same pattern. Once the journey has begun, there is no looking back.

## ▷ THEME

What is the main idea of the story? Theme can be a significant underlying truth or moral fundamental to the story. One of the greatest boons of reading is the discovery and interpretation of a novel's theme. Most outstanding works of fiction, so as not to be didactic, have themes that lie just beneath the surface of the story. This elusive quality gives readers the freedom to apply their individual interpretations and experiences to the novel. Given the diversity of human beings, as well as each novel's unique combination of narrative elements, it is difficult to pinpoint a universal theme. Nevertheless, scholars and critics still work to extract and communicate to literary audiences exactly what themes a novel holds. Common themes in fantasy literature are the conflict between good and evil and making moral choices. Fantasy is especially well suited to deal with these themes because it considers moral questions on a cosmic and spiritual level.

While one branch of fantasy, beginning with Tolkien's *The Lord of the Rings* trilogy, may play out the cosmic struggle on the battlefield, other books deal with the same issues much more subtly. The book *Tuck Everlasting* by Natalie Babbitt is a fine example of a story in which fantasy is necessary to explicate a theme that raises many moral issues: What would it be like if you had the power to remain immortal? Babbitt inserts one fantasy element into an otherwise realistic setting. Bubbling up from a magic spring comes water that holds the power to make whoever drinks it immortal. The Tuck family, having unknowingly drunk the water years before, return to the site at a pre-arranged time to reunite with their two sons. Because the Tucks do not age, it is dangerous for them to stay in any one place for too long a time. On this occasion, the young girl Winnie Foster discovers their secret.

A classic scene in *Tuck Everlasting* demonstrates how the novel's theme of having to make a choice between mortality and immortality is explicated through a juxtaposition of image and moment. Old Tuck has taken Winnie Foster out on the pond. Winnie knows that the Tucks have found the secret of immortality, and Tuck is forced to explain to her why she must not drink, why she must remain mortal.

Babbitt's imagery in describing this scene is difficult to forget: "The sky was a ragged blaze of red and pink and orange, and its double trembled on the surface of the pond like color spilled from a paint box. The sun was dropping fast now, a soft red sliding egg yolk, and already to the east there was a darkening to purple." Against this backdrop, the scene plays. Tuck has chosen the perfect place to talk to Winnie about the folly of being immortal. Tuck understands that he and his family have disturbed the true cycle of life, the cycle represented by the pond. As he explains, Winnie listens quietly. Suddenly it becomes

> Most outstanding works of fiction, so as not to be didactic, have themes that lie just beneath the surface of the story. This elusive quality gives readers the freedom to apply their individual interpretations and experiences to the novel.

clear that death is a reality she must face. "Winnie blinked, and all at once her mind was drowned with understanding of what he was saying." It would be impossible to convey this theme so powerfully without the addition of the fantasy element. If the Tuck family weren't actually immortal, and if Tuck had to explain the danger of tampering with the natural cycle of life in theory rather than from experience, this scene would have no resonance whatsoever.

## ▶ STYLE

How is the story written? How are the ideas expressed? At its most basic level, style is the words the author selects. From an infinite number of words available, a writer chooses and arranges those that create a particular story. Tone, word choice, grammatical structure, devices of comparison, sound, and rhythm all contribute to style. Good literature in any genre uses rich factual details and figurative language. A story's intent, characters, events, and setting combine to create what has been termed the *universal language* (L'Engle, *Babel*, 662). The essential components of the universal language are symbolism, archetype, metaphor, simile, and other figurative devices of language that use words in a nonliteral way. Used skillfully, the components of the universal language are scarcely noticeable and can stir the reader's imagination.

Madeleine L'Engle, author of realistic and fantasy novels for children and young adults, skillfully uses language devices to convey emotion and the feel of traditional literature when it is appropriate to her stories. An example can be found in her novel *A Wind in the Door*.

> The essential components of the universal language are symbolism, archetype, metaphor, simile, and other figurative devices of language that use words in a nonliteral way.

L'Engle uses metaphor and poetic language to convey the powerful scene in which her protagonist, Meg Murray, and her companions must enter the body of her brother Charles Wallace to destroy the Echthroi that are threatening to kill him. Having become as small as the tiny mitochondria that inhabit our cells, Meg and the others struggle to combat the evil forces. To describe the vacuum and the nothingness the Echthroi create, L'Engle plays with the idea of cold: "Cold./Cold beyond snow and ice and falling mercury./Cold beyond the absolute zero of outer space./Cold pulverizing her into nothingness./Cold and pain." L'Engle effectively describes a type of cold beyond anything we can imagine by comparing it to types of cold we can imagine. The fact that the poetic rhythm created by each sentence is a separate paragraph heightens the effect and allows us to feel to some degree what Meg is feeling.

In the fantasies of Patricia C. Wrede, the style is humorous and ironic. The opening paragraph of her novel *Searching For Dragons* is a good example: "The King of the Enchanted Forest was twenty years old and lived in a rambling, scrambling, mixed-up castle somewhere near the center of his domain. He sometimes wished he could say that it was *exactly* at the center, but this was impossible because the edges and borders and even the geography of the Enchanted Forest tended to change frequently and without warning. When you are the ruler of a magical kingdom, however, you must expect some inconveniences, and the King tried not to worry too much about the location of his castle." The style here is at once conversational, much in the tradition of the tale-spinners of traditional fantasy, and humorously ironic at the same time. Her style is ironic in the sense that it gives the feel of a traditional fairy tale with a "once upon a time" sort of beginning, yet there is also immediately evident a hip, modern sense of humor. Wrede also offers nice poetic turns of phrase, such as "rambling, scrambling, mixed-up castle," which lift her style above the mundane.

In comparing the styles of L'Engle and Wrede, we see that a comic style has as much place in fantasy as a more serious and poetic one. In a more general sense, this comparison indicates a wide variety of literary styles appropriate for fantasy. It tells us that authors find individual styles appropriate for the types of stories they wish to tell. Besides the works of Patricia Wrede, a number of other recent fantasies use this more humorous, self-aware style. Among them are Jules Feiffer's classic-in-the-making *A Barrel of Laughs, A Vale of Tears*, in which he often addresses the reader directly, making editorial comments on the characters and action of the story. Another author whose works fall in this category is Vivian Vande Velde. In her book *Curses, Inc.*, a boy uses the Internet to try to place a curse on a girl who has embarrassed him. These books pay homage to traditional fairy tales, but the style is ironic; the author and the reader know that the fairy tales and fairy tale conventions being referenced are lovingly being stood on their heads.

## ▶ CONCLUSION

Contrary to what some may believe, fantasy is not created out of thin air. Authors of fantasy draw from a source that J. R. R. Tolkien called the "Cauldron of Story." In this cauldron one can find things that inform each of the elements of fiction we have discussed: real history, imagined history, fact, fancy, daydreams, nightmares, myths, legends, folktales, and ancient and modern fairy tales. All these have been blended into the immense cauldron, ready to provide inspiration to anyone willing to dive in. Writers of fantasy are always eager to jump in and swim in the cauldron. When they emerge, they bring with them people, places, or things that they then combine and recreate in their imaginations to form something fresh and modern.

On the other side of the equation is the child reader. The same elements that inspire an author can evoke powerful emotions in children. Children may not consciously realize that they are responding to elements ladled out from the cauldron of story, but it is precisely these elements that may cause them to feel something as they read. They are responding to something much deeper and older than themselves. They are responding to settings at once familiar yet alien. They are experiencing the open-eyed wonder of seeing something wonderful, exciting, and new for the first time. They are responding to heroic characters, living their adventures with them, and projecting their own hopes and dreams and wishes onto them. They are responding to stories that mirror the patterns of their own lives: The desire for home, warmth, and safety; the need to break away and establish independence; and the need to return to that safe place once more. In these stories, they are also responding to the breathless excitement of wanting to know what happens next. They are responding to ideas and moral issues. They are responding to the beauty of lan-

> They are responding to stories that mirror the patterns of their own lives: The desire for home, warmth, and safety; the need to break away and establish independence; and the need to return to that safe place once more.

guage itself. Ultimately, the literary elements that come together to create a great work of fantasy are transcended by a more intangible quality of spirit and feeling that comes only in those moments a book is being read.

## WORKS CITED IN CHAPTER 3

Alexander, Lloyd. *The Book of Three.* New York: Holt, 1964.

—. *The Iron Ring.* New York: Dutton, 1997.

Babbitt, Natalie. *The Search for Delicious.* New York: Farrar, Straus and Giroux, 1969.

—. *Tuck Everlasting.* New York: Farrar, Straus and Giroux, 1975.

Baum, L. Frank. *The Wonderful Wizard of Oz.* Illustrated by W. W. Denslow. Chicago: Reilly and Lee, 1900.

Campbell, Joseph. *The Hero With a Thousand Faces.* Second edition. Princeton, New Jersey: Princeton University Press, 1968.

Cooper, Susan. *The Dark Is Rising.* New York: Atheneum, 1973.

Duane, Diane. *So You Want to Be a Wizard.* New York: Delacorte, 1983.

Feiffer, Jules. *A Barrel of Laughs, A Vale of Tears.* New York: HarperCollins, 1995.

Foley, Louise Munro. *Ghost Train.* (Choose Your Own Adventure 120). Illustrated by Frank Bolle. New York: Bantam, 1992.

Juster, Norton. *The Phantom Tollbooth.* Illustrated by Jules Feiffer. New York: Random House, 1961.

Levine, Gail Carson. *Ella Enchanted.* New York: HarperCollins, 1997.

McGraw, Eloise. *The Moorchild.* New York: McElderry, 1996.

Pearce, Philippa. *Tom's Midnight Garden.* Illustrated by Susan Enzig. New York: Lippincott, 1988.

Pullman, Philip. *The Subtle Knife.* New York: Knopf, 1997.

Sendak, Maurice. *Where the Wild Things Are.* New York: HarperCollins, 1963.

Sauer, Julia L. *Fog Magic.* New York: Viking, 1943.

Tolkien, J. R. R. *The Hobbit: Or There and Back Again.* Boston: Houghton Mifflin, 1966.

Vande Velde, Vivian. *Curses, Inc.* San Diego: Harcourt, Brace, 1997.

## FURTHER READING

Alexander, Lloyd. "Fantasy as Images: A Literary View." *Language Arts* 55 (1978): 440-446.

—. "The Flat-Heeled Muse." *Horn Book* 41.2 (1965): 141-46.

—. "Future Conditional." *Children's Literature Association Quarterly* 10.4 (1986): 164-66.

—. "High Fantasy and Heroic Romance." *Horn Book* 47 (1971): 577-584.

—. "Identifications and Identities." *Wilson Library Bulletin* 45.4 (1970): 144-48.

—. "Literature, Creativity and Imagination." *Childhood Education* 47 (1971): 307-10.

—. "Newbery Award Acceptance." *Horn Book* 45 (1969): 378-381.

—. "Travel Notes." *Innocence and Experience: Essays and Conversations on Children's Literature.* Edited by Barbara Harrison and Gregory Maguire. New York: Lothrop, Lee and Shepard, 1987. 59-65.

—. "Truth About Fantasy." *Top of the News* 24 (1968): 168-74.

—. "Wishful Thinking — or Hopeful Dreaming." *Horn Book* 44 (1968): 383-90.

Cooper, Susan. "Address Delivered at the Children's Round Table Breakfast." *Texas Library Journal* 52.2 (1976): 52-54.

—. *Dreams and Wishes: Essay on Writing for Children.* New York: Simon & Schuster, 1996.

—. "Nahum Tarune's Book." *Innocence and Experience: Essays and Conversations on Children's Literature.* Edited by Barbara Harrison and Gregory Maguire. New York: Lothrop, 1987. 76-85.

Horning Kathleen T. *From Cover to Cover.* New York: Harper Collins, 1997.

L'Engle, Madeline. "Before Babel." *Horn Book* 42.6 (1966): 661-670.

—. "The Danger of Wearing Glass Slippers." *Elementary English* 41.2 (1964): 105-11, 153.

—. "The Expanding Universe." *Horn Book* 39.4 (1963): 351-52.

—. "The Key, the Door, the Road." *Horn Book* 40.3 (1964): 260-268.

Lukens, Rebecca J. *A Critical Handbook of Children's Literature.* Fifth edition. New York: Harper Collins, 1995.

Tolkien, J.R.R. *Tree and Leaf.* Boston: Houghton Mifflin Co., 1965.

# CHAPTER 4

# Connecting Fantasy

## SUGGESTIONS FOR INTEGRATING FANTASY INTO THE CURRICULUM

This chapter is based on the general premise that children's trade books should be integrated into the school curriculum and made a natural part of the learning process. Many schools already use children's books as tools in different variations of the "whole language" approach to language acquisition. However, children's books can and should be used for more than just this one purpose. The use of fantasy literature in the classroom presents special challenges but also unique rewards to the teacher willing to give it a chance. The wide variety of fantasy books available in formats accessible to children on all grade levels means opportunities to expand children's horizons and develop their imaginations.

Be imaginative as you consider how fantasy might fit into your curriculum. For example, don't feel as if you are limited to using picture books with young children and chapter books with older children. You can effectively use picture books such as David Wiesner's *Free Fall* with all ages, and many chapter books are accessible to young children when read aloud. Use novels to help spark curiosity in a subject, then let the children discover more.

> The wide variety of fantasy books available in formats accessible to children on all grade levels means opportunities to expand children's horizons and develop their imaginations.

There are two main approaches to integrating a book into the curriculum. The most obvious is to start with your already established subject areas, and search out books to enrich them. The second is to start with good books and find ways to fit them into your curriculum. We have found the second technique generally to work best when integrating fantasy literature. To apply this approach, keep your curriculum plan in mind as you read. Also, look for elements, big or small, and decide if you can use them to illustrate an idea in your lesson plans. Use books as a jumping off point. Many of the activities here represent ideas that can be generated from books when they become the starting point for a journey into learning that may take children in directions you and they had never anticipated. They are designed to expand upon the ideas generated by the books to provide a total integrated learning experience. The activities suggested here range from the very simple, such as suggestions for discussion and further research, to the more elaborate, such as classroom activities. Feel free to adapt them to your abilities, interest, and budget.

To help you get started, we have chosen some fantasy novels that can be used in various subject areas. We give basic information about each book, followed by a short paragraph of ideas on how you can use the book in your curriculum. Full information for each book is included in the annotated book list at the end of this manual. The suggestions are divided by subject area: Science, Social Studies, Humanities, Mathematics, and Language Arts. This chapter ends with four sample lesson outlines.

# Science

## PLANTS

**Wiesner, David. *June 29, 1999.***
Becky's science project is to send up plants in balloons to see the effects of high altitude on growth. Large vegetables begin descending on the earth. We discover that they are not her vegetables at all but an accidental discharge from the galley of an alien ship.

**Dahl, Roald. *James and the Giant Peach.***
A little man gives James a bag filled with curious green things. When James spills them at the base of an old peach tree, an enormous peach grows and magical things begin to happen that propel James into a series of madcap adventures.

Discuss things plants need to grow (soil, water, air, sunshine). Plant vegetable or flower seeds in pots. Experiment by withholding water, air, or light from some of the plants and see what happens. Check the plants daily and keep a log of how they grow. Experiment with different kinds of fertilizer to see which ones make the plants grow better. Experiment with talking to plants. Does talking to them have any effect on their growth? Have the children talk nicely, scold, or not speak at all to different plants and record your results.

## ANIMALS AND ANIMAL HABITATS

Young people can use fantasy books to learn more about animals, their habits and habitats. Use a book with an animal protagonist to try out some of these ideas:

- Have the students compile a list of animal facts they learned from the book. Take the children to the library and have them research other facts about the animal in the book.

- Discuss the setting. Do the animals in the books live in the same place that they do in the book? If not, where do they live, and why do they live there? Have the children construct a diorama of a typical landscape in which that animal would live. Using a world map, identify the different places where a certain animal would live and mark them.

- Discuss characteristics of the animal. Do the animals in the books live alone or in groups? Is that what they would do in the wild? Are the other animals in the book ones that those animals would really have as friends or enemies? What do the animals eat? What are some special characteristics of the animal? Do they hibernate? Do they migrate? How do they care for their young?

- Learn the scientific names and classes for the animal, and make comparisons among animal groups.

- Invite an expert on an animal into the classroom to speak.

- Visit a museum, farm, zoo, or animal sanctuary where the children can see animals.

Here are some fantasies with animal protagonists to get you started:

### Mammals:
**Adams, Richard. *Watership Down.***
The story of the adventures a group of rabbits have while searching for a safe place where they can live in peace.

**Van de Wetering, Janwillem. *Hugh Pine.***
A porcupine genius named Hugh Pine works with his human friends to save his fellow porcupines from the deadly dangers of the road.

### Rodents:
**Brett, Jan. *Town Mouse, Country Mouse.***
Mice learn to appreciate their environs after a harrowing trip.

**Ivimey, John W. *Complete Story of the Three Blind Mice.***
The full story of just how those mice went blind and lost their tails.

### Birds:

**Mayne, William. *Antar and the Eagles.***
A young boy who was abducted and raised by eagles is sent on a quest to rescue a lost egg and save the race of eagles.

**White, E. B. *The Trumpet of the Swan.***
Louis, a voiceless trumpeter swan, is determined to learn to play a stolen trumpet.

### Ocean Life:

**Duane, Diane. *Deep Wizardry.***
Nita and her friend Kit assist a whale wizard named S'ree to combat an evil power during their summer vacation to the beach. Sequel to So You Want to be a Wizard.

**Senn, Steve. *A Circle in the Sea.***
Through the power of a ring, a 13-year-old girl enters an undersea world where she becomes a dolphin and aids the whales in retaliating against slaughter of the whales by hunters.

## THE HUMAN BODY

**Butterworth, Oliver. *The Trouble With Jenny's Ear.***
A young girl named Jenny gains the remarkable power to hear peoples' thoughts.

- Use a model or drawing of the inside of the ear to help children learn and label the different parts of the ear.
- Invite an otolaryngologist or audiologist to speak to the class about how we process and interpret sound.
- Using tape recorders and cassette tapes, have the children go on a sound scavenger hunt. Divide the children into groups and have them collect different sounds around the school and classroom. When they are completed, have the groups switch tapes and engage in a contest to see which groups can identify the most sounds. Learn some sign language.

**Christopher, John. *Empty World.***
A teenage boy tries to survive in a seemingly empty England when a deadly virus kills off most of the world's population.

- Bacteria are all around us. Discuss with the children how bacteria get into our bodies. Make a list of ways that we can prevent this from happening.
- Antibiotics help us to fight bacteria. Discuss how antibiotics work. Invite a physician or microbiologist to class to speak about bacteria and antibiotics. Have the speaker discuss how bacteria are identified, the types of bacteria, and which antibiotics effectively destroy them.
- Bring in lab equipment that helps scientists to identify bacteria, and let the children examine it.
- Make bacteria cultures. Take samples from all over the classroom or school. Have the children predict how many bacteria will come from each place and then see how close they came.

**L'Engle, Madeleine. *A Wind in the Door.***
Meg Murry and the creature Proginoskes travel into galactic space and finally into the small world of a mitochondrion to save Meg's brother Charles Wallace and the universe.

- Have the students research the human cell. What is a cell? What are its component parts? What is the purpose and function of each of the parts? What is the appearance and location of each of these parts? How are DNA molecules constructed? How and why do cells duplicate? Where in the process can something go wrong? How and when do cancer-causing agents disrupt the DNA's replication? Why is good nutrition essential for proper DNA duplication?
- Have the students construct a model or draw a picture of a cell, a DNA molecule, or a cell undergoing mitosis.
- Discuss how scientists can use cells and DNA to produce clones. Discuss the ethical pros and cons of cloning.

## TECHNOLOGY

**Dickinson, Peter. *Heartsease.***
*At a future time in England when anyone knowledgeable about machines is severely punished as a witch, four children aid the escape of one such witch who has been left for dead.*

Fantasy often deals not only with the good things technology provides, but with its negative consequences as well. Divide the class into two groups. Assign one group to research the benefits of technology and the other to research the negative effects. Have the students prepare to defend their side in a debate. Allow each side a set amount of time to present their arguments. Select another class or a group of teachers to act as judges and have them select the side that offers the more persuasive arguments.

**Cooper, Susan. *The Boggart.***
*Twelve-year-old Emily finds that she has accidentally brought back a boggart (an invisible and mischievous spirit with a fondness for practical jokes) after her family visits a castle in Scotland. Her brother is a computer geek, and it is through the computer that the Boggart learns to speak to the children, and that he is eventually sent back home.*

**Peck, Richard. *Lost in Cyberspace.***
*Josh and his friend Aaron use the computer at their school to travel through time where they learn secrets about the school's past and find help to improve their home situations.*

Use these fantasy books to introduce children to the Internet or to enhance the knowledge they already have.

- For a beginning class, discuss what the Internet is, how it started, how it is used, and what type of things you can find on the Internet.
- Also discuss some of the controversial issues relating to the Internet, such as copyright and access to certain types of materials.
- For a more advanced class, discuss how information is transferred on the Internet, what types of formats and protocols are used to ensure that information gets from one place to another, how information is stored and retrieved, types of software used to retrieve information, and how information is kept secure.
- Also have children compare and contrast different types of software. Which are the best, the worst? How fast do they work? Which gives you "the best" information?
- Continue the discussion of Internet issues. Have the students use current magazines and newspapers to write reports on how these issues are being addressed locally and nationally.

## ECOLOGY

**Farmer, Nancy. *The Ear, the Eye and the Arm.***
*When General Matsika's three children are kidnapped and put to work in a plastic mine where garbage is recycled, three mutant detectives are hired to use their special powers to find them. This story takes place in a Zimbabwe of the future.*

Discuss general information about recycling.
- How do materials break down in the environment?
- What materials are suitable for recycling?
- What impact does recycling have on the environment?
- What new products can be made from the old products?
- How are recycled materials remanufactured into new products?

Discuss landfills.
- Where does your trash go?
- What do landfills cost?
- When will current landfills close?
- Have the students brainstorm ways that they can start a recycling program at home and at school.
- Use the phone book or local newspapers to find the locations of recycling centers.
- Take a field trip to some of these centers.
- Set up a recycling center in the classroom.

# Social Studies

## GEOGRAPHY AND GEOLOGY

**Alexander, Lloyd. *The Book of Three.***
*When the oracular pig HenWen escapes into the woods, Taran, assistant pig keeper at Caer Dallben, begins a mighty quest in which he must face the forces of evil. The book includes a map of Prydain. Series: Chronicles of Prydain, Book 1.*

Help the students develop skills related to reading and making maps.

- What important kinds of information should you have on a map?
- Have the children make maps.
- Discuss the different types of maps (i.e., road, topographical) and their purposes. What kind of map will yours be?
- What information do you need on your map?
- Have students develop a legend that covers the symbols used for mountains, castles, and roads. Ensure that the children label their maps clearly.
- Help the children develop a scale for their maps.
- How well do the maps convey information?
- Invite a surveyor or map maker to speak to the class about his or her job and the skills needed.

**Osborne, Mary Pope. *Afternoon on the Amazon.***
*Eight-year-old Jack, his seven-year-old sister, Annie, and Peanut, the mouse, ride in their tree house to the Amazon rain forests, where they find giant ants, flesh-eating piranhas, hungry crocodiles, and wild jaguars. Series: Magic Tree House.*

Assign topics to research aspects of the Amazon jungle.

The land:
- Where is the Amazon? How big is it? How much land does it cover?
- What is the climate of the Amazon?
- How many rivers are there in the Amazon?

The animals:
- How many species of animals and birds are there in the Amazon jungle?
- What are some of the animals and birds that live in the Amazon?

The plants:
- How many species of plants are there in the Amazon?
- What are some of those plants?
- How are plants from the Amazon being used in medicine today?

The people:
- Who lives in the Amazon?
- How do they live?
- What do they eat?
- What do they do for a living?
- How do they build their houses?

**Wrightson, Patricia. *The Dark Bright Water.***
*A young Australian Aborigine is urged by tribal elders to investigate the strange events occurring in the interior of the vast continent.*

Use the library and other classroom resources to answer some or all of these questions about Australia. Have the children draw a map or create a topographical map of the continent using clay.

- How big is Australia?
- Where is its center?
- Is Australia the biggest or smallest continent?
- Is it the lowest or the highest?
- How many deserts are there in Australia?
- Which is the highest or lowest mountain?
- Which is the largest or smallest lake?
- Which is the longest or shortest river?
- Which is the tallest or shortest waterfall?
- What is the farthest point from the sea?
- Is Australia the world's largest island?

**Osborne, Mary Pope. *Dinosaurs Before Dark.***
*Jack and his sister Annie find a magic tree house that takes them back to the time when dinosaurs roamed the earth. Series: Magic Tree House.*

Discovering dinosaurs and fossils. (See Sample Lesson Outline Number One at the end of this chapter).

# CULTURE

Fantasy novels offer a great starting point for you to introduce children to the different cultures of the world. To start the children on a journey into world cultures, have them research the culture the book is based in. Have them present the facts they have learned to the class. You can also focus on only one aspect of a particular culture. If you are studying a culture's art, for example, have the children create artwork in the same style. If you are studying dress, have the children make paper dolls with clothing from that culture. Incorporate in a culture day the things you learn. Have the children prepare exciting displays about the culture. Set them up in the hallway or gym and let other classes come and look at them. Invite native members of the culture to speak in class. Have them bring artifacts and pictures if possible. Learn some words in the language of the culture you are reading about. The following list of fantasy books, divided into cultural groups, should help you get started.

## *English, Celtic, Irish, Welsh:*

Alexander, Lloyd. **The Book of Three.**
*When the oracular pig HenWen escapes into the woods, Taran, assistant pig keeper at Caer Dallben, begins a mighty quest in which he must face the forces of evil. The book includes a map of Prydain. Series: Chronicles of Prydain, Book 1.*

Cooper, Susan. **The Dark Is Rising.**
*On his eleventh birthday, Will Stanton discovers that he is the last of the Old Ones and that he is destined to seek the six signs that will enable the Old Ones to triumph over the evil forces of the Dark*

King-Smith, Dick. **Paddy's Pot of Gold.**
*After making friends with Paddy, the leprechaun Brigid wonders if he has a pot of gold.*

### Asian:
Alexander, Lloyd. **The Remarkable Journey of Prince Jen.**
*On a perilous quest to find the legendary court of T'ienkuo, Prince Jen must face his destiny and engage in a grim struggle from which he emerges triumphantly into manhood.*

Sleator, William. **Dangerous Wishes.**
*Fifteen-year-old Dom and his friend Lek search for a jade carving that must be returned to appease a Thai spirit, with the hope it will end the bad luck that Dom and his parents have been having since their arrival in Thailand.*

### Australia:
Wrightson, Patricia. **The Nargun and the Stars.**
*An ancient stone creature threatens the lives of a family on a sheep farm in Australia.*

### Native American:
Vick, H. H. **Walker of Time.**
*A 15-year-old Hopi boy and his friend travel back 800 years to the world of the Sinagua, a group of people plagued by drought and illness and in need of a leader. (See other books in same series.)*

# HISTORY

## *Prehistoric Times*
Scieszka, Jon. **Your Mother Was a Neanderthal.**
*The Time Warp Trio find themselves in prehistoric times, where cave art is a form of graffiti, and "rock" music is something entirely different. Series: Time Warp Trio.*

Have the children study cave paintings. Some of the best cave paintings are located at Lascaux, France and Altamira, Spain.

- What kinds of things do they show?
- How do archeologists and scientists learn about these ancient people from their pictures?
- What kind of pictures would you paint to let people in the future know about you?
- Have the children paint their own cave pictures, patterning them after the ones they have studied.

## Europe:

**Osborne, Mary Pope. *The Knight at Dawn.***
*Jack and his younger sister Annie use their magic tree house to travel back to the Middle Ages, where they explore a castle and are helped by a mysterious knight. Series: Magic Tree House.*

Research medieval tournaments.

- Have the children plan and carry out a tournament day.
- Have them invent games to substitute for jousting and other medieval games.
- Have the children prepare food or make costumes.
- Choose kings and queens and switch them every hour so that everyone gets a chance.

Study medieval coats of arms and other symbols used to identify knights and their houses.

- Have children make banners and coats of arms that represent them.
- Have a parade of banners around the school grounds.

**Norton, Andre. *Red Hart Magic.***
*A brother and sister travel back to the time of King James I in England, where they find solutions that help them to deal better with some serious peer problems in their own time.*

- Have the students make a biography of King James I: Where he was born, his childhood, his teen years, his reign in England, the important historical events during his reign, his death.
- Have the students identify some of the matters of political importance at the time.
- Discuss with the students the historical and social climate of the time of James I, the Tudor and Stuart periods in England.
- Divide the class into groups and have each group study a different aspect of the times: The architecture, food, clothing, politics, transportation, and industry.
- Have the students report their findings to each other.

## United States:

**Bond, Nancy. *Another Shore.***
*While working in a reconstructed colonial settlement in Nova Scotia, 17 year-old Lyn is suddenly transported back to 1744, when the French inhabitants are at war with England.*

Use general reference sources in the school library to find information about the historical period, diplomatic relationships, economics, and important events of the period in France, England, and the Americas. Focus on the period between 1744 and 1748, when these countries were fighting King George's War to gain control over the American and Canadian lands.

- Have the students present the information they found in different forms, such as maps, timelines, or reports comparing the countries.

Have the students answer such questions as

- Why did both France and England want these lands?
- How did the quarrels between these European powers affect local disputes?
- What was the outcome of the war?

**Vande Velde, Vivian. *Dragon's Bait.***
*Fifteen-year-old Alys, wrongly condemned of witchcraft, finds an ally in the dragon to which she has been sacrificed when she is tempted to take revenge on her accusers.*

Discuss with the students how the Salem witch trials began, what caused them, and the outcome. Have the students research answers to the following questions.

- Who were the people accused of being witches? Men or women? Rich or poor?
- Ask the students to discuss why they think these people were the ones accused.
- What did others have to gain or lose by accusing these people of witchcraft?
- What kinds of evidence were used to convict those accused?
- Was the evidence fair?

- Did the accusers really have proof that these people were witches?
- Do you see any parallels between the Salem witch trials and modern history?
- How are the situations the same or different?
- Have the students write biographical essays on some of the major players in the Salem witchcraft trials: Rev. Samuel Parris, Bridget Bishop, Cotton Mather, and Sir William Phips.

### Africa and the Orient:

**Peck, Richard. Blossom Culp and the Sleep of Death.**
*High school freshman and possessor of second sight, Blossom Culp helps an Egyptian princess recover her tomb and saves a suffragette teacher from losing her job in 1914.*

Have the children research the ancient Egyptian practice of mummification.
- How did the ancient Egyptians make a mummy?
- What did the Egyptians believe about the afterlife?
- Where were mummies put?
- What things were placed in the pyramid tombs?
- Why were these things put there?
- What kind of ceremony did the Egyptians hold before the mummy was placed in the tomb?

Have the students research some of the famous Egyptian archeological digs.
- What kind of things did the archeologists find?
- What did they learn from the artifacts that they recovered?
- Invite an archeologist to the class to speak.
- Take a field trip to a museum that displays Egyptian artifacts.

**Osborne, Mary Pope. Night of the Ninjas.**
*Jack and his younger sister Annie travel in their magic tree house back in time to feudal Japan where they learn about the ways of the Ninja. Series: Magic Tree House.*

Have students research the Heian-kyo era of Japanese history. Describe the feudal system of nobles and lords of Japan at this time. Compare and contrast the Japanese system with that of Europe in the middle ages. Have the students research the Shogun lords and the Samurai warriors. Instruct them to investigate as many different aspects of their lifestyle as possible. Discuss the Samurai's Bushido, or code of conduct.
- How did the Bushido govern the lives of the Samurai?
- What was good about the code?
- What was bad?
- How did the Samurai determine if they lived up to the Bushido.
- Have the class develop a Bushido, or a set of classroom rules, for themselves.

## PSYCHOLOGY AND SOCIOLOGY

**King-Smith, Dick. Three Terrible Trins.**
*Ignoring the class system separating the rodents in the farmhouse, three mouse brothers befriend a mouse from a lower class and form a team to fight the cats.*

Discuss the following questions with the students:
- What do we mean by social class?
- What decides social class? Income? Wealth? Occupation?
- What are some of the social class divisions in the United States?
- What names do we have for them?
- What is "the upper class"?
- What is "the lower class"?
- What are the characteristics of these groups?

Study some of the differences in class inequality in the United States and in other parts of the world. Decide on some of the things that determine to what class you belong.

- Is there a way to move from one class to another?
- Why do class inequality and poverty exist in our society?
- Do we need them or not?
- What can we do to change?

Have the students consider their perceptions of class divisions. Ask these questions:

- What is the most money you can make and still be considered poor?
- How many more rooms does the home of an upper-class person have compared to a middle-class one?

Have the students compare and contrast their perceptions of "official" definitions from government and social agencies.

### Sherman, Josepha. *Child of Faerie, Child of Earth.*

*The half-human son of a queen of Faerie, named Percinet, falls in love with the daughter of a mortal medieval count. He leaves his realm to profess his love to her and to defend her against her cruel stepmother.*

Discovering stereotypes. (See Sample Lesson Outline Number Four at the end of this chapter.)

### Sleator, William. *House of Stairs.*

*Five 15-year-old orphans are placed in a house of endless stairs as subjects for a psychological experiment on conditioned human response.*

Discuss the work of behaviorists such as Pavlov.

- What is classical conditioning?
- How does it work?
- Present the students with various experiments conducted by Pavlov and others.
- Have them identify the conditioned stimulus and response as well as the unconditioned stimulus and response.
- Have the students develop and write about an experiment in classical conditioning they might conduct.
- Instruct them to identify the various stimuli and responses in their experiment.
- Discuss ideas related to classical conditioning, such as extinction.

# Humanities

## ART

**Alcock, Vivien. *The Sylvia Game.***
*During a trip to the seaside with her artist father, 12-year-old Emily befriends a gypsy's son and the young heir to a stately home, who are struck by her resemblance to a girl in a painting by Renoir.*

Study some of the paintings of Renoir.

- Select one of his paintings and research what critics have said about it.
- Study the painting for the ways Renoir used color, form, texture, and perspective.

Study the impressionist movement.

- What is it?
- What characterizes impressionist paintings?
- Collect biographical information on other famous impressionists.
- Have the students create paintings in the impressionist style.

**Bang, Molly. *Tye May and the Magic Paint Brush.***
*A poor orphan girl acquires a magic brush that makes the things she paints come alive. Everyone tries to cash in on her ability, but Tye May paints a boat, has the wicked emperor board it, then paints a storm that sinks it.*

Tye May uses a paintbrush to create her pictures, but you can use many other things to make pictures.

- Have the children collect various objects that will not be harmed by putting paint on them. All types of sponges, cotton balls or swabs, old toothbrushes, pieces of wood, or even potatoes are good items.
- Have the children select an item and then paint a picture using it.
- Compare the different styles, textures, and results from each tool.
- Have a "Cool Tools" art show.

Artists not only use different tools but different media to create art.

- Have the children list as many different things they can think of that people use to create art work—oil paint, watercolor paint, crayons, markers, colored pencils, paper, stone, wood.
- Have the children find different examples of artwork that uses these media. Children's picture books are an especially rich place for artwork in different media.
- Go to the library and have a scavenger hunt to find as many books as possible that use different media of artwork. The medium used for the artwork is usually listed on the verso of the title page.

## BOOKS, LIBRARIES, AND LANGUAGE

**Alexander, Lloyd. *The Jedera Adventure.***
*Vesper Holly and her faithful guardian Brinny travel to the remote country of Jedera, where they brave dangers while trying to return a valuable book borrowed many years ago by Vesper's father.*

Invite the school librarian to speak to the children about the library. Touch on the following areas:

- What the library contains.
- How to find things in the library.
- Rules of the library.
- How to check out and return books and other materials.
- How to care for library books.

This discussion could also extend to a discussion of different types of research sources (dictionaries, encyclopedias, atlases), the Dewey decimal classification system, and the Library of Congress system.

- Define fiction and nonfiction.

- Take a field trip to a local library that has a special collection of rare or old books.
- Ask the librarian to speak on what makes books rare and how he or she preserves books.

### Asch, Frank. *Journey to Terezor.*
*Matt and his parents are transported to a mysterious planet after their home has been destroyed by a devastating flood, inhabited by other misplaced earthlings, and ruled by robots. Matt teams up with two young geniuses and a robot in an effort to escape back to Earth.*

Discovering nouns. (See sample lesson outline number two at the end of this chapter.)

### Babbitt, Natalie. *The Search for Delicious.*
*When compiling a dictionary, the prime minister comes to a screeching halt when no one at court can agree on the meaning of "delicious"; to settle the controversy the king sends his 12-year-old messenger to poll the country.*

- Discuss the use of dictionaries, the parts of a dictionary, how to read the abbreviations and symbols, and different kinds of dictionaries (foreign language, medical, slang).
- Have the children start their own dictionary.
- In a notebook, have them write words and definitions of words as they learn them.
- Younger children can draw pictures explaining words.
- Older children can write their own definitions.
- Bind their dictionaries together as a class dictionary.

## MUSIC

### Bethancourt, T. Ernesto. *Tune in Yesterday.*
*Two teenage boys who have a passion for jazz and big band music inadvertently find a way to go back in time to 1942.*

- Explore different genres of jazz: bebop, boogie woogie, Dixieland, ragtime, or swing.
- Have the students cover the major characteristics as well as prominent composers and performers of each genre.
- Have the students present their information to the class with examples of each type.
- Collect and make a book of biographical information of famous jazz composers, singers, musicians, and band leaders.
- Have a 1940s dance. Hire a band and invite a local dance specialist to teach the students some dances to the big band jazz music of the 1940s.
- Invite a local nursing home or center for the elderly to the dance. Have the students dance with the senior citizens.
- Invite a local tap dance troupe or other dance group to perform at your school.

### Jones, Diana Wynne. *Cart and Cwidder.*
*Three children become involved in rebellion and intrigue when they inherit a lute-like cwidder from their father, a traveling minstrel, which has more than musical powers.*

### White, E. B. *The Trumpet of the Swan.*
*Louis, a voiceless trumpeter swan, is determined to learn to play a stolen trumpet.*

- Have the students make a list of all the string and brass instruments they know.
- Include on the list how the instruments are played (by plucking, using a bow, pressing keys, blowing into a reed or mouthpiece).
- Play recordings of different types of instruments.
- Have the students guess what each instrument is.
- Invite a local musician to speak and perform for the class.
- Invite the school or local orchestra to perform.
- Have time at the end of the performance for the students to ask questions of the performers and if possible to look at the instruments.

# Mathematics

**Juster, Norton. *The Phantom Tollbooth.***
*When Milo journeys through a tollbooth into another world, he learns the importance of words and numbers and discovers the cure for his boredom.*

Discovering polygons. (See Sample Lesson Outline Number Three at the end of this chapter.)

**Alexander, Lloyd. *The Book of Three.***
*When the oracular pig HenWen escapes into the woods, Taran, assistant pig keeper at Caer Dallben, begins a quest in which he must face the forces of evil. The book includes a map of Prydain. Series: Chronicles of Prydain, Book 1.*

Use the situations in Lloyd Alexander's Prydain Chronicles to make math word problems.

- For example, one of the characters, Gurgi, is given a magic pouch that always has food in it. Create a word problem from this situation. If four people are going on a trip with Gurgi and his magic food pouch, and if everyone eats 6.3 ounces of food three times a day, how many ounces of food will Gurgi's wallet have to produce to feed the party for one week?

Another situation in Alexander's Prydain Chronicles deals with Fflewddur Fflam, who has a harp with strings that break every time he extends the truth. Construct a word problem to help children learn about adding money and percentages.

- If Fflewddur's harp strings cost $1.34 each, how much would it cost Fflewddur to replace them if one day he broke the strings nine times?

- What about 30 times?

- If the harp string store was having a 50 percent off sale, what would it cost him to replace 10 strings?

- What if the sale were 75 percent off? How much would he have to pay to buy 11 strings?

**Bowden, Joan Chase. *The Bean Boy.***
*A cumulative tale in which an old lady carves a boy from a bean. The bean is then eaten by a rooster, who is then eaten by a cat, and so on.*

**Kent, Jack. *The Fat Cat.***
*A cumulative Dutch folktale about a cat that eats everything that comes across its path.*

These and other cumulative tales are excellent places to start teaching number sequences.

- For younger children, have the students count each item as it appears in the tale. First we read about it once, then twice, then three times.

- Lead them to discover how the things that appear later in the tale only appear once or twice.

- Have the children look for patterns in the numbers.

- For older children, use this as a starting point to teach other number sequences (Fibonacci sequence, for instance) as well as number bases (base 2, hexadecimal, and so on).

# Language Arts

### Alexander, Lloyd. *The Illyrian Adventure.*
*Sixteen-year-old Vesper Holly and her guardian Brinny become trapped in a dangerous rebellion when they travel to a remote European kingdom in 1872 to research an ancient legend.*

Read the first paragraph of Lloyd Alexander's *The Illyrian Adventure*, which describes Vesper Holly.

- Have the students list all the things that they know about Vesper.
- How does Lloyd Alexander use few words to tell us many things about Vesper?
- Why does he use such descriptive language instead of more ordinary language?
- Does the language describing Vesper make you like or dislike her? Why?
- Rewrite the introductory paragraph introducing Vesper. Include all the things that Lloyd Alexander has told us, but use the plainest language you can.
- Which do you think is better and why?
- Continue to read the book and have the children make notes of other places Lloyd Alexander uses descriptive language.
- Have them look for examples of hyperbole, understatement, allusion, symbols, onomatopoeia, alliteration, assonance, consonance, and rhythm.
- How does Lloyd Alexander use these devices?
- Do we understand more or less about the situation or character because Alexander uses descriptive language?

### Babbitt, Natalie. *Tuck Everlasting.*
*When a 10-year-old girl and a malicious stranger discover their secret spring whose water gives the drinker everlasting life, the Tuck family is confronted with an agonizing situation.*

After reading *Tuck Everlasting*, have the children discuss what they would do if they could not die, or get older.

- Have the children write an essay on where they would go and what type of things they think would be important to them if they had to live forever.
- Divide the class into two groups and have them debate whether or not they would drink the water if given the choice. Have one side be for drinking the water and the other side against it.

### Cooper, Susan. *Silver on the Tree.*
*Will Stanton, Bran, and the Drew children try to locate the crystal sword, the only object that can vanquish the strong forces of Dark. Series: The Dark Is Rising, Book 5.*

Have the students read some of the speeches and essays that Susan Cooper has written to answer some of the following questions: Where does Susan Cooper get her ideas?

- Which passages in which of her books came from dreams she had?
- Compare and contrast the description in the books and the description she gives of the dreams in the essays.
- How does Cooper use imagery?
- How does her imagery make us feel?
- What kinds of words does she use to make us "see" what we are reading about?
- Draw a picture of the images you "see" in one or more of Cooper's books.
- Compare her place images (especially the Lost Land sequence in *Silver on the Tree*) to the woodcuts and lithographs of M. C. Escher.

### Kennedy, Richard. ***Amy's Eyes.***

*Young Amy, a girl who has been changed into a doll, sails the high seas with her sea captain doll that has changed into a man, and a crew of stuffed animals brought to life, in search of gold treasure.*

Have the students select some sentences from the text that are examples of personification. Instruct the children to rewrite the sentences taking out the personification.

- Was the process hard or easy?
- How was the writing affected?
- What did personification add to the text?

Have the students select a character from the novel and make a list of the human characteristics and abilities it has been assigned.

- How does the personification help readers relate to the character?
- Ask the students to identify the most likable and dislikable characteristics and abilities of the character.
- What does the personification tell about the human traits the author values or admires?

### Norton, Mary. ***The Borrowers.***

*By borrowing things from the humans who live above them, tiny people are able to live in an old country house until they are forced to emigrate.*

- Have the children go on a scavenger hunt around the classroom or the school to find things the Borrowers could use in their house.
- Divide the class into groups, assigning each one a different room (living room, bedroom, bathroom).
- Using a shoebox, have the children build a diorama of their assigned room using the items they found for the furniture and fixtures.

### VanAllsburg, Chris. ***The Mysteries of Harris Burdick.***

*A series of mysterious pictures with only titles and captions to explain them.*

With only a pictures, titles, and captions, this book entices you to make up the rest of the story.

- Have the children select a picture that intrigues them.
- Have them write a story with the same title, using the caption of the picture somewhere in it.
- Have the children read their stories aloud to the class.

# SAMPLE LESSON OUTLINES

## OUTLINE 1

# Discovering Dinosaurs and Fossils

**SUBJECT:** Geology and animals

**GRADES:** Two through four

**PURPOSE:** To discover the nature of dinosaurs when they roamed the earth; to discover how plants and animals preserved as fossils help scientists know about life in the past.

## NOVEL TO INTEGRATE:

Osborne, Mary Pope. *Dinosaurs Before Dark.*

Jack and his sister Annie find a magic tree house that takes them back to the time when dinosaurs roamed the earth.

## ADDITIONAL MATERIALS:

- Science textbook appropriate for grade level.
- Materials for making fossil models for each child: Empty dry milk carton, seashells, petroleum jelly, plaster of Paris.
- A small notebook or papers stapled together to form a notebook for each child.
- Textbooks used for the development of this lesson plan:

Abruscato, Joseph, et al. *Holt Science 2.* Teachers' Edition. Austin, TX : Holt Rinehart and Winston, 1989. 35-45.

_____. *Holt Science 3.* Teachers' Edition. Austin, TX : Holt Rinehart and Winston, 1989. 96-113.

*State of Utah Second Grade Science.* Utah: B.K. Hixson/The Wild Goose Company. 1990. 60-63.

## PRE-LESSON ACTIVITIES:

Prepare materials for making fossil models and notebooks for each child.

## LESSON STRUCTURE:

Discussion, library research, art and craft activities

## DISCUSSION

Life began on our earth billions of years ago. Since then, the earth has changed. Today things look very different than they did long ago. Even the animals that lived on the earth were very different. We are going to read a book in which Annie and Jack travel back in time and find out just how different earth was billions of years ago.

Read Dinosaurs Before Dark

We can't travel back in time to learn about how the earth was billions of years ago. How do scientists working today learn about the past without traveling back in time? Accept the children's answers to this question. Lead them to the concept of fossils by asking leading questions such as

- What if the animals of the past left something behind for us to find?
- What if they left their bones?

The things that the plants and animals of the past left behind are called fossils. Fossils are made of rock. To become a fossil, a plant or animal must have hard parts such as bone, shell, or wood. These hard parts were quickly covered by sediment like sand and remained undisturbed as the sediment turned to rock. So even when the hard parts were gone, copies of them were still in the rock.

Many types of fossils were made from this process. Some are just impressions or imprints left in the mud, such as footprints or copies of leaves of plants. Other types of fossils were created when an animal was buried in the mud, and minerals and water replaced the parts of the animal and hardened in the same shape of the animal.

## CRAFT ACTIVITY

Have the children make their own fossil models.

- Mix up some plaster of Paris as directed on the package.
- Take an empty milk carton and fill it about two-thirds full with the plaster. Let the milk carton sit for a while to allow the plaster to set up slightly.
- Meanwhile, thoroughly grease some seashells with petroleum jelly.
- When the plaster is slightly set, press the seashell into the plaster. Set aside and allow the plaster to completely harden.
- Remove the seashell. This should be easy because of the petroleum jelly on the shell.
- Peel off the milk carton from the plaster fossil model.

Dinosaurs are some of the animals that lived billions of years ago that scientists learn about by using fossils. In the book Dinosaurs Before Dark, Annie and Jack came face-to-face with several dinosaurs.

- Do you remember which dinosaurs Annie and Jack saw? Use the pictures in the book if necessary to help the children identify some of the dinosaurs they read about in the book (Pteranodon, Triceratops, Anatosauruses, Tyrannosaurus).

## LIBRARY RESEARCH

How did Annie and Jack learn more about the dinosaurs they saw? The children will probably answer, "They saw them," "They read about them in their book," "Jack took notes on them." Even though we can't go and see dinosaurs, we can learn about them just as Jack and Annie did by reading books and taking notes. Take the children to the school library. Have each child use dinosaur books, encyclopedias, and dictionaries to find as many facts about different types of dinosaurs as he or she can. Instruct the children to write down short factual notes in their notebooks based on what they read, exactly as Jack did with his notebook. This activity could also be conducted in groups. The teacher could assign each child or group a dinosaur to research instead of having them take notes on all of the dinosaurs they can find.

## ART ACTIVITY

After the children have completed taking their notes, return to the classroom.

- Have the children compile a chart of all the facts they gathered about the dinosaurs. This activity can be done individually or in groups, depending on how the previous activity was structured.
- Have the children give their chart a title.
- First list in a column the names of the dinosaurs.
- Then have the children list the other information they found in corresponding columns. For example, one column could indicate whether the dinosaur was a plant or meat-eater; another column could tell how big the dinosaur was; and a third column could say how they got around (four legs, two legs, wings).
- Have the children decorate their charts with pictures copied from books or their own drawings.
- Display the charts in the classroom or on a school bulletin board for the entire student body to see.

**OUTLINE 2**

# Discovering Nouns

**SUBJECT:** English grammar

**GRADES:** Five through seven

**PURPOSE:** To discover nouns by defining them, creating them, and placing them into categories of person, place, thing, or idea; to discover the difference between common nouns and proper nouns and the uses of each.

## NOVEL TO INTEGRATE:

Asch, Frank. *Journey to Terezor.* When a devastating flood destroys their home, Matt and his parents are transported to a mysterious planet inhabited by other misplaced earthlings and ruled by robots. Matt teams up with two young geniuses and a robot in an effort to escape back to Earth.

## ADDITIONAL MATERIALS:

Language textbook appropriate for grade level. Textbooks used for the development of this lesson plan:

Strickland, Dorthy S., et al. *HBJ Language 6.* Medallion Edition. Orlando, FL : Harcourt Brace Jovanovich, 1993. 78-80

Strickland, Dorthy S., et al. *HBJ Language 7.* Medallion Edition. Orlando, FL : Harcourt Brace Jovanovich, 1993. 79-81

## LESSON STRUCTURE:

Discussion, group activities

## DISCUSSION

*Define nouns:* Words that stand for a person, place, thing, or idea

In the book *Journey to Terezor*, Matt spends some time in the Galator Colony learning the customs and language of the Dar. Matt's teacher and friend from Dar, Vaata, teaches Matt how to speak the Dar language. Some of the words Matt learns are irepta (chair), moafoa (garden), turba (love), and lotanga (bundles). Do these nouns stand for persons, places, things, or ideas?

- Write "Person," "Place," "Thing," and "Idea" at the top of the blackboard, leaving columns underneath.
- Write the Dar words under the appropriate heading as the students identify them.

## GROUP ACTIVITY

Frank Asch shows us very few other Dar nouns, so why don't we create some of our own to increase our Dar vocabulary?

- Divide the children into groups.
- Instruct the students to make up Dar nouns for people, places, things, and ideas in their classroom. For example, one group may decide that retoba means "desk".
- Have the students write down the Dar nouns they come up with, with their definitions.
- Encourage the students to come up with nouns in all the categories (people, places, things, and ideas).
- Instruct the students to come up with as many nouns as they can. It may be necessary to require that they have at least five nouns in each category.

- Give the students plenty of time to come up with as many nouns as possible.
- Circulate around the room to encourage those who have a hard time thinking of nouns, who have a hard time making up words, or whose imaginations may be rusty.
- After sufficient time, regain students' attention and bring the groups back into the whole class setting.
- Ask each group to read four or five of the nouns they came up with.
- Ask the class: Is that a noun? Have them answer yes or no, and make corrections as needed.
- If one of the words is not a noun, ask the students to read another until they have given four or five nouns from their list.
- Ask the class: What type of noun is _____ (one of the nouns the students just read off their lists). Is it a person, place, thing, or idea?
- Have the students classify the noun and write it in the appropriate column on the blackboard.
- Continue with these questions until each group has four or five nouns from their lists in the right category on the blackboard.
- Again separate the students into groups and have them classify all the nouns on their lists into the right categories.

*Define common and proper nouns.* Common nouns name things in general—any person, place, or thing. Proper nouns name particular things—an individual person, a specific city, a particular school. Proper nouns always begin with a capital letter.

- Instruct the students to look on their list of Dar nouns and find two common nouns.
- Then have each group read the two common nouns they have selected, making corrections as needed.
- If one of the words is not a common noun, ask the students to read another until they have given two from their list.
- Again instruct the students to look on their list of Dar nouns and find two proper nouns.
- Have each group read their proper nouns using the same procedure as above.
- Separate the students into their groups and have them identify all the nouns on their lists as either common or proper nouns.
- Have them capitalize the proper nouns.
- When this is completed, give each child a sheet of paper.
- Instruct the child to create a Dar noun dictionary by copying his or her list and putting the Dar noun, the definition, the category (person, place, thing, or idea), and its identity (common or proper noun) all together.
- Encourage the students to decorate their Dar noun dictionary.

## FURTHER PROJECTS:

This lesson plan may be extended to teach all parts of speech and other grammatical ideas.

- Have the students create verbs.
- Help them conjugate their verbs into present, past and future tenses.
- Have them continue to develop their verbs, dividing them into their four basic forms (present, present participle, past, and past participle).
- Continue with adjectives, pronouns, and other parts of speech.
- Use the grammatical patterns and form of English to structure the Dar language.
- Have the students create a dictionary at the end of each lesson. This exercise will help them understand the English language and its grammatical structure while strengthening their creative abilities.

**OUTLINE 3**

# Discovering Polygons

**SUBJECT:** Mathematics

**GRADES:** Five through seven

**PURPOSE:** To discover polygons and polyhedra by defining them, classifying them, naming them, and creating them.

## NOVEL TO INTEGRATE:

Juster, Norton. *The Phantom Tollbooth.* When Milo journeys through a tollbooth into another world, he learns the importance of words and numbers and discovers the cure for his boredom.

## ADDITIONAL MATERIALS:

Straws, a model or picture of a triangular prism, a rectangular prism, a square pyramid and a triangular pyramid, pencil or other straight object, construction paper or cardboard, scissors, tape. Textbooks used to create this lesson plan:

Bolster, L. Carey, et al. *Invitation to Mathematics.* Glenview, IL : Scott Foresman, 1988. 134-35

Champagne, Ruth I. Mathematics: *Exploring Your World.* Morristown, NJ : Silver Burdet Ginn, 1995. 274-75

**PREREQUISITE:** Students should understand and be able to define parallelogram and parallel.

## LESSON STRUCTURE:

Lecture, discussion, group projects, crafts

## LECTURE AND GROUP PROJECT

**Define polygon:** A closed plane figure bounded by straight lines or a flat shape made of straight lines that are all connected.

- Show various shapes (or draw them on the blackboard), some that are polygons some that are not.
- Show (or point to) each shape and have the students identify whether it is a polygon or not.
- Have the students justify their answers. Why is this a polygon? Why is this not a polygon?
- Explain that polygons can be made up of any number of straight lines.
- Divide the class into groups. (This may also be done individually.)
- Give each group up to 20 plastic straws, pencils, or other straight objects.
- Instruct the students to use the straws to construct as many different kinds of polygons as they can.
- Encourage the students to use their imaginations to construct various shapes and sizes of polygons. Students may also want to cut their straws for shorter lengths to use in their construction projects.

- Once they have constructed a polygon, ask the students to draw on paper the polygons they have just put together.
- Instruct them to write in the center of each polygon the number of sides or edges that it has.
- Allow sufficient time for children to explore this idea.
- Explain that polygons are given special names, depending upon the number of sides or edges they have. Define triangle (three sides), quadrilateral (four sides), pentagon (five sides), hexagon (six sides), octagon (eight sides), and so forth.
- Instruct the children to write the name of the polygon next to, on top of, or under the drawings of polygons they created in the previous activity.
- Show the students a prism and a pyramid.
- Explain that we can combine the same or different kinds of polygons to make space figures (or solids) called polyhedra.

Define:
- *Polyhedron (plural: polyhedra):* A solid formed by plane faces. One kind of polyhedron is a pyramid.
- *Pyramid:* A geometrical figure having for its base a polygon and for its sides several triangles meeting at a common point. Explain that another kind of polyhedron is a prism.
- *Prism:* A solid whose sides are parallelograms and whose ends are parallel and alike in shape and size.
- Show students a model or drawing of a square pyramid, triangular pyramid, triangular prism, and rectangular prism.
- Have the students identify each as a pyramid or a prism and justify their answers.
- Ask what polygons are used to make up these polyhedra. (Referring to the square pyramid, triangular pyramid, triangular prism, and rectangular prism.)

*Define faces:* Surfaces of the polyhedron that are flat.
- Ask how many faces these polyhedra have. (Refer to the square pyramid, triangular pyramid, triangular prism, and rectangular prism.)
- Explain that the polyhedra we have looked at are constructed using triangles and quadrilaterals. You can make polyhedra out of other polygons besides triangles and quadrilaterals. One polygon, called a dodecahedron, is constructed using pentagons.
- Read the section from The Phantom Tollbooth where Milo meets the Dodecahedron.
- Using colored paper or cardboard, have the students construct a model of a dodecahedron.

### OUTLINE 4

# Discovering Stereotypes

**SUBJECT:** Psychology

**GRADES:** Seven through nine

**PURPOSE:** To define stereotype, prejudice, and discrimination; to discuss issues related to these ideas; and to develop ways in which these negative beliefs can be overcome.

## NOVEL TO INTEGRATE:

Sherman, Josepha. *Child of Faerie, Child of Earth.*

The half-human Percinet, son of a queen of Faerie, falls in love with the daughter of a mortal medieval count. He leaves his realm to profess his love to her and to defend her against her cruel stepmother.

## ADDITIONAL MATERIALS:

Psychology textbook appropriate to the grade. Textbooks used for the development of this lesson plan:

Kalat, James W. *Introduction to Psychology.* Fourth edition. Pacific Grove, CA : Brooks/Cole Pub. Co., 1996. 700-703

McMahon, Judith, Frank McMahon, and Tony Romano. *Psychology and You.* Second edition. Minneapolis, MN: West Pub. Co., 1995. 599-602

Before the lesson, read the novel aloud or have the students read it privately. Ask them to identify and think about the beliefs and attitudes that Graciosa has about Percinet and his people and to keep a reading journal in which they record answers to this question as well as their own thoughts about the book. One to two days before the lesson, assign the appropriate pages from the textbook dealing with stereotype, prejudice, and discrimination. Ask students to read about and gain an understanding of the ideas presented.

## LESSON STRUCTURE:

Lecture and discussion, writing activities

## LECTURE AND DISCUSSION

*Define stereotype:* A set of fixed beliefs about a group that may or may not be true. What are some of Gracioca's stereotypes about Percinet and his people?

- All magic is evil (p. 22).
- Faeries are akin to demons (p. 23).
- Faeries are creatures of enchantment with no heart or feeling (p. 24).
- Faeries do not keep their word (p. 35).
- People of Faerie can create with a wave of their hand anything they possibly need (p. 41).
- Magical things lead to a hideous Underworld (p. 43).
- Faeries kidnap humans and keep them in perpetual hopeless slavery ( p. 62).
- The land of Faerie is perilous, unfeeling and profane (p. 69).
- Faeries hate humans (p. 71).
- The people of Faerie never lie (p. 71).
- Humans will crumble into dust from old age if they set foot on mortal soil after being in Faerie ( p. 73).
- Eating or drinking while in the land of Faerie binds a human there forever (p. 73).
- Humans who agree to stay in the inhuman land of Faerie have committed a grievous error (p. 85).

- Humans yield to temptation when they are caught by the lures of smiles, magic, and unseemly freedom of Faerie (p. 86).
- When the people of Faerie die, there is no paradise for them, only extinction (p. 87).
- Faeries are empty-headed little sprites with nothing on their minds but the thoughts of dancing in pretty rings (p. 92).

What experiences and evidence does Graciosa gain that show how some of the things she believes about Faeries are incorrect?

- Faeries do not keep their word (p. 35). Percinet always keeps his word. He promises that the beating Graciosa is given by the guards will not harm her, and it does not (p. 35). Percinet always comes to her aid, just as he had promised, even when she believes he will not (pp. 47, 58-59, 108, and 119).
- Faeries kidnap humans and keep them in perpetual hopeless slavery ( p. 62). Humans will crumble into dust from old age if they set foot on mortal soil after being in Faerie (p. 73). Eating or drinking while in the land of Faerie binds a human there forever (p. 73). None of these things happen to Graciosa when she enters and leaves the land of Faerie.
- Faeries hate humans (p. 71). Both Percinet and his mother loved humans (p. 71).

It is obvious that most of what Graciosa believes about Faerie is untrue, so why was she taught to believe these things? What purposes do stereotypes serve?

- Stereotypes solidify and increase a group's self-esteem by making the stereotyped group seem inferior.
- Because a group wants to stay the way it is, stereotypes reduce the possibility that different ways will take over.
- Stereotypes serve to keep people in their "proper" places or ranks. (Count's daughters knew their place and stayed there, accepting the responsibilities that came with their position.)

# DISCUSSION AND WRITING ACTIVITIES

Using references to and quotations from the novel, discuss how the stereotypical beliefs about Faerie served their purpose in Graciosa's world.

- How did they make Faerie seem inferior to mortals?
- How did they discourage the possibility of the different ways of Faerie taking over?
- How did they keep people in their places?

*Define prejudice.* A judgment made about people based on the group to which they belong, rather than on their individual characteristics.

- Because of her stereotypical beliefs, what prejudicial judgments did Graciosa make against Percinet?
- He was evil (p. 22).
- He was a demon (p. 23).
- He had no heart or feeling (p. 24).
- He did not keep his word (p. 35).
- He could create with a wave of his hand anything he needed (p. 41).
- He never lied (p. 71).
- He was an empty-headed sprite with nothing on his mind but dancing and pleasure (p. 92).

*Define discrimination:* Denying rights to or mistreating people because of their membership in a particular group.

- In what ways, if any, did Graciosa discriminate against Percinet?
- When Graciosa was in Percinet's land, was she discriminated against because she was a mortal?
- Extending beyond the novel's bounds, what are some ways in which Percinet and Graciosa could have been denied rights or mistreated while in the other's world?

In what ways did Graciosa overcome her stereotypical beliefs and prejudices against Percinet and his people?

- Through exposure, the longer she lived in his culture, the more her negative beliefs about that culture began to fade.
- She got to know Percinet, his mother, and his people better.
- She stopped now and then and tried to reflect on her prejudices to see if they were incorrect.
- She tried to put herself in their situation.
- She worked together with Percinet and his mother toward a common goal.

What can we learn from Graciosa's experiences? Try to identify in your own life some stereotypical beliefs you may have. Identify some concrete ways that you can work to overcome them.

## FURTHER ACTIVITIES:

People tend to resist new information that contradicts a stereotypical belief. We often see relationships that match our set beliefs and ignore the ones that do not match. This is called illusory correlation. We tend to remember unusual events more than ordinary ones. So when relationships match (correlate), we think we have seen the two events or behaviors together more often than is really the case (illusion). This habit makes our stereotypical beliefs even stronger.

- Have students discuss or write about this idea in relationship to the novel.
- Have them determine ways in which beliefs based on this principle were overcome in the novel.
- Have them suggest ways in which they can overcome these beliefs in their own lives.

# CHAPTER 5

# Programming Fantasy

This chapter contains programming ideas most suitable for use in libraries, both school and public. We have given you all the information you need to present these programs. Patterns for the art activities and puppet shows are included. The programs are divided into the following categories: booktalks, a series of theme programs for middle to upper elementary age students; and storytimes using fantasy for toddlers, preschoolers, and older elementary-age children.

## ➢ SOME NOTES ON PROGRAMMING

We want to emphasize that each of these program ideas has been successfully presented in a library setting. Depending on your situation, talents, and resources, you may feel that some of these programs are overly elaborate, or hard to pull off without extensive planning. Remember that any program worth doing requires some planning.

On the other hand, you may find them to be overly simplistic. We have tried to keep things as simple as possible. Remember that these ideas are to be used as a springboard for your own particular situation in planning programs that revolve around fantasy. Some of you may want to simplify; others may want to expand upon these ideas. We also tried to provide craft and activity ideas that were specifically linked to the books in some way.

> **Creatively dramatizing a story or book is a sure-fire way to generate interest, and many stories beg to be acted out.**

Creatively dramatizing a story or book is a sure-fire way to generate interest, and many stories beg to be acted out. When considering the programs in which creative dramatization is a suggested activity and for which scripts are provided, please keep in mind the following:

First of all, putting on a play does not mean that the scripts must be memorized, or even that you must have sets. Your sets, costumes, and props can be as simple or as complicated as you want, depending on your budget and abilities. All you really need is space and imagination.

- You can do a readers' theater production in which cast members read from their scripts with minimal movement or staging.
- You can do creative dramatization on the spot, and hand out scripts as children come to the program.
- You can lead the children in acting out a particular scenario, which allows for a lot of spontaneity as you guide the children through the story.
- If you want to be more elaborate with sets, an option that has been used with success is to obtain funding through foundations or grants to bring in a local theatre artist.

To put on a play for an audience in a library setting, you might consider making the presentation part of a theater workshop held on a weekly or more frequent basis over a period of time. This has been done by having a group of students come for an after-school program each week. The students themselves chose the play they wanted to produce and even came up with excellent costumes on their own.

## BOOKTALKING FANTASY

Booktalks are a way to present books to children with the hope that they will be interested enough to actually read the book. The best booktalks function like a good movie trailer. They entice you to see the movie, or in this case read the book. A good booktalk gives just enough information to entice without giving away the story. Booktalks should be a mainstay of both public librarians in their school visits and programs, and school librarians, with classes that visit the library. Classroom teachers can also do booktalks. What better way to get a child to read than to say, "I just read the greatest book. You ought to try it!" This, accompanied by a few juicy plot details, may be just enough to get a child excited about a book. The following are some booktalk ideas along with accompanying activities. The booktalks can be used on their own, or you can combine them with the activity ideas to create an entire program.

### BOOKTALK 1

# White, E.B. *Charlotte's Web*

**BOOKTALK:** Fern's father leaves the house one morning with an axe, and of course Fern wants to know where he is going. During the night some pigs were born, and her father was going to kill the runt of the litter. Fern can't bear to see the little pig killed, so she agrees to take care of it. Fern names him Wilbur and loves him more than anything in the world. After five weeks, she has to sell Wilbur to her uncle, who lives on a farm down the road. (Read Chapters 4 and 5.)

This book is all about how Charlotte proves to be a loyal and true friend as she saves Wilbur from a terrible fate.

## ACTIVITY 1: Which Character Am I?

Place character names (Fern, Wilbur, Charlotte, Mr. Zuckerman, Mrs. Zuckerman, Lurvy, Mr. Arable, Mrs. Arable, Avery, Old Sheep, Goose, Ms. Fussy, Henry Fussy, Templeton) on the back of each child. Play 20 Questions. Each child tries to guess who he is.

## ACTIVITY 2: Weaving a Spider Web

Have children weave a web with black yarn on a piece of construction paper.

- Start with a cross that divides the paper into quarters, and then go from corner to corner to form an X, then between each spoke.
- Use tape or staples to anchor yarn ends behind the paper.
- Children start at the center and weave yarn in a circular pattern, alternating yarn over and under base threads. (You can also let the children weave words, as Charlotte did.)
- You can also use glue for the lines of the web and sprinkle glitter on the glue for a jazzy-looking web.
- You can have the children make spiders out of a pom-pom, with wiggle eyes and pipe cleaner legs. Put them on the web.

**VARATION:** You or the children can make this web on a bulletin board and use the area to display art. Make sure these base lines are taut. Use staples instead of glue to attach yarn. Make a border to cover the staples and yarn ends.

**FIGURE 5-1** Booktalk 1, Charlottes Web, A Spiderweb

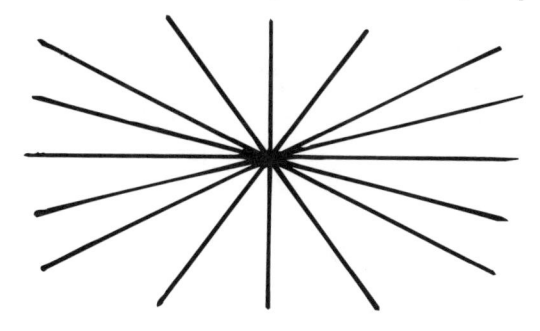

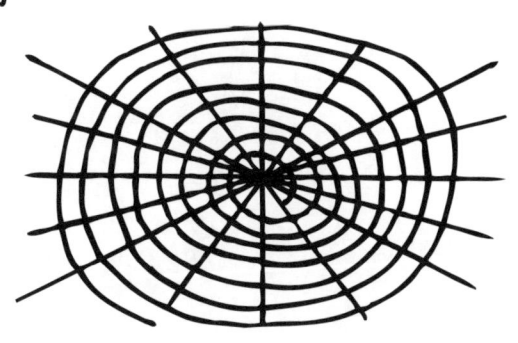

### BOOKTALK 2

# Cooper, Susan. *The Dark Is Rising.*

**BOOKTALK:** (Read first 12 paragraphs of Chapter 2.)

Will Stanton is not just an ordinary kid. When he wakes up on this Christmas morning, he is about to find out that he is the last of the Old Ones, a group of people who have a special mission—that of defeating the forces of evil in the world. To accomplish this, they must find some ancient objects that will give them the needed power. Will's mission is to find the six signs—a Celtic symbol of a circle quartered by a cross, each one made out of one of the primary elements: wood, bronze, fire, water, stone, and iron. Will tries to find these signs while learning of his newfound powers as an Old One.

## ACTIVITY: Making a Circle of Signs

Have the children make a circle of signs like the one Will made (Figure 5-2, Circle of Signs).

- Have the children trace the pattern and cut out six signs.
- Use a different color of paper to represent each element (wood, bronze, fire, water, stone, and iron), or trace them all on white paper and color them to look like the different elements.
- Each child needs to cut six strips of paper about 1" x 4", preferably from a gray paper (representing metal).
- Slip the strip of paper through the sides of two signs and glue. (This is somewhat like a paper chain, except you will be using the chain part to attach two signs together.)
- Continue until you have joined all the signs together into a circle.

**FIGURE 5-2** Booktalk 2, *The Dark is Rising*, Circle of Signs

## BOOKTALK 3

# L'Engle, Madeleine. *A Wrinkle in Time.*

**BOOKTALK:** Meg Murray's father has disappeared. He was working on a secret government project dealing with something called the *Tesseract*. Meg, her friend Calvin O'Keefe, and her precocious younger brother Charles Wallace want to find him, and get help from Mrs. Whatsit, Mrs. Who, and Mrs. Which, three unusual ladies whom Charles Wallace first met in the "old shingled house back in the woods that the kids won't go near because they say it's haunted."

These three weird ladies take Meg, Calvin, and Charles Wallace to a planet near where their father is. They explain that their father has been transported to a dark planet taken over by an evil force called simply "It." They explain that it is through the Tesseract that their father traveled there, and it is how they got where they are. (Read the explanation of "tesseract" in Chapter 5, beginning with "If a very small insect..." through "That is how we travel." Rather than reading it, you could visually explain it, using a chalkboard or other visual aid.)

Meg, Calvin, and Charles Wallace have to rescue Mr. Murray from this dark planet called Camazotz. When they arrive on the planet itself, they quickly begin to realize just how much the evil force has taken over. (Read from Chapter 6 just after the three asterisks beginning with "Below them the town was laid out in harsh, angular patterns" through "The doors clicked shut behind them.")

## ACTIVITY 1:
Show the video *Madeleine L'Engle: Stargazer* (Ishtar, 1990. 30 min.)

## ACTIVITY 2:
Use a long piece of paper to make a timeline of events that happened in the story.

## BOOKTALK 4

# Levine, Gail Carson. *Ella Enchanted.*

**BOOKTALK:** Did you know that "Cinderella" is one of the most popular stories in the world? Almost every country has a version of it. In Gail Levine's version of the story, Ella was enchanted at birth by the fairy Lucinda with a curse that should would always have to obey any command anyone gave her. Unlike the Disney cartoon, in which Cinderella had mice to help her, in this version Ella has to rely on her own wits.

Things get a little dicey when Ella gets captured by a band of ogres who want her for dinner. (Read from the beginning of Chapter 14 on page 96 through "The bubble burst" on page 98). Read the rest and find out if Ella is able to escape from this predicament, and from her curse.

### ACTIVITY 1: Play "Simon Says"

Let the children feel what it would be like to be cursed to obey every command. You could make the commands things the stepsisters would make her do, like sweeping or scrubbing the floor.

### ACTIVITY 2: Magic Slippers

Have the children bring a pair of old tennis shoes, and let them use glitter, markers, fabric paint, sequins, and buttons to design "magic slippers."

# BOOKTALK 5

# McKinley, Robyn. *Beauty.*

**BOOKTALK:** You probably have heard the story of "Beauty and the Beast." This book gives you the whole story. Beauty did not have that name at first. Her mother named her Honor. (Her two older sisters were named Grace and Hope.) When she was five, her father tried to explain to her what her name meant, but he couldn't make her understand. She said, "Huh, I'd rather be Beauty," and the name stuck.

Beauty is different from her sisters. She's the smartest and certainly the most bookish. Her father is a wealthy merchant, but the family's fortunes are ruined when his ships are sunk at sea. Where once they lived in a grand house with maids and servants, they now have to auction off all their belongings to pay off debts and move to a cottage near a forest with Gervain, who marries one of Beauty's sisters. They learn how to care for the house themselves and go on as best they can, but Beauty gets restless. (Read Chapter 3 from the beginning through the first three asterisks—"Tell your sisters I'll be in in a minute.") Of course, Beauty does go into the woods, and finds out the true nature of the beast who lives there.

## ACTIVITY 1: Picture the Beast

Show different versions of "Beauty and the Beast."

- Note the different ways the beast has been depicted.
- Have the children draw a picture of the way they think the beast should look.

## ACTIVITY 2: Design a Castle

- What would it look like?
- How many rooms would it have?
- What would the servants do?
- How many would there be?
- Would it be a modern castle, or an old one?

### BOOKTALK 6

# Banks, Lynne Reid. *The Indian in the Cupboard.*

**BOOKTALK:** Omri is not terribly pleased when his brother Patrick gives him a secondhand, plastic Indian for his birthday. He already has lots of plastic figures. He also gets a present from Gillon, his other brother, "a small white metal cupboard with a mirror in the door" that Gillon found with the trash in the alley. Omri finds a key that will make the cabinet lock. It's one of his mother's, which she got from her mother and which fits a jewelry box. Omri puts the Indian in the box, and as he drifts off to sleep that night, he hears a noise. (Read in Chapter 1 from the break where it begins, "In the morning there was no doubt about it..." through the end of the chapter.)

So what do you do with a tiny live Indian? How do you keep it a secret? What do you do when you realize that the Indian has to be treated like a human being? That's what this book is all about.

## ACTIVITY 1: A Shoebox Diorama

Make a shoebox diorama depicting a scene from *The Indian in the Cupboard*. (The bottom of the box will be the back, the side the bottom.)

- Cut a piece of paper to fit the bottom of the box.
- Draw a background and glue it in.
- Draw pictures of Omri, Little Bear, and any scenery you desire, and cut them out, leaving about 1/2" on the bottom.
- Fold this piece back, and use it to glue to the side of the box.
- If needed, make a brace by cutting a small strip of paper and gluing one end to the back of the figure and the other end to the box behind the figure.
- If desired, you can use plastic figures and add sticks, cotton, and fabric.
- All the children could participate in making one large diorama, or could make their own individual ones.
- These dioramas could be displayed in the library.

## BOOKTALK 7

# Cassedy, Sylvia. *Behind the Attic Wall.*

**BOOKTALK:** Maggie has been thrown out of more boarding schools than you can imagine, and is finally dispatched to live with her Uncle Morris. When she arrives at his house, she thinks it looks like all the other institutions and schools she's been in and out of. Maggie is not amused. She doesn't eat; she just plays with her food and makes terrible, yucky messes.

Uncle Morris says, "I think you are the right one after all." What does he mean by that? Maggie remains obstinate, not wanting to play with any toys when her aunts are around. When she is alone, she talks with five imaginary friends she calls "The Backwoods Girls"—all poorer, uglier, dirtier, and dumber than herself. As time passes, she begins to realize that she and her aunts and uncle are not alone in the house. (Read Chapter 12.) This is a suspenseful novel that doesn't resolve itself until the very last sentence of the book.

## ACTIVITY 1: An Anniversary Party

Have a party like the anniversary party Maggie has in Chapter 29. Serve cupcakes and play Blindman's Bluff. One person is blindfolded and tries to catch someone else.

## ACTIVITY 2: Imaginary Friends

Have the children draw pictures of imaginary friends. Have them describe the personality attributes of their imaginary friends.

### BOOKTALK 8

# Wrede, Patricia C. *Searching For Dragons.*

**BOOKTALK:** This is one of the four books in Patricia Wrede's "Enchanted Forest Chronicles." Mendanbar, King of the Enchanted Forest, becomes disturbed when parts of the forest appear to have been drained of all their magical power. He goes to Kazul, the King of the Dragons, only to find that Kazul is not in. However, her chief cook and librarian, Cimorene, is. (Kings can be male or female in the Dragon community.)

Kazul has, in fact, disappeared on a trip to visit her grandchildren, and Cimorene is about to set out in search of Kazul. Together, Mendabar and Cimorene travel on a magic carpet through the Enchanted Forest trying to unravel the mystery. At one of their stops, they meet Herman, who is a relative of a character you may recognize.

Read from Chapter 9, "In Which They Discover the Perils of Borrowed Equipment," beginning on page 114 with "ABSOLUTELY NOT!" through "...but they keep finding me anyway" on page 118. Herman's relative is, of course, Rumpelstiltskin.

## ACTIVITY 1: Guessing Game

Have children come up individually or in groups to act out a fairy tale character. The other children guess which character they are. A variation is to have a child choose a fairy tale character and play 20 Questions. The other children ask questions that can be answered only "yes" or "no" until the identity of the character has been guessed.

# PROGRAMMING WITH FANTASY: "OH, THE PLACES YOU'LL GO!"

In a library setting it is difficult to program for the same group of children in a regular weekly program. Public librarians do not have the captive audience that school librarians are blessed with. On the other hand, public librarians have more freedom in what they can do in terms of programming. It is possible to bring a regular group of children to the public library for programming, but it requires some flexibility and ingenuity. Many schools offer regularly scheduled after-school programs. If transportation is available, schools and agencies can tie in with your program. You can also contact child-care agencies and recreation centers that provide after-school care for school-age children. These groups can sometimes provide a ready-made audience for a weekly program. With good publicity, you should also get word of mouth, as well as fans of the particular books you'll be highlighting.

One challenge can be disparity in age ranges. It is difficult and awkward to do the same program for a first grader that you would do for a third or fourth grader. Because of this, it is advisable to advertise an age range for your program, or plan stories and activities that will appeal to the widest age range of children possible.

The joy of doing a weekly program for school-age children is that it provides the librarian with an opportunity to make a lasting impression on a group of children. It is fun to be able to have a group with whom you can share school-age materials and program in a little more sophisticated way than you can with preschool storytimes. You are able to introduce kids to books they might otherwise never have encountered and give them a positive identification with the library that will last a lifetime.

The following is a suggested series of weekly programs focusing on fantasy literature for school-age children under the umbrella title "Oh, the Places You'll Go!" This was the National Children's Book Week Theme for 1996 and seems especially appropriate for fantasy. These programs were designed to take children to a different place each week so that they could explore a fantasy book in their imagination.

## PROGRAM 1: "We're Off to See the Wizard"

The following are suggested elements for an Oz program. The book *The Wizard of Oz* will be 100 years old in the year 2000, which makes this an appropriate time for programming on this theme. You might consider playing music from the soundtrack of the movie *The Wizard of Oz* as the children are coming in. Reading aloud a chapter from the "Oz" books may encourage children to explore the series and will provide a good listening experience. Here are some suggested chapters from some of the Oz books that make good read-aloud sharing:

"A Highly Magnified History." *The Land of Oz.* Chapter 13.

"The Girl in the Chicken Coop." *Ozma of Oz.* Chapter 1.

"Tiktok the Machine Man." *Ozma of Oz.* Chapter 4.

"The Musiker." *The Road to Oz.* Chapter 8.

"The Nine Tiny Piglets." *Dorothy and the Wizard of Oz.* Chapter 17.

"How the Cuttenclips Lived." *The Emerald City of Oz.* Chapter 10.

"How They Matched the Fuddles." *The Emerald City of Oz.* Chapter 12.

"How Dorothy Visited Utensia." *The Emerald City of Oz.* Chapter 16.

"How They Came to Bunnybury." *The Emerald City of Oz.* Chapter 17.

"How They Encountered the Flutterbudgets." *The Emerald City of Oz.* Chapter 23.

"The Loons of Loonville." *The Tin Woodman of Oz.* Chapter 4.

### ACTIVITY 1: A Map of Oz

Give children a copy of the map of the Land of Oz. (See Figure 5-3, Map of Oz.) Have them color each country the appropriate color.

### ACTIVITY 2: Creative Dramatization

The following are two dramatizations to use in Oz programs with children. The first is an adaptation of the first book, *The Wizard of Oz*. The second is a scene from *The Land of Oz*, a hilarious take on communication problems. There are a number of possibilities for presenting the following scenes. The characters with speaking parts have been listed, but a number of characters without speaking parts can be added as your situation merits. You might consider asking kids from a high school drama class to come in to perform. You could have children take parts and read from the scripts. If you choose to present these plays more formally with rehearsals, you can make the costumes as simple (masks) or as complex as you like. Descriptions of the characters are found in *The Land of Oz*. This could also work as a puppet show.

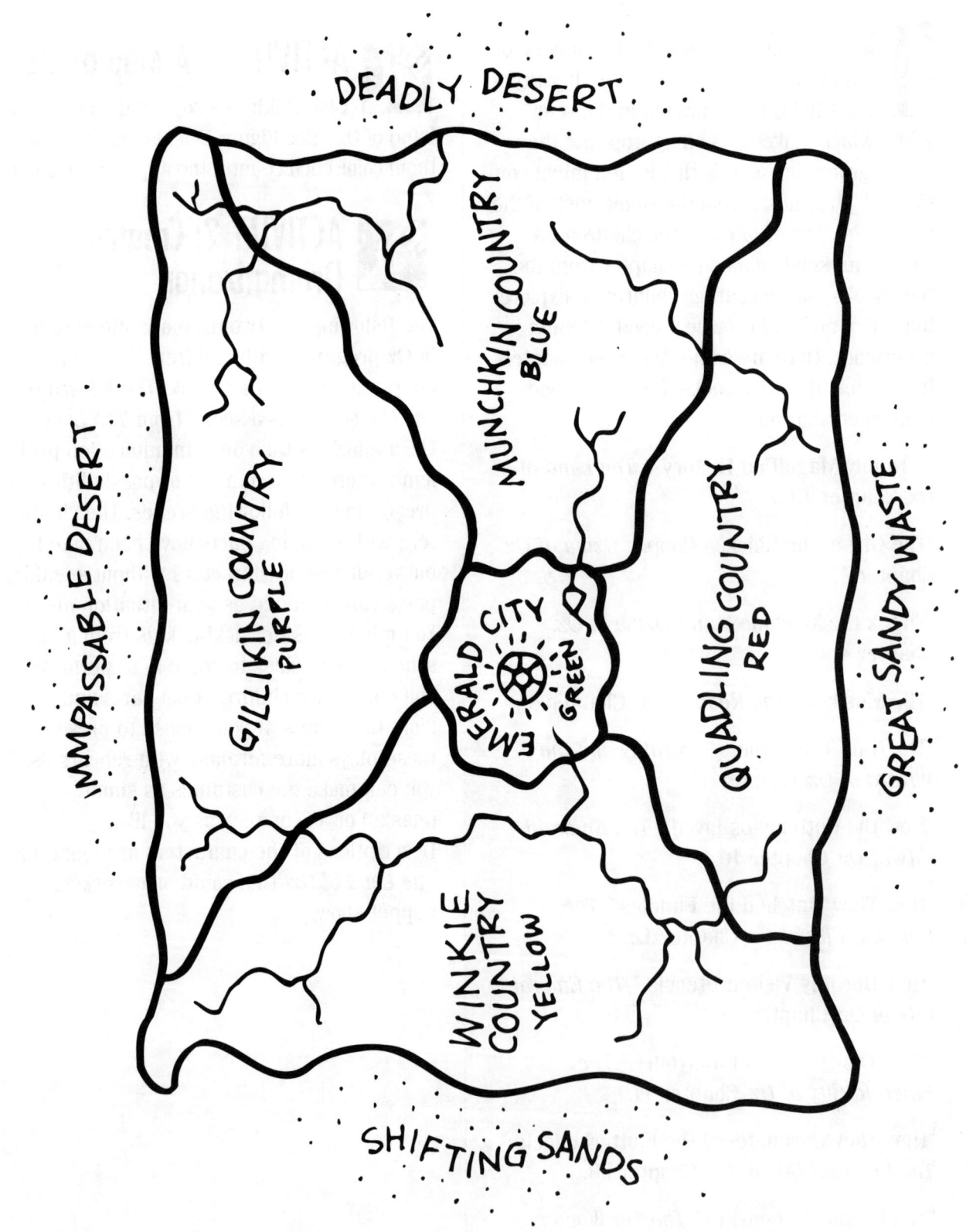

**FIGURE 5-3** Program 1, "We're off to See the Wizard", The Land of Oz

# The Wizard of Oz

Adapted from *The Wizard of Oz* by Tim Wadham

**CHARACTERS:**

Narrator
Dorothy
Glinda, the Good Witch
Scarecrow
Tin Man
Cowardly Lion
Wizard of Oz
Wicked Witch

**NARRATOR:** Dorothy lived in the middle of the great Kansas prairies with Uncle Henry, who was a farmer, and Aunt Em, his wife. One day a strange thing happened. From far north they heard a low wail on the wind. It was a cyclone coming. Dorothy couldn't get to the storm shelter because her dog Toto had run away, and when she caught him the wind was blowing too hard. The house whirled around two or three times and rose slowly in the air. Dorothy felt as if she were going up in a balloon. The wind howled terribly around her, but Dorothy soon closed her eyes and fell fast asleep.

*(Dorothy enters with Toto. She is rubbing her eyes as if she had just awakened.)*

**NARRATOR:** The cyclone had set her house down in the midst of a country of marvelous beauty.

**DOROTHY:** This doesn't look like Kansas anymore. *(Toto barks.)*

*(Munchkins gather around her, and then Glinda, the good witch, steps up to her.)*

**GLINDA:** Are you a good witch or a bad witch?

**DOROTHY:** I'm Dorothy Gale, from Kansas.

**GLINDA:** We are so grateful to you, Dorothy Gale from Kansas, for having killed the Wicked Witch of the East.

**DOROTHY:** There must be some mistake, I have not killed anything.

**GLINDA:** Your house did, anyway. She made the Munchkins her slaves for many years. Now they are all set free, and grateful to you for the favor.

**DOROTHY:** Who are the Munchkins?

**GLINDA:** They are the people who live in this land of the East. I am the witch of the North.

**DOROTHY:** Oh, gracious! Are you a real witch?

**GLINDA:** Yes, but I am a good witch.

**DOROTHY:** : I am anxious to get back to my Aunt Em and Uncle Henry. Can you help me?

**GLINDA:** The Land of Oz is surrounded on all sides by a deadly desert. You must go to the Emerald City to see the great Wizard of Oz.

**DOROTHY:**

**ALL:** Follow the yellow brick road!

**GLINDA:** Take these silver slippers. They will keep you from harm. Goodbye, my dear!

*(Dorothy and Toto skip down the yellow brick road. Soon they meet the Scarecrow.)*

**SCARECROW:** Good day.

**DOROTHY:** Did you speak?

**SCARECROW:** Certainly, how do you do?

**DOROTHY:** I'm pretty well, thank you. How do you do?

**SCARECROW:** I'm not thinking well. I don't have any brains.

**DOROTHY:** I'm going to see the wonderful Wizard of Oz. Maybe he can give you brains. *(She helps him down)*

**DOROTHY AND SCARECROW:** We're off to see the Wizard.

*(They soon come to the Tin Woodman)*

**TIN WOODMAN:** Oil can!

**DOROTHY:** Did you groan?

**TIN WOODMAN:** Oil can!

**SCARECROW:** I think he's saying "oil can."

*(Dorothy picks up the oil can that is sitting at the Tin Woodman's side and proceeds to oil his joints.)*

**TIN WOODMAN:** This is a great comfort. I have been holding this axe in the air ever since I rusted. I might have stood there always if you had not come along. How did you happen to be here?

**DOROTHY:** We are on our way to the Emerald City to see the great Oz. I want him to send me back to Kansas, and the Scarecrow wants him to put a few brains in his head.

**TIN WOODMAN:** Do you suppose Oz could get me a heart?

**DOROTHY:** Why, I guess so.

**ALL:** We're off to see the Wizard...

*(Cowardly Lion comes out and roars. Toto runs barking to him. The lion tries to bite him. Dorothy slaps the lion on the face.)*

**DOROTHY:** Don't you dare bite Toto! You ought to be ashamed of yourself. You are nothing but a big coward.

**COWARDLY LION:** I know it, but how can I help it?

**SCARECROW:** I am going to the great Oz to ask him to give me some brains.

**TIN WOODMAN:** And I am going to ask him to give me a heart.

**DOROTHY:** And I am going to ask him to send Toto and me back to Kansas.

**COWARDLY LION:** Do you think Oz could give me courage?

**DOROTHY:** Of course. Come along with us.

**ALL:** We're off to see the Wizard...

**NARRATOR:** After a long journey through a country that was sometimes pleasant and sometimes dark and terrible, our band of adventurers finally came to the Emerald City and were admitted to the presence of the great Oz.

*(Slide of Oz appears on the screen.)*

**VOICE OF OZ:** I am Oz, the great and terrible. Who are you, and why do you seek me?

**DOROTHY:** I am Dorothy, the small and meek. I have come to ask you to send Toto and me back to Kansas.

**SCARECROW:** I have come to ask you for brains.

**TIN WOODMAN:** *(so scared that his tin is clattering):* I have come to ask you for a heart.

**COWARDLY LION:** *(his knees beating together in fright):* And I have come. . . I have come. . . Aaaaaaargh!

*(He runs away.)*

**VOICE OF OZ:** Kill the Wicked Witch of the West, and I will grant you your desires.

**ALL:** What?

**VOICE OF OZ:** You heard what I said. Now go, and do not ask to see me again until you have done your task.

*(Oz disappears)*

**DOROTHY:** What shall we do now?

**COWARDLY LION:** There is only one thing we can do, and that is seek out the Wicked Witch and destroy her.

**DOROTHY:** But suppose we cannot?

**COWARDLY LION:** Then I shall never have courage.

**SCARECROW:** And I shall never have brains.

**TIN WOODMAN:** And I shall never have a heart.

**DOROTHY:** And I shall never see Aunt Em and Uncle Henry. I suppose we must try it, then.

**NARRATOR:** Therefore, the adventurers decided to start upon their journey the next morning. *(They go off. On the other side of the stage, the Wicked Witch enters with her crystal ball.)*

**WITCH:** I see them coming. When they get here, I will have my flying monkeys tear them to pieces! All except the girl. I want her silver slippers. *(She cackles her very best witch cackle.)*

*(Dorothy and the others arrive at the Witch's castle.)*

**WITCH:** Come in, my pretty.

*(The witch has set a trap for Dorothy. She has placed an iron bar in the middle of the floor, and as Dorothy walks toward the Witch she trips over it and loses her shoe. The witch grabs it.)*

**DOROTHY:** Give me my shoe!

**WITCH:** I will not, for now it is my shoe and not yours.

**DOROTHY:** You are a wicked creature! You have no right to take my shoe away from me.

**WITCH:** I shall keep it, just the same. And some day I shall get the other one from you, too.

*(This makes Dorothy very angry. She grabs a bucket and throws its contents on the witch.*

*Note: Since you can't have real water, fill the bucket with blue confetti.)*

**WITCH:** See what you have done! In a minute I shall melt away. Didn't you know water would be the end of me?

**DOROTHY:** Of course not. How should I? I am very sorry, indeed.

**WITCH:** Help! I'm melting, I'm melting...
*(She lets out one last scream.)*

**NARRATOR:** The travelers returned to the Emerald City, where they were received as heroes. Word that the Wicked Witch had been killed by a small, simple girl from Kansas had spread quickly. They were once again received into the presence of the great Oz. *(Slide of Oz appears on the screen again.)*

**VOICE OF OZ:** I am Oz, the great and terrible. Who are you, and why do you seek me?

**DOROTHY:** We have come to claim our promise, oh great Oz.

**VOICE OF OZ:** What promise?

**DOROTHY:** You promised to send me back to Kansas.

**SCARECROW:** You promised to give me brains.

**TIN WOODMAN:** And you promised to give me a heart.

**COWARDLY LION:** And you promised to give me courage.

**VOICE OF OZ:** Is the Wicked Witch really destroyed?

**DOROTHY:** I have brought back her broomstick, just as you asked.

**VOICE OF OZ:** Dear me. I shall have to have time to think this over.

*(During this last conversation Toto has seen something at the side of the stage. He opens*

*the door and reveals the real wizard, a small man who looks out in horror at the others.)*

**WIZARD:** I am Oz, the great and terrible.

**DOROTHY:** You're just a humbug.

**WIZARD:** Exactly so. I am a humbug.

**TIN WOODMAN:** But this is terrible. How shall I ever get my heart?

**COWARDLY LION:** Or I my courage?

**SCARECROW:** Or I my brains?

**DOROTHY:** Or I to Kansas? I think you are a very bad man.

**WIZARD:** Oh no, my dear. I'm really a very good man; I'm just a very bad wizard.

**NARRATOR:** But the Wizard was as good as his word. He gave the Scarecrow a diploma in recognition of his intelligence; he gave the Tin Man a heart that ticked; and he gave the Cowardly Lion a medal for bravery. Getting Dorothy back to Kansas was another matter entirely. The Wizard turned out to be a balloon artist from Kansas, and he had come to Oz accidentally in his balloon. He decided to fix it and travel back to Kansas with Dorothy. But just as they were about to lift off, Toto ran out. Dorothy ran to catch him, but before she could get back to the balloon, the great humbug wizard was already flying away. Just when Dorothy thought she would never get back to Kansas again, Glinda, the good Witch, appeared.

**GLINDA:** Your silver shoes will carry you across the desert. You have had the power to go home right with you all the time. All you have to do is click your heels together three times and say, "There's no place like home!"

*(Dorothy waves goodbye to all her friends and clicks her heels three times, saying the words Glinda told her. Blackout. When the lights come back up, Dorothy is back in Kansas. She runs back into the waiting arms of Aunt Em.)*

**DOROTHY:** Oh, Aunt Em, I've been to the Land of Oz, and oh, Aunt Em, I'm so glad to be home again!

# I Do Not Understand You

Adapted from Chapter 7 of *The Land of Oz* by Tim Wadham

**CHARACTERS:**
Narrator
Soldier
Scarecrow
Jellia Jamb
Jack Pumpkinhead

**NARRATOR:** I'll bet you might not know that L. Frank Baum wrote a total of 14 books about Oz. In the second book, *The Land of Oz,* the Scarecrow is now ruler of Oz. In the north part of Oz there is a boy named Tip who lives as a prisoner of the old Witch Mombi. Tip has built a wooden man with a pumpkin head to scare Mombi, but instead, she used the pumpkin man to try out a new magic potion she has acquired, the Powder of Life. She uses it to bring the pumpkin-headed man to life.

Later, Tip escapes with the man, whom he's named Jack Pumpkinhead. They steal Mombi's powder and use it to bring a wooden sawhorse to life, and Jack rides the Sawhorse to the Emerald City with Tip at his side. As they near the Emerald City, Tip gives the Sawhorse the command to "Trot," which the Sawhorse remembers as a command to go as fast as he can, and he does, leaving poor Tip in the dust. Jack Pumpkinhead arrives in the Emerald City with the Sawhorse and is immediately escorted into the presence of the Scarecrow.

*(Scene: The Throne Room of the Emerald City)*

**SCARECROW:** Where on earth did you come from, and how do you happen to be alive?

**JACK:** I beg your Majesty's pardon, but I do not understand you.

**SCARECROW:** What don't you understand?

**JACK:** Why, I don't understand your language. You see, I come from the country of the Gillikins, so I am a foreigner.

**SCARECROW:** Ah, to be sure. I myself speak the language of the Munchkins, which is also the language of the Emerald City. But you, I suppose, speak the language of the Pumpkinheads?

**JACK:** Exactly so, your Majesty. So it will be impossible for us to understand one another.

**SCARECROW:** That is unfortunate. Certainly we must have an interpreter.

**JACK:** What is an interpreter?

**SCARECROW:** A person who understands both my language and your own. When I say anything, the interpreter can tell you what I mean; and when you say anything, the interpreter can tell me what you mean. For the interpreter can speak both languages as well as understand them.

**JACK:** That is certainly clever.
*(Enter the Soldier with the Green Whiskers.)*

**SCARECROW:** Soldier, I command you to search among my people until you find one who understands the language of the Gillikins as well as the language of the Emerald City, and bring this person to me at once.
*(Soldier bows and departs.)*

**SCARECROW:** *(to Jack Pumpkinhead again):* Won't you take a chair while you are waiting?

**JACK:** Your Majesty forgets that I cannot understand you. If you wish for me to sit down, you must make a sign for me to do so.

*(The Scarecrow looks puzzled. Not knowing what to do, he goes over to Jack and pushes him into a sitting position.)*

**SCARECROW** *(politely):* Did you understand that sign?

**JACK:** Perfectly.

*(Jellia Jamb enters.)*

**SCARECROW:** Why, it's little Jellia Jamb! Do you understand the language of the Gillikins, my dear?

**JELLIA JAMB:** Yes, your Majesty, for I was born in the North Country.

**SCARECROW:** Then you shall be my interpreter and explain to this pumpkinhead all I say, and also explain to me all that he says. Is this arrangement satisfactory?

**JELLIA JAMB:** Very satisfactory, indeed.

**SCARECROW:** Then ask him to begin with what brought him to the Emerald City.

**JELLIA JAMB** *(to Jack):* You are certainly a wonderful creature. Who made you?

**JACK:** A boy named Tip.

**SCARECROW:** What did he say? My ears must have deceived me. What did he say?

**JELLIA JAMB:** He says that your Majesty's brains seem to have come loose.

**SCARECROW** *(sighing):* What a fine thing it is to understand two different languages. Ask him, my dear, if he has any objection to being put in jail for insulting the ruler of the Emerald City.

**JACK:** I didn't insult you.

**SCARECROW:** Tut, tut! Wait until Jellia translates my speech. What have we got an interpreter for?

**JACK:** All right, I'll wait. Translate the speech, young woman.

**JELLIA JAMB:** His Majesty inquired if you are hungry.

**JACK:** Oh, not at all! It is impossible for me to eat.

**SCARECROW:** It is the same with me. What did he say, Jellia, my dear?

**JELLIA JAMB:** He asked if you are aware that one of your eyes is painted larger than the other?

**JACK:** Don't believe her, your Majesty.

**SCARECROW:** Oh, I don't. (to Jellia) Are you quite certain you understand the languages of both the Gillikins and the Munchkins?

**JELLIA JAMB:** Quite certain, your Majesty.

**SCARECROW:** Then how is it that I seem to understand them myself?

**JELLIA JAMB:** Because they are one and the same! Does not your Majesty know that in all the land of Oz but one language is spoken?

**SCARECROW:** Is it indeed so? Then I might have easily been my own interpreter!

**JACK:** It is all my fault, your Majesty. I thought we must surely speak different languages since we came from different countries.

**SCARECROW:** Ah, as we have now resolved the matter, let us be friends.

*(Jellia Jamb and Soldier are dismissed. When they are gone, Scarecrow takes his new friend by the arm and they exit.)*

# PROGRAM 2: Camelot: Stories of King Arthur

**BOOK:** Shannon, Mark. *Sir Gawain and the Green Knight*

## ACTIVITY 1: Calligraphy

Teach the children basic calligraphy strokes. Have them write their own names in the style of writing that would have been used in King Arthur's time. They can write their names with the title Lord or Lady, Duke or Duchess, or Knight. A great book for reference is Drogin, Marc. *Yours Truly, King Arthur: How Medieval People Wrote, and How You Can Too* (New York: Taplinger, 1982).

## ACTIVITY 2: Round Table

Discuss with the children stories of King Arthur. They may already be familiar with the story of the sword in the stone and how Arthur became king. They may not be as familiar with the stories of the knights of the round table, nor of the stories of Arthur's death and his prophesied return. One good way to do this program is to have the children sit around a large round table, if one is available.

## PROGRAM 3: The Enchanted Forest–Fairy Tales

### BOOKS:

Wrede, Patricia. *Book of Enchantment*

Levine, Gail Carson. *The Princess Test*

"The Slow Ogre" from *Fantastic Stories* by Terry Jones

### ACTIVITY 1: Magic Kitchen Utensils

Read "Utensile Strength," a hilarious story that takes about 30 minutes to read, so allow for time. In the story, a young man named Tamriff comes to visit King Mendanbar and Queen Cimorene of the Enchanted Forest. He is at a loss as to what to do with a frying pan, on which his enchanter father has accidentally cast a spell. It is now a dangerous weapon, "The Frying Pan of Doom." It is decided that a cooking contest will be held in conjunction with a tournament which all knights and heroes will attend in order to find out who may rightfully wield "The Frying Pan of Doom." As it turns out, this weapon has the power to turn people into poached eggs!

- Bring a frying pan and other common kitchen utensils.
- Tell the children that the frying pan is "The Frying Pan of Doom."
- The one in the story is hot to the touch, so make sure you bring a hot pad or mitt.
- Then show the other utensils.
- Ask the children to tell you what each of these might be called if it were a weapon, and what it might do. For example, children might dub a fork "The Fork of Fear" and decide that it would turn you into scrambled eggs.

- At the end of the story, Wrede includes a recipe for "Quick After-Battle Triple Chocolate Cake." If you are so inclined, you may wish to make this recipe for a refreshment after the program.

### ACTIVITY 2: A Princess Test

After reading or retelling Gail Levine's short novella, *The Princess Test*, discuss how this story compares to Hans Christian Andersen's original tale, "The Princess and the Pea." In *The Princess Test*, the King and Queen make the prospective princesses undergo a number of tests beyond feeling a pea under a mountain of mattresses, such as finding a sprig of parsley in a bouquet of flowers, and finding an uncooked noodle in a salad.

- Have the kids develop their own prince or princess tests and act them out.
- If you meet regularly in the same location, you might introduce this activity by changing the location of a piece of furniture or other object.
- Then have the children try to determine what is different.

### ACTIVITY 3: Walk Like an Ogre

Read or tell "The Slow Ogre" from *Fantastic Stories* by Terry Jones. This is a story especially suited for telling if you have the time to learn it.

- The kids might have fun acting out the Ogre's slow walk.
- The Ogre's favorite foods are cabbages, sausages, and radishes. You might consider cole slaw or finger sausages as a refreshment.

**PROGRAM 4**

# The Imagination of Chris VanAllsburg

**BOOK:** VanAllsburg, Chris. *The Mysteries of Harris Burdick*

**ACTIVITY: Build a Story**

Use the new portfolio edition of *The Mysteries of Harris Burdick*.
- Have the children sit in a circle.
- Tell the children the title of one of the pictures and read the caption.
- Using the caption as a starting point, hand the picture to the child next to you and have that child add a sentence or two to the story.
- That child in turn hands it to the next child, and so on.
- You might start the program by telling children about Chris VanAllsburg and showing the children some of his other books.

**PROGRAM 5**

# A Birthday Party for Pooh

**BOOKS:** Milne, A. A. *Winnie the Pooh* and *The House at Pooh Corner*

**ACTIVITY: Pooh and Friends**

Read Chapter 2 "In Which Pooh Goes Visiting and Gets Into a Tight Place," the account of the time Pooh visited Rabbit but ate so much honey that he got stuck in Rabbit's hole trying to get out.
- Play Pin the Tail on Eeyore.
- Have appropriate birthday refreshments and sing "Happy Birthday" to Pooh.
- You might also want to share some of the delightful poems from *When We Were Very Young* (New York: Puffin, 1992) and *Now We Are Six* (New York: Puffin, 1992). Some of our favorites from the first book are "Happiness," "The Four Friends," "Disobedience," and "Politeness."

## PROGRAM 6: Scotland and Canada

**BOOKS:** Cooper, Susan. *The Boggart* and *The Boggart and the Monster*

### ACTIVITY 1: Picture the Boggart

The Boggart is a mischievous poltergeist who lives in a castle in Scotland. When the owner dies, the closest relatives, the Volnicks of Toronto, inherit the castle. They travel to Scotland and ship things back that can be sold in their antique business. Unfortunately, they also unknowingly ship the Boggart to Toronto. The Boggart has never experienced modern wonders, such as electricity.

- Read the scenes in which the Boggart discovers pizza and ice cream (pages 62-65), or in which the Boggart steals a peanut butter and jelly sandwich (pages 70-73).
- Since the Boggart is never really described but moves about invisibly playing his tricks, have the children draw a picture of what they think he might look like.

### ACTIVITY 2: Decorate a Loch Ness Monster

Introduce *The Boggart and the Monster* by explaining that in the book, the Loch Ness monster is discovered to be a Boggart who has taken on the shape of the monster and cannot return to his original form.

- Have the children decorate a Loch Ness monster. You can create one as you would a piñata, with newspaper strips dripped in flour paste, placed over the form of the monster created with balloons.
- If you want to have this done beforehand, then all the children would have to do is decorate it.
- Display the monster in your school or library.

## PROGRAM 7: London

**BOOK:** Smith, Dodie. *The Hundred and One Dalmatians*

### ACTIVITY: Pet Care

Read the first chapter up to the appearance of Cruella De Ville.

- Ask the children what differences there are between the novel and the Disney version.
- Ask someone from the local SPCA or a kennel club to bring a Dalmatian and talk about how to care for dogs in general.

## PROGRAM 8: Narnia

**BOOKS:** Lewis, C. S. "The Chronicles of Narnia"

### ACTIVITY: Creative Dramatization

Read the new picture book versions of the Narnia stories: *The World of Narnia: Lucy Steps Through the Wardrobe* (Illustrated by Deborah Maze. New York: HarperCollins, 1950, 1997) and *The World of Narnia: Edmund and the White Witch.* (Illustrated by Deborah Maze. New York: HarperCollins, 1950, 1997).

- Have the children act various scenes from *The Lion, the Witch and the Wardrobe.* A published dramatization is also available to help you, as well as a graphic novel adaptation.
- You might consider a few simple props. A bell that signals the White Witch's approach is nice, as are simple crowns, when the children are crowned rulers of Narnia.

## PROGRAM 9: Outer Space

**BOOK:** L'Engle, Madeleine. *A Wrinkle in Time.*

### ACTIVITY: A Coordination Exercise

You can use the activities suggested with the booktalk mentioned above. In addition, you might ask your local recreation center if you can borrow some balls and jump ropes.

- Have the children stand in two straight lines facing each other.
- See if they can bounce the balls and jump rope in unison. It's more difficult than it sounds.

## PROGRAM 10 | The Internet

**BOOK:** Vande Velde, Vivian. "Curses, Inc.," from *Curses Inc. and Other Stories.*

**ACTIVITY: Design a Web Page**

Read the story, which is about Bill Essler trying to get revenge on Denise Bainbridge after she embarrasses him in front of the whole school. In fact, she does this with good reason, because Bill has backed out of his invitation to the graduation dance at the last moment. He goes home and discovers a site on the World Wide Web called Curses, Inc., that allows him to order curses and hexes and place them on anyone he chooses. But none of his curses have the intended effect. This story has a terrific trick ending, which we won't spoil by revealing it.

- Have the children design home pages for the Curses, Inc. site, or for their own sites.
- They can draw these on paper, or if you have access to computers with drawing programs or an actual program that creates Web pages such as Web Workshop, the children can accomplish this on the computer.

## PROGRAM 11 | Earth

**BOOKS:** Applegate, K. A. *The "Animorphs" Series*

**ACTIVITY: An "Animorphs Fan Club" Program**

If you have Internet access, the Animorphs site at <www.scholastic.com> has updates on new books and transcripts of Applegate's answers to children's questions. You might want to begin with a discussion of why the children like the Animorphs books, which ones they like best, and which characters or scenes are their favorites.

- Have each child choose the animal he or she would most like to morph.
- Have children draw pictures of themselves morphing into the animal they choose.
- An Animorphs fan club program could develop into a monthly event with discussions of the newest entries in the series.

## PROGRAM 12 | Hogwarts

**BOOKS:** Rowling, J. K. *Harry Potter and the Sorcerer's Stone* and *Harry Potter and the Chamber of Secrets*

**ACTIVITY: Brewing a Wizard's Potion**

Pretend you're at Hogwarts School for Witchcraft and Wizardry attending your potions class. Here's a simple recipe for a "wizard's potion" that will create a little fizz.

- Fill a cup or bottle about halfway with white vinegar.
- Add two to three tablespoons of baking soda, making sure you have a pan underneath to catch the overflow.

Scholastic has created a Harry Potter Web site at <www.scholastic.com/tradebks/harrypotter> that includes a helpful discussion guide and biography of the author, J. K. Rowling.

## PROGRAM 13 | Redwall

**BOOKS:** Jacques, Brian. The "Redwall" books

**ACTIVITY: A Great Redwall Feast**

This is a good activity to end your program. The book *The Great Redwall Feast* can be read in one sitting with a few judicious cuts to make the story flow more quickly. Display the Redwall map available in *the Redwall Map and Riddler* (1998), available from Philomel, the publisher of the "Redwall" books. This package includes a quiz book that includes riddles, questions, puzzles and "cryptic conumdrums" that young Redwall fans will enjoy. For the feast itself, get foods that small animals would eat, such as nuts, cheese, and berries.

# FANTASY STORYTIMES FOR YOUNGER CHILDREN
## Sharing Traditional Fantasy

### STORYTIME 1

## Animal Fables: All the Miles of a Hard Road Are Worth One Moment of True Happiness.

**BOOKS:** Lobel, Arnold. *Fables*
Aesop. *Fables*

**FILMS:** *Aesop's Fables.* (Films Incorporated, 1975. 27 min).
*The Tortoise and the Hare.* (Walt Disney Educational Media, 1984)

### ACTIVITY 1: Act Out a Fable

Have props ready and act out some of the fables.

- For example, in "The Bear and the Crow" from Lobel's *Fables*, a bear is dressed in his finest hat, coat, vest, and shiny shoes to go to town.
- He meets a crow, who tells him that the gentlemen in town are wearing frying pans on their heads, bed sheets wrapped around them, and paper bags on their feet.
- The bear, eager to be in fashion, changes before going into town, where everyone laughs at him.
- He goes back to the crow, who tells him, "I told you many things, but never once did I tell you that I was telling the truth."
- The moral of the story is, "When the need is strong, there are those who will believe anything."
- For props use dress shoes, a sheet, two paper bags and a frying pan.

(Other favorites are "The Bad Kangaroo," "The Pelican and the Crane," "The Hippopotamus at Dinner," or "The Mouse at the Seashore.")

### ACTIVITY 2: Matching Fables to Morals

Have the children draw a moral from a hat and read it. Tell some fables (without telling the morals) and have the children try to guess which fable matches their moral. The best known Aesop fables for this are

- "Androcles and the Lion" (Gratitude is the sign of noble souls.)
- "The Ant and the Grasshopper" (It is best to prepare for the days of necessity.)
- "The Dog in the Manger" (People often begrudge others what they cannot enjoy themselves.)
- "The Fox and the Grapes" (It is easy to despise what you cannot get.)
- "The Hare and the Tortoise" (Slow but steady wins the race.)
- "The Lion and the Mouse" (Little friends may prove great friends.)
- "The Shepherd's Boy" (A liar will not be believed, even when he speaks the truth.)
- "The Wolf in Sheep's Clothing" (Appearances are deceptive.)
- "The Town Mouse and the Country Mouse" (Better beans and bacon in peace than cakes and ale in fear.)

**VARIATION:** Note that several of these stories have been adapted as picture books, notably "The Town Mouse and the Country Mouse." James Daugherty's *Andy and the Lion* (New York: Viking, 1938) is a modern retelling of "Androcles and the Lion". One of the best Aesop fables for creative dramatization is "The Hare and the Tortoise."

- You can stage the race in an auditorium, or even around the library.
- You could also have the children try writing their own fable or illustrating a fable.

## STORYTIME 2

# Trip Trap, Meow, Huff Puff.

**STORIES:** "The Three Billy Goats Gruff," "The Three Little Kittens, and "The Three Little Pigs"

Any version of these stories will do. We prefer Marcia Brown's version of "The Three Billy Goats Gruff" and Paul Galdone's versions of "The Three Little Kittens" and "The Three Little Pigs."

### RHYME: Pussy Cat, Pussy Cat

Pussy cat, pussy cat,
Where have you been?
I've been to London
To look at the Queen.
Pussy cat, pussy cat,
What did you there?
I frightened a little mouse
Under her chair.

### ACTIVITY 1: Color Cutout Mittens

After reading "The Three Little Kittens," have the children color paper cutout mittens. (See Figure 5-4, Mittens). For variety, They could dip Q-tips in paint to make polka dots on their mittens.

### ACTIVITY 2: Playhouses

Use appliance boxes to make a simple straw house, stick house, and brick house. After telling the story of "The Three Little Pigs," let the children play in the houses or use the houses as props and have the children act out the story.

**VARIATIONS:**

Any of the classic fairy tales in simple editions can be introduced at this point.

- James Marshall's are certainly among the choicest and funniest of the newer adaptations for slightly older children. His "Three Bears" adds some amusing touches to the basic story. His "Little Red Riding Hood" is also nice.

- For a storytime for older children, you could pair familiar fairy tales with multicultural variants, or compare and contrast the two versions. The best examples are Ed Young's *Yeh Shen: A Cinderella Story from China* and the Caldecott winner, *Lon Po Po: A Red Riding Hood Story from China.*

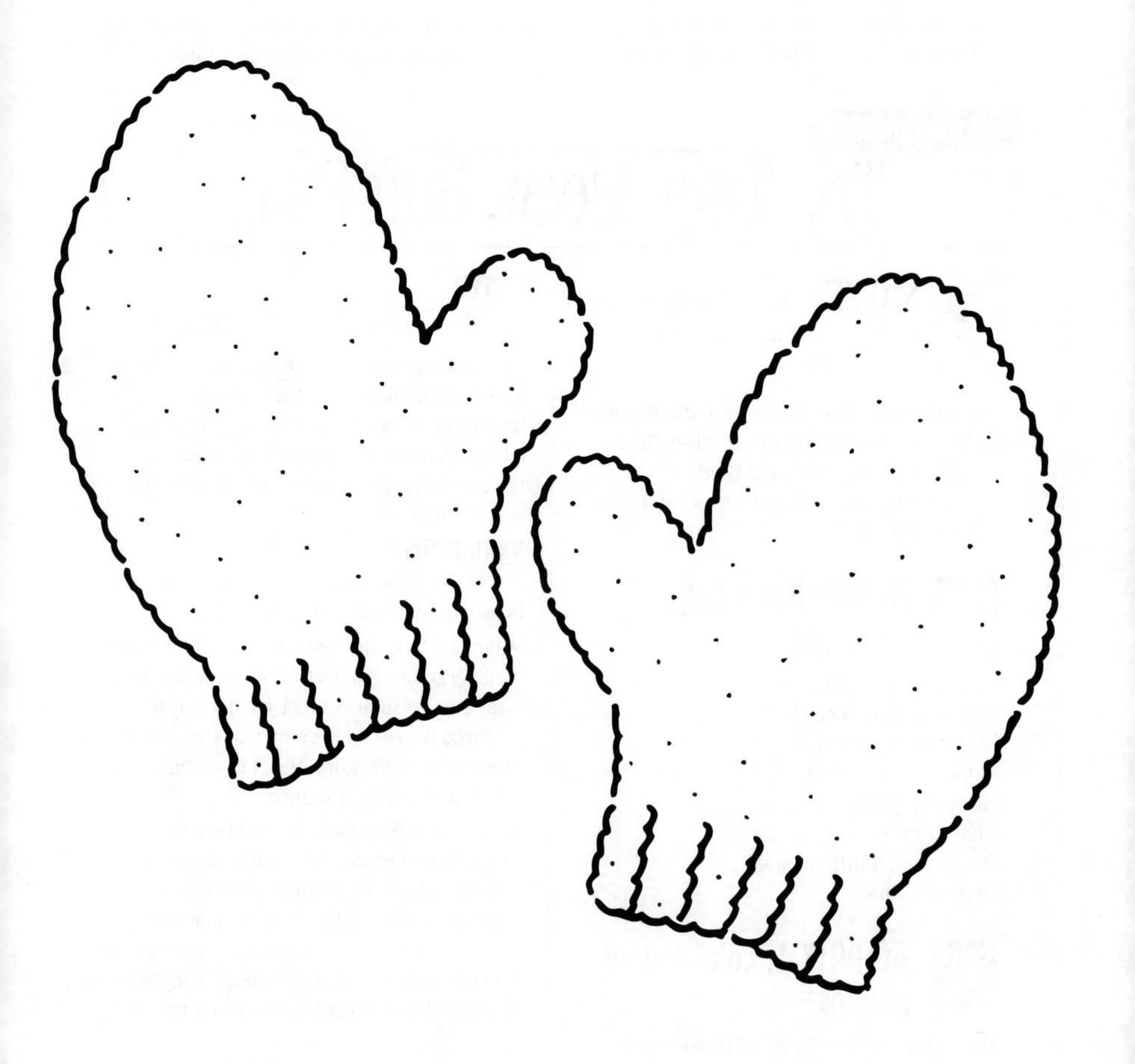

**FIGURE 5-4** Storytime 2, Trip Trap, Meow, Huff Puff, Mittens

## STORYTIME 3
# The Sky Is Falling! The Sky Is Falling!

### STORIES: "Henny Penny," "The Little Red Hen," and "Chicken Little"

We like Steven Kellogg's version of "Chicken Little," which is a bit more modern. It could be paired with Paul Galdone's "Henny Penny," which is a more traditional retelling. Paul Galdone and Margot Zemach have illustrated two good versions of "The Little Red Hen".

### RHYME: Hickety, Pickety, My Black Hen

Hickety, pickety, my black hen,
She lays eggs for gentlemen;
Gentlemen come every day
To see what my black hen doth lay.

### RHYME: Cock a Doodle Doo! My Dame Has Lost Her Shoe

Cock a doodle doo!
My dame has lost her shoe,
My master's lost his fiddling stick
And knows not what to do.

Cock a doodle doo!
What is my dame to do?
Till master finds his fiddling stick
She'll dance without her shoe.

Cock a doodle doo!
My dame has found her shoe,
And master's found his fiddling stick
Sing doodle doodle doo.

Cock a doodle doo!
My dame will dance with you,
While master fiddles his fiddling stick
For dame and doodle doo.

### RHYME: The Cock's on the Rooftop

The cock's on the rooftop
Blowing his horn,
The bull's in the barn
A-threshing the corn,
The maids in the meadow
Are making the hay,
The ducks in the river
Are swimming away.

### ACTIVITY 1: Make Bread

After reading "The Little Red Hen," let the children help you make some bread.

- For quick easy bread, use a bread mix made for bread-making machines and follow the manual directions.
- If you prefer, use your own recipe, but there won't be enough time for it to rise and bake, so have some already made.
- If you do not have cooking facilities, bring several types of bread for the children to taste.
- Ask a local bakery or grocery store to donate supplies.
- Bring in wheat grains to show the children.

### ACTIVITY 2: The Sky Is Falling

Before reading "Chicken Little" or "Henny Penny," let the children use a marker to draw faces on acorns.

- As you tell the story, let the children hold their acorns over their heads.
- When the acorn falls in the story, they drop their acorns on their heads. (They leave their acorns in their hands and just touch their heads with them.)

### STORYTIME 4

# She Ate it All!

### 📖 BOOKS:
Bonne, Rose. *I Know an Old Lady*
Bowden, Joan Chase. *The Bean Boy*
Domanska, Janina. *The Turnip*
Kent, Jack. *The Fat Cat*
Ness, Evaline. *Mr. Miacca*

### RHYME: Jack Sprat
Jack Sprat would eat no fat,
His wife would eat no lean,
And so between them both, you see,
They licked the platter clean.

### RHYME: Little Tommy Tucker
Little Tommy Tucker
Sings for his supper:
What shall we give him?
White bread and butter.
How shall he cut it
Without e'er a knife?
How will he be married
Without e'er a wife?

### POEMS:
"Boa Constrictor" and "I Must Remember" from Silverstein, Shel. *Where the Sidewalk Ends*

### ACTIVITY 1: Creative Dramatization
After reading *The Turnip*, have the children help you dramatize the story.

### ACTIVITY 2: Picture the Animals
After reading *I Know An Old Lady*, have the children draw a picture of all of the animals inside the old lady.

**VARIATIONS:** *Mother, Mother I Feel Sick* (New York: Parent's Magazine Press, 1966) by Remy Charlip and Burton Supree could be used as a creative dramatization or shadow play. Basic to either one is a box of ordinary junk under a table.

- A sheet in front of the table hides the box.
- The child is sick, so the mother takes him to the doctor.
- The doctor puts him on the table and operates.
- He pulls things out of the box, but it looks as if they are coming out of the boy.

To do the shadow play, set up the same way except

- Hang the bed sheet in front of a table.
- Place a very strong lamp behind the table and actors.
- The audience, seated in the dark on the other side of the sheet, will see only the shadows.
- You can make up things to say based on what sort of junk you have in the box.

Two other storytimes offer variations on this theme using books that are not folktales, but contain elements of fantasy.

- The first is to expand on the idea to create an "Enormous Foods" storytime. Books you can use are David Weisner's *June 29, 1999*; *The Enormous Vegetable Garden* by Nadine Bernard Westcott; and *Cloudy With a Chance of Meatballs* by Judi and Ron Barrett.
- The other option is to add Aliki's *Keep Your Mouth Closed, Dear* to *The Fat Cat* and *I Know an Old Lady*. Or you can gear the storytime to table manners and use *Dinner at Alberta's* by Russell Hoban.

**STORYTIME 5**

# We Mice Are the Greatest of All

### BOOKS:
Brett, Jan. *Town Mouse, Country Mouse*

Ivimey, John W. *Complete Story of the Three Blind Mice*

Morimoto, Junko. *Mouse's Marriage*

Steptoe, John. *The Story of Jumping Mouse*

Young, Ed. *Seven Blind Mice*

### RHYME: John Watts

Pretty John Watts,
We are troubled with rats.
Will you drive them out of the house?
We have mice too in plenty
That feast in the pantry,
But let them stay
And nibble away;
What harm is a little brown mouse?

### RHYME: Six Little Mice

Six little mice sat down to spin;
Pussy passed by and she peeped in.
What are you doing, my little men?
Weaving coats for gentlemen.
Shall I come in and cut off your threads?
No, no, Mistress Pussy, you'd bite off our heads.
Oh, no, I'll not; I'll help you to spin.
That may be so, but you can't come in.

### ACTIVITY 1: Guess What This Is

After reading *Seven Blind Mice*, blindfold several children.

- Bring in several objects and let children feel different parts of each object.
- Based on the part they felt, have them guess what it is.
- Do this with several objects so that each child can have a turn.
- Could they guess by only touching one part?

**NOTE:** Many young children do not like to be blindfolded; instead, put the objects in a pillowcase and ask the children to reach into the bag, feel an object, and describe it.

### ACTIVITY 2: A Puppet Show

Put on the puppet show *The Greatest of All*, or use the script to put on a play. (Figures 5-5 through 5-12 are patterns for simple puppets.)

- Color and mount on lightweight cardboard.
- Cut out puppets.
- Attach craft sticks to the backs.

**FIGURE 5-5** Storytime 5, We Mice Are the Greatest of All, Father Mouse

**FIGURE 5-6** Storytime 5, We Mice Are the Greatest of All, Cloud

**FIGURE 5-7** Storytime 5, We Mice Are the Greatest of All, Daughter

**FIGURE 5-8** Storytime 5, We Mice Are the Greatest of All, Wind

Bringing Fantasy Alive for Children and Young Adults | 99 | Chapter 5: Programming Fantasy

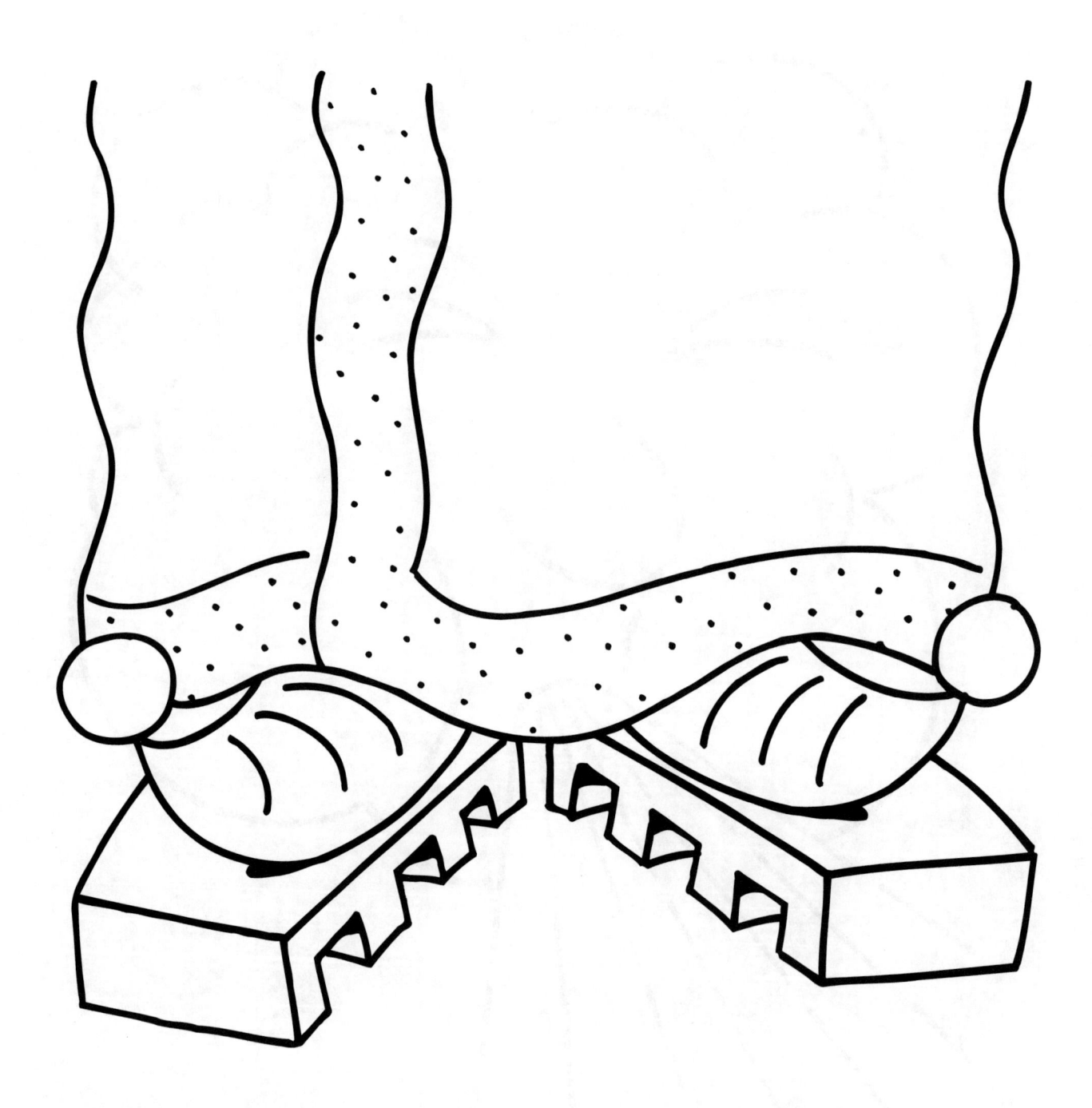

**FIGURE 5-9** Storytime 5, We Mice Are the Greatest of All, Emporer

**FIGURE 5-10** Storytime 5, We Mice Are the Greatest of All, Wall

**FIGURE 5-11** Storytime 5, We Mice Are the Greatest of All, Sun

**FIGURE 5-12** Storytime 5, We Mice Are the Greatest of All, Field Mouse

Bringing Fantasy Alive for Children and Young Adults — Chapter 5: Programming Fantasy

# The Greatest of All

Based on a Japanese folk tale. Adapted by Tim Wadham.

## CHARACTERS:
Father Mouse
Cloud
Daughter
Wind
Emperor
Wall
Sun
Field Mouse

**FATHER MOUSE:** Oh, most honorable audience, I welcome you. This is the Emperor's palace where I live with my family. I dine off crumbs from the Emperor's table; I dress in silk from the Emperor's wardrobe. I am the most splendid of mice!

*(Enter Father Mouse's daughter)*

**DAUGHTER:** Father, I met a handsome field mouse today. He asked me to marry him, but he is too shy to ask your permission. Please say yes. I like him very much.

**FATHER MOUSE:** My daughter marry a mouse? A humble field mouse! That will never be! You deserve the best. Your husband must be the greatest of all.

**DAUGHTER:** Who is the greatest of all?

**FATHER MOUSE:** You will see.

*(Daughter and Father Mouse leave. The Emperor rises up with appropriate fanfare. Father Mouse enters and approaches him humbly.)*

**FATHER MOUSE:** Oh, most mighty Emperor. My daughter wishes to marry. She can have only the best for her husband. We have chosen you, because you are the greatest of all.

**EMPEROR:** I am sorry, Father Mouse. I cannot marry your daughter. There is one who is greater than I.

**FATHER MOUSE:** Who is that?

**EMPEROR:** The sun. When the sun beats hot at noon, even an emperor must seek shade.

**FATHER MOUSE:** Thank you for telling me. I will go to the sun.

*(Father Mouse and the Emperor leave. The sun arises. Father Mouse reappears and approaches it.)*

**FATHER MOUSE:** Sun, I bring good news. My daughter wishes to marry. She can have only the best for her husband. We have chosen you because you are the greatest of all.

**SUN:** I am sorry, Father Mouse, I cannot marry your daughter. There is one who is greater than I. His name is cloud. When cloud covers the sky, even the sun must hide his face.

**FATHER MOUSE:** Thank you for telling me. I will go to the cloud.

*(Father Mouse and the Sun leave. The cloud drifts in from the side of the stage. Father Mouse reappears and approaches him.)*

**FATHER MOUSE:** Cloud, I bring good news. My daughter wishes to marry. She can have only the best for her husband. We have chosen you because you are the greatest of all.

**CLOUD:** I am sorry, Father Mouse, I cannot marry your daughter. There is one who is greater than I. His name is wind. When wind blows, clouds scatter.

**FATHER MOUSE:** Thank you for telling me. I will go to the wind.

*(Father Mouse and the Cloud leave. The wind blows in, and Father Mouse approaches, trying to keep himself from being blown away.)*

**FATHER MOUSE:** Wind, I bring good news. My daughter wishes to marry. She can have only the best for her husband. We have chosen you because you are the greatest of all.

**WIND:** I am sorry, Father Mouse, I cannot marry your daughter. There is one who is greater than I. His name is wall. Wall stands firm. I cannot blow him down, no matter how hard I try.

**FATHER MOUSE:** Thank you for telling me, I will go to the wall.

*(Father Mouse and Wind leave. The wall rises up. Father Mouse approaches it.)*

**FATHER MOUSE:** Wall, I bring good news. My daughter wishes to marry. My wife and I want only the best for her husband. We have chosen you because you are the greatest of all.

**WALL:** I am sorry, Father Mouse, I cannot marry your daughter. There is one who is greater than I. He is a humble field mouse. He tunnels inside me, here and there. I can do nothing to stop him. One day he will bring me down.

**FATHER MOUSE:** I did not know that. Thank you for telling me.

*(The wall disappears. The field mouse appears.)*

**FIELD MOUSE:** Father Mouse!

**FATHER MOUSE:** So you are the famous field mouse. I came to tell you that I have made up my mind. Our daughter shall marry a mouse. You may marry my daughter. I should have known it all along. We mice are the greatest of all!

# TODDLER TIME (18 MONTHS-2 YEARS)

**STORYTIME 6**

# "May We Come Too?" Animals All Crowd In

## BOOKS:
Allen, Pamela. *Who Sank the Boat?*
Burningham, John. *Mr. Gumpy's Outing*
Lillegard, Dee. *Sitting in My Box*

## FINGER PLAY: "Meet the Boats"
from Judy Nichols' *Storytimes for Two-Year-Olds* (Chicago: American Library Association, 1987)

## SONG: Row, Row, Row Your Boat

Row, row, row your boat
Gently down the stream.
Merrily, merrily, merrily, merrily
Life is but a dream.

## ACTIVITY 1: Celery Boats

**NOTE:** This is a messy activity, so have plenty of wipes, paper towels, or wash clothes handy for cleaning up. This activity can also be done with peanut butter (but be aware that many young children are allergic to peanuts. If you choose to use peanut butter, check with the parents or caregivers first.)

- Before the program, cut processed cheese slices into eight pieces. Cut each slice in half horizontally, vertically, and on each diagonal.
- Cut celery into sticks about four inches long.
- Have the children either press a piece of cheese onto the top of a pretzel stick for their sail, or use some of the spread to "glue" it to the stick.
- Have them fill their celery with cheese spread.
- Have the children stick their sails in the middle of the pieces of celery to finish their boat.
- A knife, even a plastic one, can be awkward for young children to use. We suggest that you put a small amount of filling on a paper plate for each child and let the children use their fingers.

## ACTIVITY 2: What Floats?

- Have a pan of water and a variety of different objects.
- Have the children place the objects in the water.
- See which ones float and which ones sink.

## STORYTIME (3-8 YEARS)

### STORYTIME 7
# Royalty: The King Said "Hello," and the Queen Said "Wheee!"

### 📖 BOOKS:
DePaola, Tomie. *Helga's Dowry*
De Regniers, Beatrice. *May I Bring A Friend?*
Kahl, Virginia. *The Duchess Bakes a Cake*
Shulevitz, Uri. *One Monday Morning*
Wood, Audrey and Don. *King Bidgood's in the Bathtub*

### RHYME: Sing a Song of Sixpence

Sing a song of sixpence,
A pocket full of rye.
Four and twenty blackbirds,
Baked in a pie.
When the pie was opened,
The birds began to sing.
Now wasn't that a dainty dish to set before the king?

### RHYME: Old King Cole

Old King Cole was a merry old soul,
And a merry old soul was he.
He called for his pipe,
And he called for his bowl,
And he called for his fiddlers three.
Every fiddler he had a fiddle,
And a very fine fiddle had he;
Oh, there's none so rare,
As can compare,
With King Cole and his fiddlers three.

### ACTION RHYME: The Grand Old Duke of York

Oh, the grand old Duke of York, *(squat)*
He had ten thousand men.
He marched them up to the top of the hill, *(stand)*
And he marched them down again. *(squat)*
And when you're up, you're up; *(stand)*
And when you're down, you're down. *(squat)*
But when you're only halfway up, *(stand up part way)*
You're neither up nor down.

### ✋ ACTIVITY 1: Make a Crown

Have each child make a crown. You will need a piece of paper about 6" x 18" for each child.

- Make a pattern (See Figure 5-13) by copying the crown on a piece of light cardboard or poster board. Extend each end beyond the pattern so it will be long enough to go around the child's head.
- Have the children trace the pattern on their paper, cut it out, and decorate it with markers, stickers, buttons, glitter, or scraps of fabric or paper.
- Staple to fit the child.
- For preschool children, you may want to have the crowns precut and let them decorate.

## ACTIVITY 2: Make a Scepter

- Cover an empty paper towel holder with construction paper, or have the children paint the cardboard tubes.
- Take a piece of tissue paper about 12" x 6" and cut streamers about every half inch or so; cut to about 1" from the end of the paper.
- Depending on the direction you cut your streamers, when you wrap them around the tube you will have one row of 1" streamers, or two rows of 5" streamers. Decide which you like better before you cut them.
- Tape or staple the tissue paper around the end of the tube.

## VARIATIONS:

- If you use *Helga's Dowry*, have the children find the Troll King who is hiding in almost every picture, watching what Helga is doing.
- You can use Ed Emberly's book *Klippity Klop* as an audience participation story. Simply have the children make the sounds along with you as indicated in the story.
- The video adaptation of *King Bidgood's in the Bathtub* (Random House Video, 1988, 8 min.) is staged as an operetta, and it is an absolute delight.

**FIGURE 5-13** Storytime 7, Royalty, Crown

### STORYTIME 8

# Witches and Ghosts: "Let's Frighten Somebody."

### BOOKS:
Ahlberg, Janet and Allan. *Funnybones*
Bright, Robert. *Georgie to the Rescue*
Calhoun, Mary. *The Witch of Hissing Hill*
Devlin, Wende and Harry. *Old Black Witch*
Thayer, Jane. *Gus Was A Friendly Ghost*

### ACTION RHYME: Boo!

See my great big scary eyes. *(Hold fingers around eyes.)*
Look out now for a big surprise.
Oo-oo-ooo! *(Walk like a ghost.)*
I'm looking right at you. *(Point at someone.)*
BOO! *(Everyone)*

### POEM: Ah-Ha!

Whatever is inside that sheet,
Just gave a dreadful shout.
Aha, but what about those feet,
That I see sticking out?
They help me guess who's hiding there,
Whose eyes are peeking through.
And how could anyone be scared
of YOU?

### POEM: Three Little Ghostesses

Three little ghostesses
Sitting on postesses
Eating buttered toastesses
Greasing their fistesses
Up to their wristesses
Oh, what beastesses
To make such feastesses!

### POEM: There Was An Old Woman

There was an old woman all skin and bones.
Oooh, oooh, oooh, ooh, ooh.
She went to the graveyard all alone.
Oooh, oooh, oooh, ooh, ooh.
She looked up and she looked down
Oooh, oooh, oooh, ooh, ooh.
Rotting corpses all around
Oooh, oooh, oooh, ooh, ooh.
And the worms crawled here, and the worms crawled there.
Oooh, oooh, oooh, ooh, ooh.
A putrid smell filled the air.
Oooh, oooh, oooh, ooh, ooh.
She went to the Sexton and to the Sexton she said,
Oooh, oooh, oooh, ooh, ooh.
"Will I look like that when I am dead?"
Oooh, oooh, oooh, ooh, ooh.
And the Sexton to the woman said,
"AAAArrrghhhh!"

### RIDDLE:

What kind of a pet does a ghost have?
Answer: A scaredy cat.

For more riddles, look in *Spooky Riddles* (New York: Random House, 1993.) by Marc Brown.

## ACTIVITY 1: Make a Witch

- Make copies of the pattern provided (Figure 5-14).
- Have the children color it.
- Or make stiff patterns and have the children trace them on construction paper (black hat and brim, orange hair, green face).
- Have them draw a face, cut out the pieces, and glue them together.

## ACTIVITY 2: Make a Ghost

- Use a round sucker (Tootsie Pop or Dum Dum).
- Put a white tissue over the sucker.
- Tie a piece of string or heavy thread around the "neck."
- Use a marker to make black eyes.

**VARIATIONS:**

There's a recipe for blueberry pancakes on the back cover of *Old Black Witch* that comes complete with magic words to say while stirring the mixture. You might consider this as an activity. For older children, tell the story "Smelly Sneakers" from Judith Gorog's *In a Messy, Messy Room and Other Stories*.

**FIGURE 5-14** Storytime 8, Witches and Ghosts, Witch

Bringing Fantasy Alive for Children and Young Adults — Chapter 5: Programming Fantasy

### STORYTIME 9

# A Monster Is Coming!
# A Monster Is Coming!

## BOOKS:

Bang, Molly. *Wiley and the Hairy Man*
Harper, Wilhemina. *The Gunniwolf*
Heide, Florence Parry and Roxanne. *A Monster Is Coming! A Monster Is Coming!*
Howe, James. *There's a Monster Under My Bed*
Seymour, Peter. *What's in the Cave?*

## ACTION RHYME:

"The Monster Stomp" from Hayes, Sara. *Stamp Your Feet: Action Rhymes* (New York: Lothrop, Lee and Shephard, 1988)

## POEM:

"Come See The Thing" from Prelutsky, Jack. *The New Kid on the Block* (New York: Greenwillow, 1984)

## FILMS:

*There's a Nightmare in My Closet* (Phoenix, 1987. 14 min)

*There's Something in My Attic* (Phoenix, 1991. 14 min)

## ACTIVITY 1: Draw a Monster

You'll need long sheets of butcher paper three to four feet long and boxes of crayons or markers, as well as newspapers to be placed underneath the butcher paper.

- Assemble three stations with some of each item.
- Read the first rhyme of the following poem, leaving out the last word of each phrase.
- The first person on each team responds by filling in the rhyming word and then adds that part to the monster drawing.
- Continue using the same procedure until all rhymes and parts have been completed.
- After you've completed your monster, ask the children to help make up a name for him.

*(This idea is from Brenda Robinson, formerly with the Dallas Public Library.)*

When you draw a monster, it is said,
You always begin with his *head*.

He'll be able to see when he flies,
If we draw two bright *eyes*.

To tell which way the cold wind blows,
Our monster will need a great big *nose*.

Look to the North and look to the South,
Now we can give our monster a *mouth*.

Some up above and some beneath,
Our monster has lots of *teeth*.

Now under his chin, let's just check,
That's where we should put his *neck*.

So he won't be tipsy-toddy,
Let's give him a *body*.

If he really, really begs,
I guess we could give him some *legs*.

Now to make our monster nice and neat,
We'll have to teach him to wipe his *feet*.

A notice sent by Air Mail!
We can't forget the monster's *tail*.

Now this may seem a little weird,
But on his chin let's draw a *beard*.

He isn't fierce. He isn't hairy,
But don't you think he's a little scary?

## ACTIVITY 2: Monster Repellent

- You need a bottle of "smelly stuff." Use old perfume, or any extract, such as mint, lemon, or vanilla.
- Put a bright label on your bottle that says, "Monster Repellent Concentrate."
- Provide, or have the children bring, small spray bottles.
- Put about a teaspoon of perfume in the spray bottles and fill them with water.
- You will need to adjust this according to what you are using for your "concentrate," and to the size of the spray bottles.
- The final product is mostly water and should have only a faint scent.
- Help label the child's bottle "Monster Repellent."
- Parents can spray it in the child's room at bedtime; it will keep away monsters or tigers or anything else that might frighten a child.

### VARIATIONS:

- The best monster folktale besides *The Gunniwolf* is probably Paul Galdone's *Tailypo*. Either of these stories is great for telling.
- For extra scary storytimes, add some poems from *Nightmares: Poems to Trouble Your Sleep* or *The Headless Horseman Rides Tonight: More Poems to Trouble Your Sleep*, both by Jack Prelutsky. One of the scariest is "The Zombie" from *The Headless Horseman*.
- For a humorous touch, you could read a section on an individual monster from *How to Care for Your Monster* by Norman Bridwell.

**STORYTIME 10**

# Stuffed Animals: I've Always Wanted a Friend

## BOOKS:
Freeman, Don. *Corduroy*
Freeman, Don. *A Pocket for Corduroy*
Hissey, Jane. *Old Bear*
Wahl, Jan. *Humphrey's Bear*

## POEMS:
"When a Bear Gets Mad" and "Three Bears Walking" from Yolen, Jane. *The Three Bears Rhyme Book* (New York: Harcourt Brace Jovanovich, 1987)

## FILM:
*A Pocket for Corduroy* (Phoenix, 1986. 20 min)

## ACTIVITY 1: Color Corduroy
- Make copies of Corduroy for each child. (Use Figure 5-15 for a pattern.)
- Use the pattern (Figure 5-16) to cut overalls and pockets from scraps of fabric. (Corduroy wears green corduroy, but if you don't have that, use a different type or color of fabric.)
- Let the children color the bear.
- Then they may glue on his overalls, a pocket, and two buttons.
- Younger children will need precut patterns, but older children can do their own cutting.

## ACTIVITY 2: Make a Parachute

Help Old Bear from Jane Hissey's story to parachute out of the attic.
- Provide each child with a small plastic figure (animals, cowboys, figures that have a little bit of weight to them) or have them bring their own.
- Tie the figure securely in the middle of the string.
- Tie each end of the string to one handle of a plastic grocery sack.
- Have the kids wad up the bag and toy and throw it into the air.
- The toy will parachute down.
- You can save plastic grocery bags, or pick some up at a grocery store that recycles.
- A local store may be willing to donate the plastic animals.

**FIGURE 5-15** Storytime 10, Stuffed Animals, Corduroy

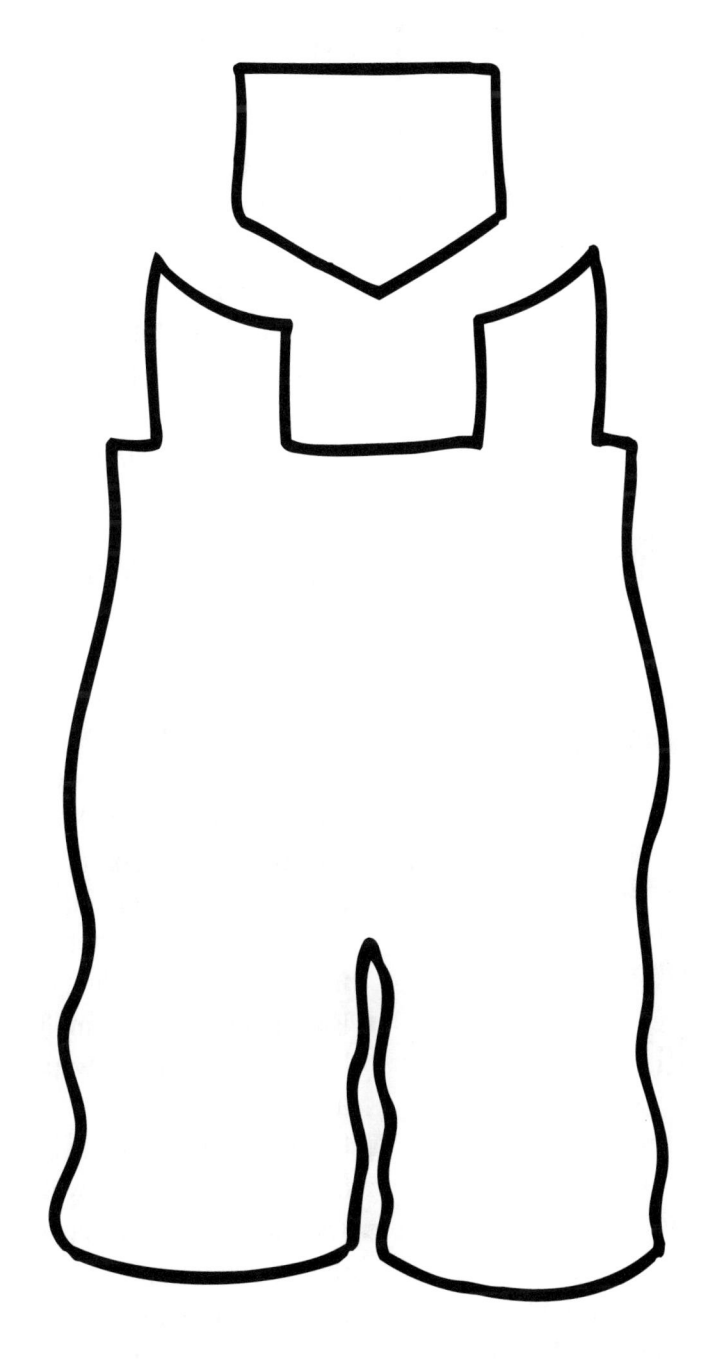

**FIGURE 5-16** Storytime 10, Stuffed Animals, Overalls

## UPPER ELEMENTARY PROGRAMS (9-12 YEARS)

**STORYTIME 11**

# Giants: Fe Fi Fo Fum, I Smell the Blood of an Englishman!

### BOOKS:

Gaeddert, Louann. *Gustav, the Gourmet Giant*
Kellogg, Steven. *Jack and the Beanstalk*
Kroll, Steven. *Big Jeremy*

### RHYME: Giant Jim

The Giant Jim, great giant grim,
Wears a hat without a brim,
Weighs a ton and wears a blouse,
And trembles when he meets a mouse.

### POEM:

"The Towering Giant" from Prelutsky, Jack.. *The Headless Horseman Rides Tonight: More Poems to Trouble Your Sleep*

### ACTIVITY 1: Make a Beanstalk

- Take a few sheets of paper (newspaper or construction paper, any size).
- Lay one sheet down.
- Lay the next sheet down next to the first sheet with only about two inches overlapping the first.
- Continue until all the paper is laid out. (The more paper you use, the higher your beanstalk will be.)
- Begin with the first sheet: Roll it toward the other sheets you put down.
- Tape the side.
- Tear or cut from the top to about one-third the way down four times.
- Reach inside and gently pull the center out.
- For more directions, look in *How to Make Flibbers, Etc.* by Robert Lopshire (Beginner Books (Random House), 1964)

### ACTIVITY 2: Paper Maché Eggs

Have the children make a golden egg out of paper maché. (This activity will take two programs to complete, or the children will have to paint them at home.)

- Just before the program, mix equal parts of flour and water for your paste. (This will dry out if made too soon. If it's too thick, add more water; if too thin, add more flour.)
- Each child needs a small, round, inflated balloon, part of a newspaper, and access to a bowl of paste.
- Have the children tear off small strips of newspaper, which they dip in the paste.
- They wipe the excess paste off and smooth the wet newspaper over the balloon.
- Continue until all the balloon is covered with two or three layers of newspaper.
- It takes at least a day to dry (depending on how much paste was left on the newspaper).
- When the eggs are dry (or the next week), paint them with gold paint. (If you can't find gold, use yellow tempera paint and sprinkle with glitter while still wet.)

**STORYTIME 12**

# Toy Stories: "We Should Fix Ourselves Up as New Toys, the Kind Kids Like."

## BOOKS:

Ardizonne, Aingelda. *The Night Ride*

Stevenson, James. *The Night After Christmas*

## ACTIVITY 1: A Toy Exchange

- Have each child bring an old toy he or she doesn't want any more (with parents' permission, of course).
- Have the children trade for a different one.
- Ask the children to bring toys that are clean and in good working order.
- Set up tables around the library or program room.
- Designate tables for games, stuffed animals, musical instruments, blocks, vehicles, and other types of toys.
- As children enter, give them a ticket in exchange for each toy they bring.
- A volunteer can then put the donated toy on the appropriate table, while the child explores the tables for a toy to take home.

## ACTIVITY 2: Video Program

Show the video *The Forgotten Toys* (Sony Wonder, 1996, 30 min.), based on *The Night After Christmas*.

## ACTIVITY 3: Produce a "Video" Show

- Cut a square out of the front of a cardboard box for a TV screen.
- Draw knobs with markers.
- After reading *The Night After Christmas* or viewing the video, have the children take turns putting the "TV" over their heads and doing TV commercials.
- Get the children to brainstorm ideas for commercials.
- Write the ideas on a large sheet of paper on the wall.
- Then ask the children to develop a commercial.
- You might ask someone in advertising or marketing in your community to talk to the children about marketing and selling a specific product.

# Appendix: Celebrating Fantasy

## ONLINE RESCOURCES TO CELEBRATE FANTASY

### General Children's Literature Sites

Children's Literature Web Guide
**www.acs.ucalgary.ca/~dkbrown/index.html**
The very best and most indispensable resource we've found on the Web for children's books. Many of the author sites below can be found on this site, but there is much, much more.

### Author Sites

These are the best Internet sites we've found for some of our favorite authors. Some are "official" sites, like the C. S. Lewis site endorsed by Lewis' stepson, and Phillip Pullman's, which is found within his publishers' Web site. Devoted fans create others. The site for Brian Jacques was created by a young fan and then endorsed by the author as the official site. All of these sites contain links to literally hundreds of other sites on the authors and related topics. We've tried to include just the highlights here.

L. Frank Baum—The Wonderful Wizard of Oz Website
**www.eskimo.com/~tiktok/index.html**

Lewis Carroll
**www.lewiscarroll.org/carroll.html**

Susan Cooper
**missy.shef.ac.uk/~emp94ms/index.html**

Roald Dahl
**www.roalddahl.org/index2.htm**

Diane Duane
**www.ibmpcug.co.uk/~owls/homeward.html**

Sylvia Louise Engdahl
**www.teleport.com/~sengdahl/**

Brian Jacques
**www.islandnet.com/~qnd/dave/jacques.html**

Tove Jansson (Moomintroll books)
**www.io.com/~fazia/Moomin.html**

Diana Wynne Jones
**suberic.net/dwj/**

Madeleine L'Engle
**www.geocities.com/Athens/Acropolis/8838**

C. S. Lewis
**cslewis.drzeus.net**

Robin McKinley
**ofb.net/~damien/mckinley/**

Philip Pullman
**www.randomhouse.com/subtleknife**

Dr. Seuss
**www.randomhouse.com/seussville**

J. R. R. Tolkien
**www.csclub.uwaterloo.ca/u/relipper/tolkien/rootpage.html**

### Other Fantasy Resources on the Web

Ask ERIC Info Guide to Folk and Fairy Tales
**ericir.syr.edu/Virtual/InfoGuides/alpha_list/folkandfairy12_96.html**
This site contains links not only to Web sites, but also to gopher, ftp, and telnet sites. Information for subscribing to relevant listserv groups is also included. This is an awesome all-in-one resource.

Joseph Campbell Foundation
**www.jcf.org/new/index.html**

Mythopoeic Society
**www.mythsoc.org/**

Of Gods and Men: The A to Z of Mythology and Legend
**www.clubi.ie/lestat/godsmen.html**
This is an excellent search engine that accesses the site author's extensive collection of information about mythological characters and themes.

Windows to the Universe
**www.windows.umich.edu**
While primarily a science site, this includes a section on the mythology related to celestial bodies. There is also an archive of mythology-related art.

## Listserv Discussion Groups

### KIDLIT-L
KIDLIT-L is a discussion list about children's literature involving teachers, librarians, students, and others interested in the field. To subscribe, send e-mail to
*listserv@bingvmb.cc.binghamton.edu*
Your message should contain the following line:
*subscribe KIDLIT-L [your first name] [your last name]*
You will receive a confirming message from the listserver (the computer that reads such messages automatically and adds or removes people from the mailing list) providing further information about the list, including how to temporarily or permanently unsubscribe. You should retain that message for future reference. To send a message to the membership of the list, send e-mail to *kidlit-l@bingvmb.cc.binghamton.edu*

### CHILDLIT
Children's Literature: Criticism and Theory. A list devoted to discussion and critical analysis of children's literature. Its subscribers tend to approach children's literature in a somewhat more academic way than KIDLIT-L does. To subscribe, send e-mail to *majordomo@email.rutgers.edu*. Your message should contain the following line:
*subscribe child_lit [your e-mail address]*
You will receive a confirming message from the listserver. To send a message to all subscribers of the list, e-mail *child_lit@email.rutgers.edu*
CHILDLIT's Web address is:
**www.rci.rutgers.edu/~mjoseph/childlit/about.html**

### PUBYAC
A discussion list for Children's and Young Adult Librarians in Public Libraries. To subscribe, send e-mail to *listserver@nysernet.org*. Your message should contain the following line:
*subscribe PUBYAC [your first name] [your last name]*
You will receive a confirming message from the listserver. To send a message to the membership of the list, send e-mail to *pubyac@nysernet.org*
The Web address for PUBYAC is:
**www.pallasinc.com/pubyac/**

### FOLKLORE
A folklore discussion list. To subscribe, send e-mail to: *listserv@tamvm1.tamu.edu*.
Your message should contain the following line:
*subscribe folklore [your first name] [your last name]*
You will receive a confirming message from the listserver. To send a message to the membership of the list, send e-mail to *folklore@tamvm1.tamu.edu*

# SELECTED AUTHOR BIOGRAPHIES

Fantasy could not exist without the authors from whose rich imaginations these books spring. The best way of celebrating fantasy is to celebrate the authors who have given us cherished books. With that in mind, here are some mini-biographies of our very favorite authors. We've included references for more information on some of the authors for whom books are available. Information on all these authors can be found in the series *Something About the Author*.

## Alexander, Lloyd

*"I see no conflict between realism and fantasy. Both try to illuminate human relationships, conflicts, and moral dilemmas. I do admit that I much prefer fantasy. To me, it has the emotional strength of a dream, it works directly on our nerve endings, whatever age we happen to be, touching heights and depths not always accessible through realism. In fantasy, my concern is how we learn to be real human beings. It's a continuing process."* (Faces of Fantasy 32)

Lloyd Chudley Alexander was born on January 30, 1924, in Philadelphia, Pennsylvania. Alexander learned to read at a very young age. He devoured the varied assortment of books that his parents had around the house. Among his favorite things to read as a child were the works of Charles Dickens and Greek and Celtic mythologies. At the age of 15, Alexander decided that he was going to become a poet. His parents were horrified. They pleaded with him to forget writing and do something "sensible" with his life.

His parents could not afford to send him to college but eventually Alexander earned enough to attend a local college. Quickly becoming dissatisfied with his studies because he was not learning anything about being a writer, he left school after one term and decided that having adventures was the best way to learn about writing.

With World War II raging, Alexander found his path to adventure by joining the army. During his time in the military, he served as an artilleryman, a cymbal player, an organist, and a first-aid man. At last he was assigned to a military intelligence center in Maryland, where he trained to be a member of a combat team. After completing their training, the group sailed to Wales and then on to Germany.

When the war ended and he was discharged, Alexander began attending the University of Paris, where he met his wife Janine. After their marriage, Alexander returned to the United States and began writing. While writing novel after novel that publishers turned down, Alexander worked as a cartoonist, an advertising writer, a layout artist, and an associate editor for a small magazine, in order to support his family. Seven years later, his fourth novel *And Let the Credit Go* was published.

Alexander spent the next 10 years writing novels for adults. He finally discovered the world of children's literature and fantasy with his novel *Time Cat*. Alexander followed *Time Cat* with his immensely popular and award-winning series, the "Chronicles of Prydain," starting with *The Book of Three*. Since that time, Alexander has written numerous fantasy adventure stories in novel and picture-book form for children.

## Babbitt, Natalie

Natalie Babbitt was born on July 28, 1932 in Dayton, Ohio. Babbit's mother encouraged her early interests in reading and writing, and together they determined that Babbitt would be an artist when she grew up. Babbitt's early drawings were influenced by Sir John Tenniel's illustrations in *Alice's Adventures in Wonderland*.

These works were produced in pen and ink, which was to become Babbitt's specialty.

Babbitt graduated from Smith College with a degree in art in 1954 and married Samuel Babbitt the same year. In the years after her marriage raising her three children kept her busy while her husband, an aspiring writer, wrote a novel. Finding that writing did not suit him, Samuel soon went back to work as a college administrator.

After a successful career as a homemaker, Babbitt decided to pursue a second career as an illustrator. Her husband wrote and she illustrated *The Forty-Ninth Magician*, which Farrar, Straus, and Giroux published in 1966. With the encouragement of Michael di Capua at Farrar, Babbitt continued to produce children's books even after her husband became too busy to write.

The ideas for Babbitt's books tend to begin with a single image. Characters tend to spring into her imagination as she thinks about a word or an image. For example, the idea for *Goody Hall* formed while she was thinking about the word "smuggler." Babbitt's best known novel is a fantasy titled *Tuck Everlasting*, the tale of a family who become immortals after they drink water from a secret spring. This book is generally considered one of the all-time classics of children's literature. Babbitt has received numerous awards including a Newbery Honor Medal in 1971 for her novel *Kneeknock Rise*.

## Baum, L. Frank

Lyman Frank Baum was born on May 15, 1856, in Chittenango, New York. As a young boy, Baum and his younger brother, Harry, put out an amateur newspaper using a hand press. This project lasted for only three years, but it gave Baum his first encouragement to write. Baum continued to write and publish homespun newspapers and magazines throughout his youth.

In 1878, Baum decided to become a professional actor and joined the Albert M. Palmer Union Square Theater in New York. From that time on, Baum spent most of his time acting and writing for the theater. Baum also managed several small theaters in New York and Pennsylvania that were owned by his father.

On November 9, 1882, Baum married Maud Gage. After leaving the theater in 1885, Baum, his wife, and two young sons moved to the Dakota Territory where he opened a store called "Baum's Bazaar." He also ran the local weekly newspaper, *The Aberdeen Saturday Pioneer*. In 1891, Baum and his family moved to Chicago, where he took a job as a reporter for the *Evening Post*. To help make ends meet, he also took a job as a traveling salesman for a china company.

Baum's first children's book, *Father Goose, His Book*, was published in 1899 and was an instant success. The next year, Baum published his now classic *The Wonderful Wizard of Oz*. With his reputation as a writer firmly established, Baum began to branch out into other areas. In 1902, he produced a musical version of the *Wizard of Oz*. The play was a major hit and ran for 293 nights on Broadway between 1902 and 1911. During this time, Baum continued to write children's books. His second book in the Oz series, *The Marvelous Land of Oz*, was published in 1904.

In 1910, Baum moved his family to Hollywood, California, where he established the Oz Film Manufacturing Company. This company produced a number of films based on the Oz books, but they were unsuccessful, and Baum sold the company to Universal. Despite failing health, Baum continued to write children's books, including one Oz book each year. Baum died on May 5, 1919. His last book, *Glinda of Oz*, was published one year after his death.

Baum, Frank J. and Russell P. McFall. ***To Please a Child: A Biography of L. Frank Baum, Royal Historian of Oz.*** Chicago : Reilly and Lee, 1961.

Carpenter, Angelica Shirley and Jean Shirley. ***L. Frank Baum, Royal Historian of Oz,*** Minneapolis: Lerner Publications, 1992.

Hearn, Michael Patrick. ***The Annotated Wizard of Oz.*** New York: Clarkson Potter, 1973.

# Cooper, Susan

"...[W]henever my imagination can run free, unencumbered by facts or commissions, the stories that it brings me always seem to be fantasies, generally of a sort published these days as novels for children. Perhaps writers of my kind are able to tell the truth only through metaphor. Or perhaps we're just greedy, wanting always not only to look in the mirror but to step through it, not only to live today but to fly in and out of yesterday and tomorrow. 'This is how life is,' says the realistic novel. The fantasy say, 'Yes, but what if—?'" (Faces of Fantasy 148)

Susan Cooper was born on May 23, 1935, in Burnham, Buckinghamshire, England. Cooper's mother taught her to love poetry and music from a very young age. Her maternal grandparents also had a great influence on her; Cooper's grandfather read to her the novels of his favorite authors, including Dickens, Thackeray, and H. G. Wells. One of Cooper's favorite pastimes as a child was listening to the radio. Her favorite program was the BBC's "Children's Hour," which presented dramatizations of books.

Cooper also read a great deal as a child, and from the age of eight she knew she wanted to be a writer. After graduating from high school, Cooper won a scholarship and entered Somerville College at Oxford University. There she majored in English and became the first woman to edit the Oxford newspaper *Cherwell*.

Cooper graduated from Oxford in 1956, and after a lucky break she began working at the *Sunday Times*, where she wrote and edited for the next seven years while also turning out short stories for ladies magazines and one novel. Cooper also began work on a second novel, *Over Sea Under Stone*, which would not be published until several years later.

At the age of 27, in 1963, Cooper married an American scientist and moved to America. *Over Sea Under Stone* was published the same year. Cooper spent the next several years raising her two children, writing biographical novels, and editing a collection of essays. Although she had no intention of doing so, Cooper began writing a sequel to *Over Sea, Under Stone*. As she began writing, the plot not only for that book but a sequence of five emerged. The result was *The Dark Is Rising* and the other four books of "The Dark Is Rising" series. Within a year of completing the last of "The Dark Is Rising" novels, Cooper began writing for the stage and screen. Collaborating with the actor Hume Cronyn, Cooper wrote a play called *Foxfire* and a teleplay for the television movie *The Dollmaker*.

Cooper continues to write children's books. Her latest novels are all about an invisible and mischievous spirit from Scottish folklore called a Boggart.

Cooper, Susan. ***Dreams and Wishes: Essays on Writing for Children.*** New York: M. K. McElderry, 1996.

# Dahl, Roald

Roald (pronounced Roo-ahl) Dahl was born on September 13, 1916, in Llandaff, South Wales, an energetic and mischievous child who loved finding and getting into trouble. On annual trips to visit relatives in Norway,

Dahl's mother would read to him the great Norse myths.

Dahl was an average student who showed no aptitude for writing in his early years. After completing high school, Dahl opted to take a job with the Shell Oil Company instead of going to college. Dahl was almost immediately shipped of to Tanzania, where he had many adventures selling oil to the owners of the diamond mines.

In 1939, he joined the Royal Air Force and began his training in Nairobi, Kenya. During World War II, he made a name for himself as a fighter pilot battling the Germans all around the Mediterranean Sea. Soon Dahl was forced to stop flying because of the frequent blackouts he had as a result of earlier injuries.

Transferred to Washington, D.C., he served as an assistant air attaché. Dahl began his writing career as a fluke soon after that, when a story he wrote about his war experiences was sold. Dahl's first children's book, *The Gremlins*, was published in 1943 and was to be the basis for a sadly unproduced Walt Disney animated film.

In 1945, Dahl returned to England and married actress Patricia Neal. Together they had five children. Dahl attributed his success as a children's author to his children. During the 1950s Dahl firmly established himself as a writer, authoring numerous short stories for adults. Dahl's career began in earnest in 1961 with the publication of his novel *James and the Giant Peach*. Two of Dahl's most famous novels, *Charlie and the Chocolate Factory* and *Charlie and the Great Glass Elevator*, have sold over one million hardcover copies in America.

Roald Dahl died on November 23, 1990, in Oxford, England.

Dahl, Roald. *Boy:* **Tales of Childhood.** New York: Farrar, Straus, Giroux, 1984.

Dahl, Roald. **Going Solo.** New York: Farrar, Straus, Giroux, 1986.

# Duane, Diane

Diane Duane was born on May 18, 1952, in New York. From early childhood she loved books. She began writing her own stories at an early age when she found that the library did not have enough of the kinds of books she liked to read. After graduating from Roosevelt Senior High School, Duane began college at Dowling College in Oakdale, New York. Duane started out studying astronomy and astrophysics, but because higher math was awkward for her, she moved into the biological sciences and ultimately nursing.

In 1970, Duane moved from Dowling to the Pilgrim State Hospital School, graduating in 1974. She started her career as a psychiatric nurse at the Whitney Psychiatric Clinic of New York, continuing to write for her own entertainment. But it was not until several years after her first novel was published in 1979 that Duane realized she could actually make a living as a writer. In 1981, Duane began to write full time. In 1987, Duane met and married Peter Morwood, a writer from northern Ireland.

To date, Duane has published over 18 novels, numerous short stories, comics, and computer games. She and her husband have collaborated on over five novels and various screenplays. Duane's work for television has included an episode of Star Trek: The Next Generation, "Where No One Has Gone Before," and a script for the animated Batman series, "Red Claw Rising." Duane's novels for children include the popular "So You Want To Be a Wizard" quartet, which chronicles the adventures of two young wizards, Nita and Kit.

## Garner, Alan

*"The job of a storyteller is to speak the truth. But what we feel most deeply can't be spoken in words alone. At this level, only images connect. And here, story becomes symbol; symbol is myth. And myth is truth."* (Faces of Fantasy 38)

Alan Garner was born on October 17, 1934, in Congleton, Cheshire, England. He spent a lonely childhood. Until the age of 11 he rarely attended school. Afflicted by spinal and cerebral meningitis, diphtheria, pleurisy, and pneumonia, Garner spent most of his childhood home alone. At school, when he did begin to attend, Garner received high grades and was an outstanding athlete. After graduation, Garner attended Magdalen College at Oxford, where he studied Homeric archaeology and British mythology.

He soon left college because he felt that formal study was diminishing his imaginative interaction with the myths and legends that he loved. From that time on, Garner devoted his life to writing. During his first few years as a professional writer, Garner published nothing and was penniless. Determined not to give up, he relied on public assistance until he was able to establish himself. Garner spent two years working on his first novel, *The Weirdstone of Brisingamen: A Tale of Alderley*. Its sequel, *The Moon of Gomrath*, followed three years later.

Although his work is published as children's literature, many find it too challenging for young people. For example, one of Garner's most challenging novels, *Red Shift*, contains three different plots, in three different settings, and there is no narrative, only dialogue. Despite their complexity, Garner's works are still enjoyed by many young people.

## Jacques, Brian

Brian Jacques (pronounced "Jakes") was born on June 15, 1939, in Liverpool, England. From an early age, he loved to read all types of adventure. Quitting school at the age of 15, Jacques set out to find adventure on the high seas by becoming a merchant seaman. After two years at sea, Jacques tired of life at sea and returned to his home in Liverpool. For the next 19 years, he worked in various occupations—railway fireman, longshoreman, long-distance truck driver, bus driver, boxer, policeman, and dock representative.

In 1980, Jacques began work in the radio broadcasting industry. His broadcasts for BBC-Radio Merseyside have included a musical program, "Jakestown"; a program for children, "Schools Quiz"; a program on movies, "Flixquiz"; and various documentaries. Jacques began his writing career as a playwright. Three of his stage plays, "Brown Bitter," "Wet Nellies," and "Scouse," have been performed numerous times. Jacques did not begin his first novel for children, *Redwall*, with publication in mind. Jacques wrote the novel for the children at the Royal Wavertree School for the Blind in Liverpool, where he is a patron. Redwall, the first in the continuing "Redwall" series, was published in 1987, after Jacques' former teacher, Alan Durband, gave the manuscript to a publisher. Currently, Jacques is still in broadcasting, continues to write, and enjoys lecturing at schools and colleges.

## Jones, Diana Wynne

Diana Wynne Jones was born on August 16, 1934, in London, England. Jones began reading at an early age and by the age of eight realized that someday she would be a professional writer. Like Susan Cooper, Jones's childhood was affected by World War II. She spent much of her time moving between Wales and England with her mother and sisters. Left by their parents to their own devices much of the time, the young girls became very attached to each other. At the age of 13, Jones began writing, reading her stories to her sisters at night.

Jones was an excellent student; in 1953 she started college at St. Anne's College at Oxford. While at Oxford, Jones spent time listening to the lectures of two great men who would later have a great influence on her writing, C.S. Lewis and J. R. R. Tolkien. Jones married John Burrow in 1956 and they had three sons.

Jones's books mix elements from various fantasy traditions. She finds inspiration in traditional European fairy tales, the Arabian Nights, and even Greek, Celtic, and Norse mythologies. Jones has written over 20 novels including two very popular series, the "Chrestomanci Cycle," starting with *Charmed Life,* and the "Dalemark Cycle," which starts with *Cart and Cwidder.* Jones has received numerous awards for her writing. These include the Guardian award in 1978 for *Charmed Life* and two Carnegie commendations, one in 1975, the other in 1977, for *Dogsbody* and *Charmed Life,* respectively.

## *L'Engle, Madeleine*

Madeleine L'Engle was born on November 29, 1918, in New York and writing and reading at an early age. She wrote her first stories at the age of five. As an only child, L'Engle enjoyed solitude and created a rich fantasy life to entertain herself. L'Engle was educated in various boarding schools, but because she was shy and introspective, was not a popular girl at any of her schools.

After completing high school, L'Engle began her studies at Smith College. During her early college years, she was active in the theater and continued acting afterwards. She took various small roles and worked as an assistant stage manager for two years, but even while pursuing a stage career, never stopped writing.

On January 26, 1946, L'Engle married Hugh Franklin, an actor she had met years earlier. At this time, L'Engle postponed her writing career to raise her family and work with her husband in their small general store in rural Connecticut. During her spare time, she continued to write short stories, submitting them to magazines, but they were invariably rejected. By 1958, L'Engle was discouraged by all her rejections and vowed to stop writing.

L'Engle spent time as a high school teacher and librarian in the 1960s, but her need to write persisted. Things changed for the author when her writing began to sell. Her novel *A Wrinkle in Time* was rejected by 26 publishers before it was accepted by Farrar, Straus, and Giroux. Despite its rocky start, *A Wrinkle in Time* was a success. It won the Newbery Medal in 1963 and the Lewis Carroll Shelf Award in 1965 and was a runner-up for the Hans Christian Andersen Award in 1964.

Hettinga, Donald R. **Presenting Madeleine L'Engle.** New York : Twayne Publishers, 1993.

## *LeGuin, Ursula K.*

"*Fantasy is the language of the inner self. I will claim no more for fantasy than to say I personally find it the appropriate language in which to tell stories to children—and others. But I say with some confidence, having behind me the authority of a very great poet, who put it much more boldly. 'The great instrument of moral good,' Shelley said, 'is imagination'*" (LeGuin 70).

Ursula Kroeber LeGuin was born on October 21, 1929, in Berkeley, California to parents who gave her an early acquaintance with folktales and myths. Her father would tell stories around a fire, and her mother kept many collections of myths around the house. LeGuin read everything she could get her hands on from a very early age. She wrote her first story at the age of nine. Her first attempt to publish a story came at age 12, when she submitted a piece to *Astounding Stories* that was promptly rejected.

After completing a bachelors degree in romance languages at Radcliff College, LeGuin went on to receive her masters from Columbia University in 1953. She promptly started work on a PhD but dropped it when she met and married Charles LeGuin. After her marriage, LeGuin worked as a secretary, taught French, and spent the rest of her time writing. For the next 10 years, she published poetry and wrote five novels, none of which were published. It was not until 1966 that LeGuin published her first novel, *Racannon's World.* The first novel in her "Earthsea" trilogy, *A Wizard of Earthsea,* was published in 1968.

Although she did not realize it at first, from the time LeGuin started writing, she was writing science fiction and fantasy. LeGuin enjoys pushing the limits of these genres outward as she discovers new ways to use language and to address themes. She has written over 30 novels and countless short stories and poems, receiving numerous awards including five Hugo Awards, three Nebula Awards, a Newbery Honor medal, the Lewis Carol Shelf Award, and the Gandalf Award as the "Grand Master of Fantasy."

LeGuin, Urusla K. ***The Language of the Night: Essay on Fantasy of Science Fiction.*** Edited with Introduction by Susan Wood. New York: Putnam, 1979.

## Lewis, C.S.

Clive Staples ("Jack") Lewis was born on November 29, 1898, in Belfast, Northern Ireland. He grew up in a house filled with books. As young men, Lewis and his older brother, Warren, felt more at home in the books that they read than in the real world. At the age of 10, Lewis began writing stories to help him deal with his grief over his mother's death. During his years at Cherbourg School in Malvern, England, he developed an attachment for Wagner's music and Norse mythology.

He began college at Oxford 1917 but soon interrupted his studies to serve in World War I. After being wounded and hospitalized several times, Lewis left the army and resumed his studies at Oxford. In 1925, Lewis was elected a fellow in English Language and Literature at Magdalen College in Oxford, where he remained until 1954.

After his conversion to Anglicanism in 1931, Lewis began writing and publishing numerous books with metaphysical and religious themes. In 1939, he became a member of the Inklings, a group that met at Magdalen College to talk and criticize each others' works. The group included W. H. Lewis, J. R. R. Tolkien, Nevill Coghill, H. V. D. Dyson, A. C. Harwood, C. T. Onions, and Robert Havard. In 1950, Lewis published *The Lion, the Witch, and the Wardrobe,* the first of his famous "Chronicles of Narnia." For the next six years, one volume of the "Chronicles of Narnia" appeared each year. It pleased Lewis that both children and adults enjoyed his Narnia books. In addition to the "Chronicles of Narnia," he published numerous works of science fiction for adults. Lewis died one week before his sixty-fourth birthday, on November 23, 1963.

## Tolkien, J. R. R.

John Ronald Reuel Tolkien was born January 3, 1892, in Bloemfontein, South Africa. Orphaned at the age of 12, he was sent with his brother to live with a kindly priest at the Birmingham Oratory in England. Both boys attended King Edward's School, where Tolkien learned the classics, Anglo-Saxon, and Middle

English. Always adept at linguistics, Tolkien began to invent his own languages after completing a study of old Welsh and Finnish.

Tolkien in 1908 entered Exeter College in Oxford, where he studied English language and literature. In 1915, Tolkien began service as a solider in World War I but was soon was stricken with trench fever and returned to England. During the war he had started to write a cycle about the myths and legends of Middle-earth, which would eventually become *The Silmarillon*. After leaving the service, Tolkien returned to Oxford and completed his degree in English. The next year he married his childhood sweetheart, Edith Bratt.

In 1925, Tolkien was elected professor of Anglo-Saxon at Oxford. He and Edith had four children, and it was to entertain them that he first created the tale of "The Hobbit." He not only told these tales; he wrote them down, and by 1936, his novel *The Hobbit* was complete. The book, published in 1927 by Sir Stanley Unwin, became an immediate success. Soon, Sir Stanley was asking for a sequel. But it was not until 1954, when Tolkien was approaching retirement, that the first two volumes of his masterpiece, *The Lord of the Rings*, were published. The last volume followed one year later in 1955.

"The Lord of the Rings" trilogy, like its predecessor *The Hobbit*, was extraordinarily popular from the beginning. After his retirement, Tolkien and his wife moved to Bournemouth, where they lived until her death in 1972. Tolkien then returned to Oxford and died after a brief illness on September 2, 1973.

## White, E.B.

Elwyn Brooks White was born on July 11, 1899, in Mount Vernon, New York, and died in 1985. He started writing at an early age, finding it an easy way to collect his thoughts and calm his childhood fears. White's father worked at the piano firm of Horace Walters and Company; he brought home musical instruments, so that White and his five brothers and sisters were surrounded by music. As a child, White learned to play the piano, the mandolin, and the cello.

A diligent student, he consistently got good grades. In 1917, he won two scholarships that paid his tuition to Cornell University. While at Cornell, White wrote for and edited the Cornell Daily Sun. After graduation, he took a job with United Press International, a syndicated news service. White spent many years moving from job to job until he began work for the New Yorker in 1927.

Two years later, 1929, was a momentous year for White. Not only were his first two books published, but in November he married Katharine Angell, an editor at the New Yorker. White's son, Joel, was born on December 12, 1930. Fatherhood suited White; after publishing a book of poems, he started work on his first children's book. *Stuart Little* was published in 1945. White's second children's book, *Charlotte's Web*, was published seven years later. It was named a Newbery Honor Book in 1953, and in 1958 it received the Lewis Carrol Shelf Award, an award given to a book that is worthy to take a place on a shelf next to Carrol's *Alice's Adventures in Wonderland*.

White was one of 38 Americans to receive the Presidential Medal of Freedom from President John F. Kennedy, in 1963. This is the highest honor a civilian can receive during peacetime. White has also received the Laura Ingalls Wilder award. In 1971, White received the National Medal for Literature for his entire body of work.

Neumeyer, Peter F. ***The Annotated Charlotte's Web: Introduction and Notes by Peter F. Neumeyer. Charlotte's Web*** by *E.B. White*. New York: HarperCollins Publishers, c1994.

## White, T.H.

Terence Hanbury White was born May 29, 1906, in Bombay, India. From the beginning, White's parents, Garrick Hanbury and Constance Edith Southcote, had an extremely unhappy marriage; consequently, White spent a relatively unhappy childhood caught in the middle of his parents violent quarrels. White's parents divorced when he was 14 years old.

Because of his unstable childhood, White developed an overwhelming need to arm himself so that if disaster struck he would be ready. To prepare for these perceived disasters, White learned carpentry; he became a pilot, plowman, equestrian, falconer, scuba diver, hunter, fisherman, painter, and concrete worker. He also believed that he must excel with his head, so he became a dedicated scholar, even learning medieval Latin shorthand. White attended Cheltenham College, a public school that also included military training. Although his time at Cheltenham was generally unhappy, he found a mentor in one of his masters, C. F. Scott, who encouraged him to be a writer.

After graduating from Queens' College, Cambridge, White taught English at Stowe School for almost four years, until at the age of 30 he decided to leave to pursue writing full-time. White's best known novel is *The Once and Future King*, which chronicles the life of the legendary King Arthur. The idea for this novel came to White while he wrote a thesis on Thomas Mallory during his years a Cambridge. Intrigued by Mallory's Morte d'Arthur, he wanted to write his own version of the classic tale. *The Once and Future King* was completed on April 17, 1957, 20 years after he had begun it.

The novel quickly became a bestseller in both the United States and England. In 1961, the musical *Camelot*, based on his book, opened on Broadway in 1961 with Julie Andrews and Richard Burton in the lead roles. White loved the show and spent every performance crawling all over the theater to find out what was going on.

White spent much of 1963 on a lecture tour throughout the United States, which he enjoyed very much. After completing the tour, White traveled throughout Europe, visiting Spain, Italy, Egypt, Lebanon, and Greece. He died of acute coronary disease at the age of 57 on January 17, 1964. He had written more than 15 novels as well as poetry, short stories, and nonfiction.

Warner, Sylvia Townsend. **T.H. White: A Biography.** New York: Viking, 1967.

## Wrede, Patricia C.

*"Most fiction is like a pane of glass, a window that we look through to see another view of the world outside ourselves. . . . Fantasy takes the window and coats the outside with the silver of wondrous impossibilities—elves, dragons, wizards, magic. And the window becomes a mirror that reflects both ourselves and all the things in the shadows behind us, the things we have tried to turn our backs on. More: In the best tradition of magic mirrors, fantasy reflects not only ourselves and our shadows, but the truth of our hearts."* (Faces of Fantasy 190)

Patricia Colling Wrede (pronounced "Reedy") was born on March 27, 1953, in Chicago, Illinois. Wrede started writing fiction in the seventh grade and would tell stories to anyone who would listen. To Wrede, writing was always a hobby. In 1974, she graduated from Carleton College with a degree in biology. After graduation, Wrede began work on her first novel, Shadow Magic, which would not be finished until five years later.

On July 24, 1976, Wrede married James M. Wrede. In 1977, she graduated with an MBA from the University of Minnesota and spent the next eight years working in various firms as a financial analyst and accountant. Her first book sold in 1980, and five years later Wrede left the business world and took up writing full-time. Wrede's most famous children's novels, the "Enchanted Forest Chronicles," came about because of a request from Jane Yolen. Yolen asked Wrede to contribute a short story to an anthology that she was editing. Challenged by the idea of writing a short story, Wrede authored a tale called "The Improper Princess." Some time later when Yolen began editing a line of children's books for Harcourt, Brace, Jovanovich, she approached Wrede and persuaded her to expand the short story into a set of novels. The result was the first of the "Chronicles" *Dealing with Dragons,* which was published in 1990.

## WORK CITED

*The Faces of Fantasy.* Illustrated by Patti Perret with Introduction by Terri Windling. New York: TOR (Tom Doherty Associates), 1996.

# Annotated Book List

**NOTES:** After the annotations, we have suggested grade levels for each book. We have also provided an index of the books by grade level at the end of the annotated book list.

Books in a series appear in series order or in order of publication rather than alphabetically by title. We've noted the series title in each case, and also when a book is a sequel to another. For series in the grade level index, we've indicated the series title only.

When a book is currently available in paperback, we've noted that fact in the citation with the abbreviation (pb). When no publisher is mentioned for the paperback edition, this means that it is from the same publisher as the hardcover. We hope this information will be useful to teachers who want to use these books in the classroom. In the case of classics like *Alice's Adventures in Wonderland*, which have been reprinted numerous times, we've listed only the most recent paperback edition.

## PICTURE BOOKS

Ahlberg, Janet and Alan. ***Funnybones***. New York: Greenwillow, 1980, 1981. Mulberry Books, 1990 (pb). Skeletons who live in a dark, dark house go cavorting at night. Grades: K-3.

Allen, Pamela. ***Who Sank the Boat?*** New York: Coward McCann, 1982, 1983. Putnam, 1996 (pb). A group of animals crowd onto a boat until it sinks. Grades: K-3

Aliki. ***Keep Your Mouth Closed, Dear***. New York: Dial, 1966, 1992. Clever, humorous story of a crocodile who keeps eating everything in sight, so his parents have to keep thinking of ways to keep his mouth shut. Grades: K-3

Ardizonne, Aingelda. ***The Night Ride***. Illustrated by Edward Ardizonne. New York: Windmill/E. P. Dutton, 1973. Dandy, Kate, and Tiny Teddy are three old stuffed toys who, when discarded, find a toy engine to help them find a new home. Grades: K-3

Bang, Molly. ***Tye May and the Magic Paint Brush***. New York: Greenwillow, 1981. Mulberry Books, 1992 (pb). Tye May is a poor orphan girl who acquires a magic brush that makes the things she paints come alive. Everyone tries to cash in on her ability, but Tye May paints a boat, has the wicked emperor board it, then paints a storm that sinks it. Grades: K-3

Bang, Molly. ***Wiley and the Hairy Man***. New York: Macmillan, 1986. Aladdin Paperbacks, 1996 (pb). Wiley tries to fool the hairy man in this adaptation of an old American folk tale. Grades: K-3.

Barrett, Ron and Judi. ***Animals Should Definitely Not Wear Clothing***. New York: Atheneum, 1970. Aladdin Paperbacks, 1988, 1989 (pb). Animals would definitely look silly if they wore the clothes depicted in this book. Grades: PreSchool-2.

Barrett, Ron and Judi. ***Cloudy With a Chance of Meatballs***. New York: Atheneum, 1978. Aladdin Paperbacks, 1982 (pb). The inhabitants of the town Chewandswallow have to deal with unusual weather conditions. Grades: K-3.

Bonne, Rose. ***I Know an Old Lady***. Illustrated by Abner Graboff. Music Alan Mills. New York: Rand McNally, 1961. Scholastic Paperbacks, 1980 (pb). Much to her detriment, the old lady tries to solve the problem of eating one thing by eating another and another. Grades: PreSchool-2.

Bowden, Joan Chase. ***The Bean Boy***. New York: Macmillan, 1989. A cumulative tale in which an old lady carves a boy from a bean. The bean is then eaten by a rooster, who is then eaten by a cat, etc. Grades: K-3.

Brett, Jan. ***Town Mouse, Country Mouse***. New York: Putnam, 1994. Two mice trade homes, and each learns to appreciate their own in the process. Grades: PreSchool-3.

Bridwell, Norman. ***How to Care for Your Monster***. New York: Scholastic, 1970. Scholastic Paperbacks, 1988 (pb). A common-sense guide to the everyday care of monsters in the home. Let Frankenstein run your vacuum cleaner, for example. Grades: K-3

Bright, Robert. ***Georgie to the Rescue***. New York: Doubleday, 1956. Georgie the Ghost rescues his friend Miss Owliver when they go with the Whitakers to the city. Grades: K-3

Browne, Anthony. ***The Tunnel***. New York: Knopf, 1989. Ignoring his sister's concerns, a young boy explores a strange tunnel. When he doesn't return, his sister is forced to overcome her fears and go into the tunnel herself where she discovers a fantasy world of fairy tales come to life. Grades: K-3

Burningham, John. ***Mr. Gumpy's Motor Car***. New York: HarperCrest, 1993. Mr. Gumpy and his entourage of children and barnyard animals go for a lovely drive through the fields, get stuck in the mud, squabble, cooperate, and go for a swim. Grades: PreSchool-3

_____. ***Mr. Gumpy's Outing***. New York: Holt, Rinehart and Winston, 1970, 1990 (pb). Mr. Gumpy invites a lot of animals to come along with him on a boat trip, as long as they don't mess around. They do anyway. Grades: PreSchool-3

Calhoun, Mary. ***The Witch of Hissing Hill***. Illustrated by Janet McCaffery. New York: William Morrow, 1964. A witch raises black cats to sell, but all of a sudden one of them is born yellow. It's an outrage. Grades: PreSchool-3

DePaola, Tomie. ***Helga's Dowry***. New York: Harcourt Brace Jovanovich, 1977. 1988 (pb). Helga tries to get a dowry to win the heart of Rich Sven, who has dumped her for Plain Inge. Her trollery gains the attention of the Troll King. Grades: K-3

DeRegniers, Beatrice. ***May I Bring a Friend?*** New York: Atheneum, 1964, 1971. Aladdin Paperbacks, 1989 (pb). The king and the queen tell a boy that any friend of his is a friend of theirs. He brings all his animal friends over for lunch. Grades: PreSchool-3

Devlin, Wende and Harry. ***Old Black Witch***. Illustrated by Harry Devlin. New York: Four Winds, 1963. Aladdin Paperbacks, 1992 (pb). Old Black Witch first hinders, then helps Nicky and his mother open a tearoom in an old New England house. Grades: K-3

Domanska, Janina. ***The Turnip***. New York: Macmillan, 1969. Everyone has to help pull the enormous turnip out of the ground. Grades: K-3

Freeman, Don. ***Corduroy***. New York: Viking, 1968, 1976 (pb), 1985. Corduroy always wanted a friend and a home. He gets them both. Grades: PreSchool-2

_____. ***A Pocket for Corduroy***. New York: Viking, 1978, 1980 (pb). Puffin, 1993, 1997 (pb). Corduroy gets lost in a laundromat while searching for a pocket. Grades: PreSchool-2

Gaeddert, Louann. ***Gustav the Gourmet Giant***. Illustrated by Steven Kellogg. New York: Dial, 1976. Gustav can't get enough of good food. When he sees a small boy's lamb, he wants it, but the boy won't let him have it. The boy decides to play a trick on the giant and persuades Gustav that eating boy is better. Grades: K-3

Galdone, Joanna. ***The Tailypo: A Ghost Story***. Illustrated by Paul Galdone. New York: Clarion, 1977. Houghton Mifflin, 1984 (pb). A man eats a tail and the creature returns, wanting it back. Grades: K-3

Harper, Wilhemina. ***The Gunniwolf***. Illustrated by William Wiesner. New York: Dutton, 1918, 1946 text, 1967 illus. A girl is told by her mother never, NEVER to go off into the woods. She does anyway to buy beautiful flowers, and meets the Gunniwolf. Grades: K-3

Heide, Florence Parry and Roxanne Heide. ***A Monster Is Coming! A Monster Is Coming!*** Illustrated by Rachi Farrow. New York: Franklin Watts, 1980. One sibling tries to warn another about an impending monster attack, but is too late. Grades: K-3

Hissey, Jane. "Old Bear Series"
***Old Bear***. New York: Philomel, 1986. Putnam, 1996 (pb). Philomel Board Books, 1998 (board book). A group of stuffed animals try to figure out how they can get Old Bear down from the attic. Grades: PreSchool-3
Sequels are: *Little Bear Lost; Little Bear's Trousers; Old Bear Tales; Best Friends: Old Bear Tales; Jolly Snow; Jolly Tall*

Hoban, Russell. ***Dinner at Alberta's***. Illustrated by James Marshall. New York: Crowell, 1975. A crocodile has to learn manners. Grades: K-3

Howe, James. ***There's a Monster Under My Bed***. Illustrated by David Rose. New York: Atheneum, 1986. Aladdin Paperbacks, 1990 (pb). A boy worries that there might be a monster, perhaps several terrible monsters, under his bed. Grades: K-3

Ivimey, John W. ***Complete Story of the Three Blind Mice***. Illustrated by Paul Galdone. New York: Clarion, 1987, 1989 (pb). The full story of just how those mice went blind and lost their tails. Grades: K-3

Kahl, Virginia. ***The Duchess Bakes a Cake***. New York: Scribners, 1955. Encore Editions, 1978. A clever rhymed story about a duchess who bakes a cake that keeps growing and growing, carrying her up with it. Grades: K-3

Kellogg, Steven. ***Chicken Little***. New York: Morrow, 1985, 1987 (pb). This is a very funny variation on the Henny Penny story. The fox disguises himself as a policeman and herds the fowl into a paddy wagon. Later, the fleeing fox is flattened by Sgt. Hippo Hefty. Grades: PreSchool-3

_____. ***Jack and the Beanstalk***. New York: Morrow, 1991. Mulberry, 1997 (pb). Kellogg's illustrations grace a traditional retelling of this favorite tale. Grades: PreSchool-3

Kent, Jack. ***The Fat Cat***. New York: Parents Magazine Press, 1971. Scholastic Paperbacks, 1987 (pb). A cumulative Dutch folktale about a cat that eats everything that comes across its path. Grades: PreSchool-3

Kroll, Steven. ***Big Jeremy***. Illustrated by Donald Carrick. New York: Holiday House, 1989. The lovable giant, Jeremy, helps his friends, the Terisons, until the day of the fire. Jeremy blows it out and literally blows the Terisons away. It takes a few heartaches before he can set things right. Grades: K-3

Lachner, Dorothea. ***Meredith The Witch Who Wasn't***. New York: North-South Books, 1997. Meredith is cast out of the witching society because she avoids the use of magic, but when the other witches find out how good things are when made by hand they reinstate her. Grades: K-3

Lillegard, Dee. ***Sitting in My Box***. Illustrated by John Agee. New York: Dutton, 1989 (pb). The box in which the little boy and all the animals are sitting gets more and more crowded until a hungry flea arrives on the scene. Grades: PreSchool-3

Lobel, Arnold. ***Fables***. New York: Harper and Row, 1980. Trophy, 1983 (pb). Lobel's *pièce de résistance* written in his typically dry witty style. The animals' predicaments are wonderful commentaries on human foibles. Grades: K-3

Morimoto, Junko. ***Mouse's Marriage***. New York: Viking Kestrel, 1985, 1988. A mouse couple searches for the best and mightiest husband in the world for their daughter. Grades: K-3

Ness, Evaline. ***Mr. Miacca: An English Folktale***. New York: Holt, Rinehart & Winston, 1967. Mr. Miacca steals a young boy who walks around the corner. He is going to cut his leg off to use for a stew, but the boy hides under his couch, holds out a wooden couch leg which Mr. Miacca mistakes for the real thing, and then escapes. Grades: K-3

Opie, Iona. ***My Very First Mother Goose***. Illustrated by Rosemary Wells. New York: Candlewick, 1996. Collection of more than 60 nursery rhymes. Grades: PreSchool-5

Scieska, Jon. ***The Stinky Cheese Man and Other Fairly Stupid Tales***. Illustrated by Lane Smith. New York: Viking, 1993. Dutton, 1998 (pb). Riotously warped versions of familiar fairy tales. Grades: PreSchool-4

Sendak, Maurice. ***Outside Over There***. New York: HarperCollins, 1981, 1987. HarperTrophy, 1989 (pb). Goblins steal Ida's baby sister, and she has to rescue her. Grades: K-3

_____. ***Where the Wild Things Are***. New York: HarperCollins, 1963. HarperTrophy, 1988 (pb). Max is sent to his room after behaving badly, and a jungle grows. A boat appears and takes him to the place where the Wild Things are, whom he tames with his magic trick. Grades: PreSchool-3

Seymour, Peter. ***What's in the Cave?*** Illustrated by David A. Carter. New York: Holt, Rinehart and Winston, 1985. Henry Holt, 1993. A lift-the-flap pop-up book that shows different things in a cave, ending with a monster. Grades: PreSchool-2

Shulevitz, Uri. ***One Monday Morning***. New York: Scribners, 1967. Atheneum, 1986 (pb). A boy living in the inner city is visited each day of the week by fantasy characters from a pack of cards. But each day, he is not home. He is out somewhere in the dreary city. Finally, on Sunday, he is home, and the royal procession drops in to say hello. Grades: K-3

Steptoe, John. ***The Story of Jumping Mouse: A Native American Legend***. New York: Lothrop, Lee and Shepard, 1984, 1985. Mulberry Books, 1989 (pb). Jumping Mouse gives away precious things, such as his sight and sense of smell, to other animals in need. Grades: K-3

Thayer, Jane. ***Gus Was a Friendly Ghost***. Illustrated by Seymour Fleishman. New York: Morrow, 1962. When Gus the Ghost's family goes away for the winter, he makes friends with a mouse. When the family returns, he has to keep them from killing him. Grades: K-3

VanAllsburg, Chris. ***The Garden of Abdul Gasazi***. Boston: Houghton Mifflin, 1979. A boy follows his dog into the mysterious garden of the magician Abdul Gasazi. Gasazi leads him to believe that he has turned the dog into a duck. Grades: 1-5

_____. ***Jumanji***. Boston: Houghton Mifflin, 1981. Peter and Judy find a jungle adventure board game that comes to life in their living room. Grades: 1-5

_____. ***The Mysteries of Harris Burdick***. Boston: Houghton Mifflin, 1984, 1996 (Portfolio Edition). A series of mysterious pictures with only titles and captions to explain them. You have to make up the rest. Grades: 5 and up

_____. ***The Polar Express***. Boston: Houghton Mifflin, 1985. The Polar Express one Christmas Eve takes a young boy who truly believes in Santa to the North Pole, where Santa gives him his heart's desire—a bell from his sleigh. Grades: 2 and up

_____. ***The Widow's Broom***. Boston: Houghton Mifflin, 1992. A witch crash-lands in a field, is tended by a kind old widow, and disappears the next morning, leaving her broom behind. The broom, it turns out, can clean the house and play the piano, among other things. Grades: K-4

_____. ***The Wreck of the Zephyr***. Boston: Houghton Mifflin, 1983. A boy hears a mysterious tale from a sailor about a boat that can fly. Grades: 2-5

_____. ***The Wretched Stone***. Boston: Houghton Mifflin, 1991. On an island, sailors find a strange glowing rock that turns them all into apes. Grades: 3-5

Wahl, Jan. ***Humphrey's Bear***. Illustrated by William Joyce. New York: Holt, Rinehart & Winston, 1987. Henry Holt, 1989 (pb). Humphrey journeys with his Teddy Bear in his dreams. His father comes into the room and tells Humphrey that the bear used to go with him as well. Grades: K-3

Westcott, Nadine Bernard. ***The Giant Vegetable Garden***. New York: Little Brown, 1981. The residents of a town grow a garden of vegetables big enough to serve as houses. Grades: K-3

Wiesner, David. ***Free Fall***. New York: Lothrop, Lee & Shepard, 1988. Mulberry Books, 1991 (pb). In this wordless picture book, a young boy dreams of daring adventures in the company of imaginary creatures inspired by the things surrounding his bed. The illustrations form one continuous picture, in which images morph from one thing to another, much like the paintings of M. C. Escher. Grades: 1-5

_____. ***Hurricane***. New York: Clarion, 1990. Houghton Mifflin, 1992 (pb). A hurricane uproots a tree in the yard of two brothers. It becomes a magical place, transporting them on adventures limited only by their imaginations. Grades: K-3

_____. ***June 29, 1999***. New York: Clarion, 1992, 1995 (pb). Becky's science project is to send up plants in balloons to see the effects of high altitude on growth. Large vegetables begin descending on the earth. We discover that they are not her vegetables at all but an accidental discharge from the galley of an alien ship. Grades: K-3

_____. ***Tuesday***. New York: Clarion, 1991, 1997 (pb). Caldecott Medal, 1992. In this nearly wordless picture book, frogs fly on their lily pads, floating through the air, and explore the nearby houses and scare dogs. Grades: K-3

Willard, Nancy. ***The Tale I Told Sasha***. Illustrated by David Christiana. Boston: Little Brown, 1999. A little girl travels in search of her lost yellow ball into the "strange adventures that shadows hide." Mystical and poetic. Grades: K-3

Wood, Audrey and Don. ***Heckedy Peg***. New York: Harcourt Brace Jovanovich, 1987, 1992 (pb). A mother with seven children named after the days of the week leaves home. While she's gone, a witch comes to the house, turns the children into food, and takes them home to eat. Mom journeys to the witch's house and breaks the spell by correctly identifying the food that each has been turned into. Grades: PreSchool-3

_____. ***King Bidgood's in the Bathtub***. New York: Harcourt Brace Jovanovich, 1985, 1993 (pb). No one can get King Bidgood out of his bath, not his wife, nor the court. Only the page who pulls the plug succeeds where everyone else has failed. Grades: PreSchool-3

Young, Ed. ***The Seven Blind Mice***. New York: Philomel, 1992. Each of the Seven Blind Mice thinks an elephant they are examining is something else, because each can feel only part of it. Grades: PreSchool-3

# CHAPTER BOOKS

Adams, Richard. ***Watership Down***. New York: Macmillan, 1972. 429 p. Avon, 1975, 1989 (pb). A group of rabbits must leave their warren when developers destroy it. This story of their quest to find a new home is a classic that has tremendous resonance because of the way Adams creates the rabbit's society complete with rabbit folklore. Grades: 6 and up

Aiken, Joan. "Wolves Chronicles"
***The Wolves of Willoughby Chase***. Illustrated by Pat Marriott. Garden City, New York: Doubleday, 1962. 168 p. Dell/Yearling, 1987 (pb). This is a first in a series set in an England with an alternate history, though it most resembles the Victorian era. Bonnie, Sylvia, and their friend Simon are pursued by wolves and face many other chilling adventures as they try to escape from the evil Miss Slighcarp and Miss Brisket, who had been charged with their care during their parents' absence. They eventually find their way to an orphanage. This story has plenty of melodramatic action. Grades: 5-7

***Black Hearts in Battersea***. Garden City, New York: Doubleday, 1964. 240 p. Laureleaf, 1987 (pb). Simon arrives in London to find his only friend there has disappeared. When he tries to find out where he has gone, he gets tangled up with a wicked group plotting against King James. Simon and his friends Dido Twite and Justin are able to discover their true family background after being kidnapped and enduring a shipwreck. Grades: 5-7

***Nightbirds on Nantucket***. Garden City, New York: Doubleday, 1966. 216 p. Dell/Yearling, 1989 (pb). When Dido Twite is rescued from a watery grave by a ship commanded by Captain Casket, she finds the ship is carrying curious cargo and soon becomes entangled in the mysterious plans of an evil woman who is concocting a plot against King James. Grades: 5-7

***The Cuckoo Tree***. Illustrated by Susan Obrant. New York: Doubleday, 1971. 314 p. Dell/Yearling, 1988 (pb). While caring for an injured friend, Dido Twite finds she has stumbled upon another Hanoverian plot. It is up to Dido to alert the King and save St. Paul's Cathedral from being put on rollers and rolled into the River Thames. Grades: 5-7

***The Stolen Lake***. New York: Delacorte, 1981. 291 p. Dell/Yearling, 1988 (pb). Dido Twite has many adventures on her way to England from Nantucket, especially when the ship is diverted to the land of New Cumbria in the southern hemisphere. Dido assists the queen to recover the titular lake. Grades: 5-7

***Dido and Pa***. New York: Delacorte, 1986. 258 p. Dell/Yearling, 1988 (pb). Her rascally father draws Dido into the middle of a dastardly Hanoverian conspiracy. Dido must break free and warn the King that there is a plot to put a pretender on the throne. Grades: 5-7

***Is Underground***. New York: Delacorte, 1993. 242 p. Dell/Yearling, 1995 (pb). Bound by a promise to her dead uncle, Is travels to the north country to discover why so many of London's children are disappearing and to find a prince and another missing boy. The children are being lured aboard trains with promises of a journey to "Playland," when in reality they are being conscripted to working in dank undersea mines. Grades: 5-7

***Cold Shoulder Road***. New York: Delacorte, 1995. 192 p. Dell/Yearling, 1997 (pb). Dido Twite and her cousin Arun tangle with hoodlums who are attempting to smuggle mastodon horns through a tunnel under the English Channel. The story is full of hair-raising adventure from the start when

Arun returns to his hometown, only to find his mother has disappeared. Grades: 5-7

***Dangerous Games***. New York: Delacorte, 1999. 288 p. This time Dido finds herself on an island where she becomes inadvertently involved in a simmering conflict. Grades: 5-7

_____. ***The Shadow Guests***. New York: Delacorte, 1980. 150 p. Dell/Yearling, 1986 (pb). Cosmo discovers that the disappearance of his mother and older brother may be attributed to a family curse. Cosmo releases a supernatural frenzy with his presence when he arrives at his cousin, Eunice's, home in England. Grades: 6-9

Alcock, Vivien. ***The Haunting of Cassie Palmer***. New York: Delacorte, 1980. 149 p. Houghton Mifflin, 1997 (pb). The seventh child of a seventh child, 13 year-old Cassie has the gift of second sight that enables her to communicate with the Other World. Unfortunately, with this power she raises a ghost from the dead who proves a nuisance. Grades: 6-8

_____. ***The Sylvia Game***. New York: Delacorte, 1982. 186 p. Houghton Mifflin, 1997 (pb). When 12 year-old Emily follows her father, a painter, on a mysterious errand to Mallerton House, she is caught up in an international art conspiracy with Oliver Mallerton, who calls her Sylvia because of her resemblance to a girl in a painting by Renoir. Together, Oliver and Emily must find out who the real Sylvia is: A girl who died one hundred years ago or Emily herself? Grades: 4-7

Alexander, Lloyd. ***The Arkadians***. New York: Dutton Children's Books, 1995. 272 p. Puffin, 1997 (pb). Delightfully funny tale of a poet who has been turned into a jackass, a young girl with mystical powers, and a young man who embark on a set of epic adventures to escape the wrath of the king and his wicked soothsayers. Grades: 4-9

_____. "Chronicles of Prydain"
***The Book of Three***. New York: Holt, Rinehart & Winston, 1964. 217 p. Dell, 1985 (pb). Taran, assistant pig keeper at Caer Dallben, begins a mighty quest in which he must face the forces of evil when the oracular pig, HenWen, escapes into the woods. Grades: 5-8

***The Black Cauldron***. New York: Holt, Rinehart & Winston, 1965. 224 p. Dell, 1985 (pb). A group of companions, including Taran, are chosen to go to the realm of Arwan Death-Lord to destroy the Black Cauldron, which Arwan uses to create an army of deathless warriors. Grades: 5-8

***The Castle of Llyr***. New York: Holt, Rinehart & Winston, 1966. 201 p. Dell, 1985 (pb). Princess Eilonwy leaves Prydain to go to Mona to be trained as a proper princess. When sinister circumstances befall her, it is up to Taran and his companions to rescue her. Grades: 5-8

***Taran Wanderer***. New York: Holt, Rinehart & Winston, 1967. 256 p. Dell, 1985 (pb). Taran goes on a quest to find out who his parents were. Along the way he meets and becomes friends with many of the common folk of Prydain, and in the end he learns some very hard lessons. Grades: 5-8

***The High King***. New York: Holt, Rinehart & Winston, 1968. 285 p. Dell, 1980, 1985 (pb). When the sword of Drnwyn falls into the hand of Arawn-Death-Lord, it is up to Taran and his companions to raise an army to defeat him. Grades: 5-8

_____. ***The First Two Lives of Lukas Kasha***. New York: Dutton, 1978. 213 p. Puffin, 1998 (pb). When a carpenter's helper pays a silver penny for a magician to perform, he is transported to a strange place where the people all call him the King of Abadan. Grades: 5-8

_____. ***Gypsy Rizka***. New York: Dutton, 1999. 176 p. Rizka lives alone in her gypsy trailer on the outskirts of Greater Dunitsa, waiting for her father to return. In the meantime she plays outrageous jokes on the townspeople, who on the surface can barely stand her and want her to leave. The truth is that deep down they really love her. Rizka is a trickster in the folktale tradition. Grades: 3-7

_____. ***The Iron Ring***. New York: Dutton, 1997. 283 p. An epic story set in India. Tamar, the king of Sundari is wakened one night by elephants. A king named Jaya visits him and plays a dice game called Aksha. Tamar loses the game and his life is now the other king's, in token of which an iron ring appears on his finger. He is driven by honor to journey to Jaya's country to pay this debt and to meet his fate, which he thinks is death. In the journey he meets a beautiful girl, gets involved in a war between two kingdoms, meets many good friends, and learns much. Grades: 6-10

_____. ***The Marvelous Misadventures of Sebastian: Grand Extravaganza, Including a Performance by the Entire Cast of the Gallimaufry Theatricus***. New York: Dutton, 1970. 204 p. Dell, 1991 (pb). Sebastian, a fiddler, after going out into the world to seek his fortune, finds that dreams can be nightmares, friends can be foes, and one's fortune is not always what he thinks it is. Grades: 4-7

_____. ***The Remarkable Journey of Prince Jen***. New York: Dutton, 1991. 273 p. Dell/Yearling, 1993 (pb). On a perilous quest to find the legendary court of T'ienkuo, Prince Jen must face his destiny and engage in a grim struggle from which he emerges triumphantly into manhood. Grades: 5-10

_____. "Vesper Holly Series"
***The Illyrian Adventure***. New York: Dutton, 1986. 132 p. Dell/Yearling, 1990 (pb). Vesper Holly has the digestive talents of a goat and the mind of a chess master. She gets her guardian, Brinnie, to go with her to Illyria, where she wants to check out the truth that might be found in that country's epic mythological poem, the Illyriad. Filled with swashbuckling adventure reminiscent of the "Indiana Jones" movies. Grades: 5-9

***The El Dorado Adventure***. New York: E.P. Dutton, 1987. 164 p. Dell/Yearling, 1990 (pb). Vesper finds out that she owns a volcano in South America. She gets a mysterious invitation from a Frenchman to go see it. He pays for a one-way passage for Vesper and her guardian, Brinnie. They arrive and find that he's going to build a canal through Vesper's land, and they discover that he wants to ever so quietly get rid of them. They also discover that the villain, Helvetius, who was their nemesis in The Illyrian Adventure, is actually controlling him. They have to deal with a handsome, Cambridge-educated chieftain and a depraved parrot. Grades: 5-9

***The Drackenberg Adventure***. New York: Dutton, 1988. 152 p. Dell/Yearling, 1990 (pb). This entry in the series centers on a trip to Drackenberg. Brinnie's wife Mary comes along this time. Helvetius, their archenemy, shows up, and it turns out he's got his claws on a lost masterpiece by DaVinci. Mary is kidnapped, they are nearly blown up by a sausage bomb, and they masquerade as gypsies. Grades: 5-9

***The Jedera Adventure***. New York: Dutton, 1989. 152 p. Dell/Yearling, 1990 (pb). Vesper Holly attempts to return a book her father checked out from the Bel Saaba library. The book ends up being the means of saving a Tawarik tribesman who has come to Vesper's aid. Vesper also flies in a machine invented by Dr. Helvetius, her evil nemesis, the secrets of which are contained in a book located only in the Bel Saaba library. Grades: 5-9

***The Philadelphia Adventure***. New York: Dutton, 1990. 150 p. Dell/Yearling, 1992 (pb). This final volume in the "Vesper Holly" series is set in Alexander's own hometown of Philadelphia against the backdrop of the 1876 Centennial Exposition. Dr. Helvetius is at it again, and his schemes take Vesper and Brinnie from downtown Philly to the Pennsylvania countryside.

_____. "Westmark Trilogy"
***Westmark***. New York: Dutton, 1981. 190 p. Dell, 1982 (pb). Theo, a printer's devil fleeing from criminal charges, escapes with the help of the outrageous count Las Bombas and his dwarf attendant. They meet Mickle, a girl disguised as a boy, who turns out to be a deposed princess. Ultimately, they arrive at the palace and help the king, who is grieving over the loss of his daughter. In a thrilling climax, Theo chases the villains up a bell tower. They jump on the bell-rope, thus making the bells ring for the first time in centuries. Soon bells are ringing all over Westmark. The central theme of the "Westmark" books is the tragedy of war. Grades: 6-12

***The Kestrel***. New York: Dutton, 1982. 244 p. Dell/Laurel Leaf, 1991 (pb). Theo and his former companions are all needed when war erupts in Westmark and Mickle assumes the throne. Grades: 6-12

***The Beggar Queen***. New York: Dutton, 1984. 237 p. Dell/Laurel Leaf, 1985 (pb). Chaos reigns when the king's uncle, Duke Conrad of Regia, plots to overthrow the new government of Westmark and bring an end to the reforms instituted by Mickle, now Queen Augusta, Theo, and their companions. Grades: 6-12

Anderson, Margaret Jean. "Time Trilogy"
***In the Keep of Time***. New York: Knopf, 1977. 149 p. A simple day exploring a ruined Scottish tower turns into a series of exciting adventures when four children from London are sent back in time to the year 1460 and then forward to the 22nd Century. Grades: 5-8

***In the Circle of Time***. New York: Knopf, 1979. 181 p. Scholastic Paperbacks, 1981 (pb). Random, 1987. Carried through the circle of time to the year 2179 it is up to two 20th century children to help a peace-loving people in their courageous struggle to protect their simple ways from a barbaric mechanized society that is bent on conquering and enslaving them. Grades: 5-8

***The Mists of Time***. New York: Knopf, 1984. 179 p. Laura Avara, who has the ability to make contact with people from other eras, is powerless when barbaric outsiders enslave her people, who refuse to answer violence with violence. In a desperate attempt to save her homeland, Laura, with the help of the mystic Lenarchus, reaches out for help to Jennifer and Robert, two time-traveling children from the 20th century. Grades: 5-8

Applegate, K. A. "Animorphs Series"
***The Invasion***. New York: Scholastic, 1996 (pb). 184 p. Jake, Rachel, Cassie, Tobias, and Marco take a shortcut home from the mall through a construction site. There they witness the landing of an alien spacecraft and the death of the Andalite, Elfangor, at the hands of the evil Yeerk, Visser Three. Before he dies, Elfangor passes on his morphing power to the five children. They are able to access the DNA pattern of any animal when they touch it, and then morph into that animal form. With this power, they are now the earth's only defense against an invasion by the Yeerks, who are sluglike creatures who need hosts to survive. They enter a person's brain and take over his thought processes. Grades 3-6

The other titles in the "Animorphs" series, in order with the "specials" listed last, are:
***The Visitor***
***The Encounter***
***The Message***
***The Predator***
***The Capture***
***The Stranger***
***The Alien***
***The Secret***
***The Android***
***The Forgotten***
***The Reaction***
***The Change***
***The Unknown***
***The Escape***
***The Warning***
***The Underground***
***The Decision***
***The Departure***
***The Discovery***
***The Threat***
***The Solution***
***The Pretender***
***The Suspicion***
***The Extreme***
***The Attack***
***The Exposed***
***The Experiment***
***The Sickness***
***Megamorphs 1: The Andalite's Gift***
***Megamorphs 2: In the Time of the Dinosaurs***
***The Andalite Chronicles***
***The Hork-Bajir Chronicles***

Asch, Frank. ***Journey to Terezor***. New York: Holiday House, 1989. 160 p. After a devastating flood destroys their home, Matt and his parents are transported to a mysterious planet inhabited by other misplaced earthlings and ruled by robots. Matt teams up with two young geniuses and a robot in an effort to escape back to Earth. Grades: 3-6

Avi. ***City of Light, City of Dark: A Comic Book Novel***. Illustrated by Brian Floca. New York: Orchard Books, 1993. 192 p. 1995 (pb). It is up to Asterel to locate a token that will prevent the Kurbs from freezing the city. A graphic novel. Grades: 4 and up

_____. ***Poppy***. Illustrated by Brian Floca. New York: Orchard Books, 1995. 146 p. Camelot, 1997 (pb). Poppy finds out that what the mice believe about the great owl is not true. They believe he protects them from the porcupine, when in reality he eats them. It begins with the owl eating Poppy's boyfriend, Ragweed, and doesn't mince words describing the fur pellet and other graphic details. Grades: 3-6

_____. ***Poppy and Rye***. Illustrated by Brian Floca. New York: Avon Books, 1998. 182 p. Avon, 1999 (pb). Poppy returns to Ragweed's family to bring them the news of Ragweed's death. She discovers that Ragweed's family's home is threatened by a band of beavers who are building a dam that will flood the mice out. Sequel to *Poppy*. Grades: 3-6

Babbitt, Natalie. ***Goody Hall***. New York: Farrar, Straus & Giroux, 1971. 176 p. Sunburst, 1986 (pb). Hercules Feltwright, an itinerant actor who is always garbling Shakespeare quotations, comes to Goody Hall to tutor a young boy named Willet Goody. Willet believes that his father is not dead, and Hercules helps him solve the mystery. Grades: 4-6

_____. ***Kneeknock Rise***. New York: Farrar, Straus & Giroux, 1970. 117 p. 1984 (pb). Young Egan, the only one in the village unafraid of the strange creature who supposedly lives at the top of Kneeknock Rise, sets out to solve the mystery. Grades: 3-5

_____. ***The Search for Delicious***. New York: Farrar, Straus & Giroux, 1969. 67 p. 1991 (pb). When compiling a dictionary, the Prime Minister comes to a screeching halt when no one at court can agree on the meaning of "delicious." To settle the controversy, the King sends his 12 year-old messenger to poll the country. Grades: 3-6

_____. ***Tuck Everlasting***. New York: Farrar, Straus & Giroux, 1975. 139 p. 1985 (pb). When 10 year-old Winnie Foster and the man in the yellow suit discover the secret spring whose water gives the drinker everlasting life, the Tuck family is confronted with an agonizing situation. They once unknowingly drank from the spring. While they share their secret with Winnie, they must persuade her not to drink as well. One of the truly great fantasy books. Grades: 4-7

Barrie, J. M. ***Peter Pan***. Illustrated by Nora S. Unwin. New York: Charles Scribner's Sons, 1950. 242 p. Bantam Books, 1994 (pb). The classic tale of the adventures the three Darling children have in Neverland with Peter Pan, a boy who would never grow up. Grades: 4-6

Baum, L. Frank. ***The Life and Adventures of Santa Claus***. Chicago: M.A. Donohue, 1902. 206 p. Signet, 1994 (pb). Tells the story of the life of Santa Claus from birth through old age. Grades: 3-8

_____. ***Little Wizard Stories of Oz***. Illustrated by John R. Neill. New York: William Morrow, 1994. 169 p. Six stories about Dorothy and Toto, Ozma, Tiktok, Jack Pumpkinhead, the Tin Woodman, and other characters from the land of Oz. Grades: 3-8

_____. "Oz Series"
***The Wizard of Oz***. Illustrated by W. W. Denslow. Chicago: G.M. Hill, 1900. 259 p. Dover, 1996 (pb). Dorothy gets carried by a cyclone from Kansas to Oz and meets the Scarecrow, Tin Man, and Cowardly Lion on her journey down the Yellow Brick Road to the Emerald City. All are on their way to meet the Wizard of Oz, who is the only one who can help her find her way back home. Grades: 3-6
Sequels are:
***The Land of Oz***
***Ozma of Oz***
***Dorothy and the Wizard in Oz***
***The Road to Oz***
***The Emerald City of Oz***
***The Patchwork Girl of Oz***
***Tik-Tok of Oz***
***The Scarecrow of Oz***
***The Lost Princess of Oz***
***The Tin Woodman of Oz***
***The Magic of Oz***
***Glinda of Oz***

_____. ***The Surprising Adventures of the Magical Monarch of Mo and his People***. Illustrated by Frank Verbeck. Indianapolis: Bobbs Merrill, 1901, 1903, 1947. 236 p. Dover, 1968 (pb). Fourteen stories about the magical land of Mo and the people and animals that live there. Grades: 3-6

Bellairs, John. "Johnny Dixon Mysteries" (selected titles)
***The Curse of the Blue Figurine***. New York: Dial Press. 200 p. Puffin, 1996 (pb). When Johnny Dixon takes a blue figurine called a Shawabti from a church, he is driven into some frightening adventures. Grades: 4-6

***The Mummy, the Will and the Crypt***. New York: Dial Press, 1983. 168 p. Puffin, 1996 (pb). Johnny Dixon and Professor Childermass are called upon to locate the will of an eccentric cereal tycoon who wanted to make things difficult for his heirs. Grades: 4-6

***The Trolley to Yesterday***. New York: Dial Press, 1989. 183 p. Puffin, 1998 (pb). Johnny Dixon and Professor Childermass discover a trolley that transports them back to 1453 Constantinople where the Turks are invading the Byzantine Empire. Grades: 4-6

_____. "House With a Clock in its Walls Trilogy"

***The House With a Clock in its Walls***. Illustrated by Edward Gorey. New York: Dial Press, 1973. 179 p. Puffin, 1993 (pb). Genuinely scary. When Lewis becomes orphaned he goes to live with his uncle, who happens to be a wizard and lives next door to a witch. Hidden in the house is a clock ticking off the seconds until Doomsday. Grades: 4-6

***The Figure in the Shadows***. Illustrated by Mercer Mayer. New York: Dial Press, 1975. 155 p. Puffin, 1993 (pb). Lewis needs courage to stand up to bully Woody Mingo. He finds it in an old magic amulet, but in the process unleashes deadly forces. Grades: 4-6

***The Letter, the Witch and the Ring***. Illustrated by Richard Egielski. New York: Dial Press, 1976. 188 p. Puffin, 1993 (pb). Lewis Barnavelt's friend Rose Rita Pottinger is upset about the prospect of a boring summer while Lewis is away at camp. It turns out to be anything but boring, as Rose Rita must decipher an unusual letter Lewis' next door neighbor, Mrs. Zimmerman, receives from her uncle on his deathbed. Rose Rita and Mrs. Zimmerman embark on a journey to solve the mystery, which involves a missing ring. Grades 4-6

_____. ***The Dark Secret of Weatherend***. New York: Dial Press, 1984. 182 p. Puffin, 1997 (pb). Fourteen-year-old Anthony Monday and the librarian, Miss Eells, must stop an evil wizard from turning earth into an icy wilderness. Grades: 4-6

Bethancourt, T. Ernesto. ***The Dog Days of Arthur Cane***. New York: Holiday House, 1976. 160 p. A teenage boy doubts the power of a witch doctor and is transformed into a dog and forced to remain that way for the entire summer. Grades: 6-9

_____. ***Tune in Yesterday***. New York: Holiday House, 1978. 156 p. Bantam, 1981 (pb). Because of their love of jazz, two friends are propelled back into the year 1942 and find their lives complicated by racial prejudice and Nazi plots. Grades: 8-10

_____. ***The Tomorrow Connection***. New York: Holiday House, 1984. 134 p. When two musicians find themselves stranded in 1906, they travel across the country arriving in San Francisco just in time for the great earthquake and enlist Harry Houdini to help them find a gate to the future. Companion to ***Tune in Yesterday***. Grades: 8-10

Bond, Nancy. ***Another Shore***. New York: Margaret K. McElderry Books, 1988. 308 p. While working in a reconstructed colonial settlement in Nova Scotia, 17-year-old Lyn is suddenly transported back to 1744, when the French inhabitants are at war with England. Grades: 7 and up

_____. ***A String in the Harp***. Allen Davis. New York: Atheneum, 1976. 370 p. Aladdin Paperbacks, 1996 (pb). An American child discovers an ancient harp-tuning key that takes him back to Wales in the time of the sixth century bard Taliesin. Grades: 7 and up

Boston, L. M. "Green Knowe Books"

***The Children of Green Knowe***. Illustrated by Peter Boston. New York: Harcourt, Brace & World 1955. 157 p. 1989 (pb). A young boy finds happiness in an old English house where he is haunted by children who lived in the house before him. Grades: 4-7

***An Enemy at Green Knowe***. Illustrated by Peter Boston. New York: Harcourt, Brace & World, 1964. 156 p. 1989 (pb). When a modern-day witch tries to find some books supposedly hidden in Green Knowe, the inhabitants of the house become involved with black magic. Grades: 4-7

***The River at Green Knowe***. Illustrated by Peter Boston. New York: Harcourt, Brace & World, 1959. 153 p. 1989. (pb). An English girl, a Polish refugee, and a boy from the Orient explore the river near Green Knowe. Grades: 4-7

***The Stones of Green Knowe***. Illustrated by Peter Boston. New York: Atheneum, 1976. 156 p. A young boy is carried through time by ancient magic while his father is building a new stone manor house to replace their old wooden Saxon hall. Grades: 4-7

***A Stranger at Green Knowe***. Illustrated by Peter Boston. New York: Harcourt, Brace & World, 1961. 158 p. 1989 (pb). A Chinese refugee makes friends with a gorilla who has escaped from the zoo. Grades: 4-7

Briggs, Katharine Mary. ***Hobberdy Dick***. New York: Greenwillow, 1975, 1977. 239 p. Although apprehensive at first, Hobberdy Dick, a hobgoblin, learns to love the new owners of Cotswold Manor. With subtle magic and impish tricks, he helps Joel, the oldest son, win his lady love, releases Martha from the village witch, and helps the children discover gold buried in the stables. Grades: 6-8

_____. ***Kate Crackernuts***. New York: Greenwillow, 1979. 223 p. Fast friends Katherine Lindsay and Kate Maxwell are overjoyed when their parents marry, but when Kate's mother, jealous of Katherine's beauty, bewitches her and she unwittingly falls into the hands of the witch Mall Gross, it is up to Kate and their trusted friend Gideon to save her. Grades: 6-9

Brittain, Bill. ***All the Money in the World***. Illustrated by Charles Robinson. New York: HarperCollins, 1979. 150 p. 1992 (pb). Quentin is granted his wish for all the money in the world, but he also gets a load of troubles. Grades: 3-6

_____. ***Professor Popkin's Prodigious Polish: A Tale of Coven Tree***. Illustrated by Andrew Glass. New York: HarperCollins, 1990. 152 p. Strange things start to happen in Coven Tree when Luther Gilpin sells Professor Popkin's magical furniture polish. Grades: 3-6

_____. ***The Wish Giver: Three Tales of Coven Tree***. Illustrated by Andrew Glass. Cambridge, Mass.: HarperCollins, 1983. 181 p. HarperTrophy, 1988 (pb). Thaddeus Blinn comes to town and offers "whatever you ask for 50 cents." For 50 cents you get a wish card with a red dot. None of the wishes turns out exactly the way people expected them, though. For example, when Rowena wishes that her traveling salesmen boyfriend would "take up roots and stay in Coven Tree," he actually sprouts roots and becomes a tree. Grades: 3-7

Brooke, William J. ***Untold Tales***. New York: HarperCollins, 1992. 164 p. 1993 (pb). Retells and continues the stories of "The Frog Prince," "Snow White," "Beauty and the Beast," and "Sleeping Beauty" from a contemporary perspective. Grades: 5 and up

Butterworth, Oliver. ***The Trouble with Jenny's Ear***. Illustrated by Julian de Miskey. Boston: Little, Brown, 1960. 275 p. 1993 (pb). A young girl named Jenny gains the remarkable power to hear peoples' thoughts. Grades: 4-7

Cadnum, Michael. ***In a Dark Wood***. New York: Orchard Books, 1998. 246 p. A retelling of aspects of the Robin Hood legend from the point of view of the Sheriff of Nottingham. Grades: 7-10

Carmody, Isobelle. ***The Gathering***. New York: Dial Books, 1994. 279 p. Viking Penguin, 1996 (pb). Fifteen year-old Nathaniel finds that he is one of the Chosen who must fight the succession of darkness in a menacing town that has been battered by ancient evil. Grades: 7-12

Carris, Joan Davenport. ***Witch Cat***. Illustrated by Beth Peck. New York: Lippincott, 1984. 154 p. Dell, 1986 (pb). A magical cat helps a young girl to learn about and accept the fact that she is a witch. Grades: 3-6

Carroll, Lewis. ***Alice's Adventures in Wonderland***. Illustrated by John Tenniel. New York: New York: Morrow Junior Books, 1993. 196 p. Scholastic, 1988 (pb). The classic tale of the adventures Alice has after she falls down a rabbit's hole and finds herself in Wonderland. The new Morrow editions (1993) of this and ***Through the Looking-glass*** have illustrations newly created from Tenniel's original wood cuts, which were found in a London bank vault. Grades: 5-8

_____. ***Through the Looking-glass and What Alice Found There***. Illustrated by John Tenniel. New York: Morrow Junior Books, 1993. 228 p. Puffin, 1996 (pb) Alice returns to Wonderland through a mirror and has an adventure resembling a chess game. Grades: 5-8

Cassedy, Sylvia. ***Behind the Attic Wall***. New York: T.Y. Crowell, 1983. 315 p. Avon/Camelot, 1994 (pb). Maggie has been thrown out of more boarding schools than you can shake a stick at. She is sent to live with her uncle and begins to hear mysterious voices in the attic of the huge, old house. In the attic she meets two dolls who are alive. There is a secret that is not revealed until the very last sentence of the novel. Grades: 6-8

Catling, Patrick Skene. ***The Chocolate Touch***. Illustrated by Margot Apple. New York: Morrow, 1952, 1979. 126 p. Dell, 1996 (pb). A boy faces many joys and sadness when he acquires a magical gift that turns everything his lips touch into chocolate. Grades: 4-6

Charnas, Suzy McKee. ***The Bronze King***. Boston: Houghton Mifflin, 1985. 196 p. Bantam, 1987 (pb). Valentine unwittingly calls a wizard from Sorcery Hall to help her fight the dreadful monster of darkness when she starts noticing things are vanishing from New York. Grades: 5-8

_____. ***The Kingdom of Kevin Malone***. New York: Harcourt, 1993. 255 p. 1997 (pb). Through gateways in New York's Central Park, Amy enters the fantasy world created in the mind of Kevin Malone. Kevin has constructed this world to escape from an abusive father, and Amy holds the power to rescue him. Grades: 7-12

Chetwin, Grace. ***On All Hallows' Eve***. New York: Lothrop, Lee & Shepard Books, 1984. 160 p. Aladdin Paperbacks, 1992 (pb). Since her attitude as a recent British immigrant grates on some of her classmates, Meg is the recipient of teasing, and worse from a bully named Kenny. On their way home from a Halloween party where Meg has turned the tables on Kenny, she and her sister fall into another world where they are involved in a life-and-death battle. Grades: 5 and up

_____. ***Out of the Dark World***. New York: Lothrop, Lee & Shepard Books, 1985. 154 p. The voice of a young boy from the Dark World first reaches in to Meg's nightmares, and then she receives a message from him on her computer. She has to devise a plan to enter into this world and rescue the boy. Grades: 5 and up

_____. "Tales of Gom Series"
***Gom on Windy Mountain: From Tales of Gom***. New York: Lothrop, Lee & Shepard, 1986. 206 p. Dell/Laureleaf, 1990 (pb). The son of a poor woodcutter named Gom finds that he has unusual powers that get him into all kinds of trouble. Grades: 5 and up

***The Riddle and the Rune: From Tales of Gom in the Legends of Ulm***. New York: Bradbury Press, 1987. 257 p. After having learned of his destiny in the first book, Gom now ventures out to fulfill it. In the course of his wanderings, he realizes that he has been given a special gift to be able to make friends. With this gift he comes to know the horse, Stormfleet, who becomes his companion. Grades: 5 and up

***The Crystal Stair***. New York: Bradbury Press, 1988. 225 p. Dell/Laureleaf, 1990. (pb). When Gom is temporarily reunited with his mother and learns the identity of his nemesis, Katak, he becomes a key figure in the battle to save Ulm from destruction. Grades: 5 and up

***The Starstone***. New York: Bradbury Press, 1989. 240 p. Dell/Laureleaf, 1990 (pb). Gom is instructed in the use of his powers so that he can help to destroy Katak and recover the lost emerald Seal. Grades: 5 and up

Christopher, John. ***Empty World***. New York: Dutton, 1977, 1978. 134 p. A teenage boy tries to survive in a seemingly empty England where a deadly virus kills off most of the world's population. Grades: 7 and up

_____. ***The Lotus Caves***. New York: Macmillan, 1969. 154 p. Two boys who live in a moon colonization bubble sneak out on a moon crawler and discover, beneath the moon's surface, "The Plant," which offers immortality and everything they could ever want. Grades: 7 and up

Christopher, John. "Tripod Series"
***When the Tripods Came***. New York: Collier Books, 1990. 151 p. Macmillan, 1990 (pb). When the Tripods descend from outer space and brainwash everyone, 14 year-old Laurie and his family try to escape. This book was written last, but tells the story that happens before the other three titles, known as the "Tripod Trilogy." Grades: 7 and up

***The White Mountains***. New York: Macmillan, 1967. 184 p. 1988 (pb). A group of freedom fighters fight against Tripods, who cap people with a metal cap at an early age to control their thinking and make them their servants. With the hope of escaping the Tripods, Will Parker and his companions journey toward the freedom of the White Mountains of Switzerland. Grades 7 and up

***The City of Gold and Lead***. New York: Macmillan, 1967. 185 p. 1988 (pb). Three young boys penetrate the city of the Tripods on a secret mission to learn more about the aliens who are ruling Earth. Grades: 7 and up

***The Pool of Fire***. New York: Macmillan, 1968. 178 p. 1988 (pb). Will Parker and a small group of people who are still free plan to stop the Tripods by destroying their great cities before the arrival of their spaceship signals the doom of the planet. Grades: 7 and up

Clapp, Patricia. ***Jane-Emily***. New York: Lothrop, Lee & Shepard, 1969. 160 p. Beach Tree Books,

1993 (pb). A chilling mystery about Emily, who is dead but seems to be alive. There is a mature romance as well. Grades: 3-6

Clarke, Pauline. **The Return of the Twelves**. Illustrated by Bernarda Bryson. New York: Coward McCann, 1963. 251 p. Dell, 1992 (pb). A young boy finds 12 wooden soldiers that once belonged to the famous Bronte children. Grades: 4-7

Cleary, Beverly. "Ralph S. Mouse Books"
**The Mouse and the Motorcycle**. Illustrated by Louis Darling. New York: William Morrow, 1965, 1989. 158 p. Avon, 1990 (pb). A mouse named Ralph makes friends with a boy who is staying in the hotel where he lives. The boy has a motorcycle, and Ralph discovers that he can make it move by making motorcycle noises. Ralph rides the motorcycle down the hall at night." Ralph had never ventured so far from home before," but he wants to see the world, or at least that wonderful place he has heard so much about, the ground floor. Grades: 2-4

**Runaway Ralph**. New York: William Morrow, 1970. 175 p. Avon, 1990 (pb). Ralph runs away from the hotel on his motorcycle and makes his way to a summer camp for boys and girls. He gets caught in a butterfly net by Garf, who is a loner, just as Catso, the evil cat, is about to pounce on him. Garf puts him in a cage, and Ralph is kept company by a hamster named Chum. A little girl leaves her watch by Ralph's cage and the cat sneaks in and makes off with it, but all the kids think Garf took it. Ralph finally is able to talk with Garf, and together they come up with a plan to put the watch back in a place where boys can't go so that his name will be cleared. All this time, Ralph is without his motorcycle, which is lost when Ralph is trying to escape from the cat. Garf finds it and gives it back to Ralph in exchange for his promise to clear Garf's name. Grades: 2-4

**Ralph S. Mouse**. Illustrated by Paul O. Zelinsky. New York: William Morrow, 1982. 160 p. Avon, 1993 (pb). 160 p. Ralph S. Mouse goes to school in this final book of the trilogy. He has befriended a boy named Ryan, whose mom works at the Mountain View Inn. Ryan takes Ralph to school, where he suddenly becomes a class project. He is supposed to run through a maze, and Ryan won't give him his motorcycle back unless he does it. A reporter comes to view the project and goes away with the mistaken idea that there's been a rat infestation in the school. Ralph's motorcycle gets accidentally broken, but later, Ryan gives him a laser XL7 race car to make up for it. Grades: 2-4

Collodi, Carlo. **The Adventures of Pinocchio**. Translated by Carol dell Chiesa and illustrated by Ava Morgan. New York: Macmillan, 1961. 206 p. Translated by Sue Kassirer. Random, 1992 (pb). The classic tale of the wooden puppet given life by the blue fairy, and the adventures he has on his quest to become a real boy. Grades: 4-8

Conly, Jane Leslie. "Rats of NIMH Series"
Note: Conly's father, Robert C. O'Brien, wrote *Mrs. Frisby and the Rats of Nimh*, the first book in this series. She continued the series after his death with these additional titles.
**Racso and the Rats of NIMH**. Illustrated by Leonard Lubin. New York: HarperCollins, 1986. 278 p. HarperTrophy, 1991 (pb). Timothy Frisby and a young rat named Racso team up to prevent the destruction of a community of rats who can read and write. Racso is the son of Jenner from the first book, and he loves candy. When he finds his way to the rats of NIMH he tries to tell them about rock music, TV, and other amusements. Grades: 5-8

**R-T, Margaret, and the Rats of NIMH**. Illustrated by Leonard Lubin. New York: HarperCollins, 1990. 260 p. HarperTrophy, 1991 (pb). Racso and his friends, Christopher and Isabella, try to ensure the survival of their secret community in Thorn Valley after its accidental discovery by two human children. Grades: 5-8

Cooper, Susan. "Boggart Books"
**The Boggart**. New York: M.K. McElderry Books, 1993. 196 p. Aladdin Paperbacks, 1995 (pb). The Boggart is a house spirit, a sort of poltergeist who lives in a castle in Scotland. When the master of the castle dies, it reverts to the heirs, a Toronto family. The daughter accidentally shuts the Boggart up in her luggage and takes him back to Toronto, where he first faces the challenges of making people believe in him in a technological world and of making sense of this new world of computers and electricity. Grades: 4-7

**The Boggart and the Monster**. New York: M. K. McElderry Books, 1997. 185 p. The Boggart has returned to his castle in Scotland, and Emily and her family come to visit. They become involved in a search for the Loch Ness Monster, who they discover is the Boggarts' cousin. He's sulking at the bottom of the loch, and has forgotten how to change his shape. Grades: 4-7

_____. "Dark Is Rising Sequence"
**Over Sea, Under Stone**. Illustrated by Margery Gill. New York: Harcourt Brace & World, 1966. 252 p. MacMillan/Aladdin,1993 (pb). Simon, Barney, and Jane Drew find an ancient manuscript in the attic of the house where they are staying while on holiday in Cornwall, England. Along with their great uncle Merry, they start on a quest for the Holy Grail and become trapped in an ancient struggle of good against evil. Grades: 5 and up
**The Dark Is Rising**. Illustrated by Alan E. Cober. New York: Atheneum, 1973. 216 p. Aladdin Paperbacks, 1993 (pb). On his eleventh birthday, Will Stanton discovers that he is the last of the Old Ones, destined to seek the six signs that will enable the Old Ones to triumph over the evil forces of the Dark. Grades: 5 and up
**Greenwitch**. New York: Atheneum, 1974. 147 p. Aladdin Paperbacks, 1993 (pb). 131 p. When Jane accepts an invitation to witness the making of the Greenwitch, a string of sinister events draws Jane and her two brothers into the quest of the Old Ones. They must recover the grail that has been stolen by the Dark. Grades: 5 and up
**The Grey King**. Illustrated by Michael Heslop. New York: Atheneum, 1975. 208 p. Aladdin Paperbacks, 1993 (pb). 208 p. While on a visit to Wales, Will Stanton is caught up in a quest to find the golden harp that will awake the ancient Sleepers. He meets the albino boy, Bran, who plays a unique part in the quest. Grades: 5 and up
**Silver on the Tree**. New York: Atheneum, 1977. Aladdin Paperbacks, 1993 (pb). Will Stanton, Bran, and the Drew children try to locate the crystal sword, the only object that can vanquish the strong forces of Dark. Grades: 5 and up

_____. **Seawa rd**. New York: Atheneum, 1983. 167 p. Macmillan/Aladdin, 1987 (pb). Both West and Cally are wrenched from their own countries into a perilous other world which they must travel through to return to the sea. Grades: 6-9

Coville, Bruce. **Jennifer Murdley's Toad: A Magic Shop Book**. Illustrated by Gary A. Lippincott. San Diego: Harcourt Brace Jovanovich, 1992. 156 p. Minstrel Books, 1993 (pb). An ordinary fifth grader has extraordinary adventures when she buys a talking toad. Grades: 3-7

_____. **Jeremy Thatcher, Dragon Hatcher: A Magic Shop Book**. Illustrated by Gary A. Lippincott. San Diego: Jane Yolen Books, 1991. 148 p. Minstrel Books, 1992 (pb). Twelve year-old Jeremy Thatcher unwittingly buys a dragon's egg. Grades: 3-7

_____. **The Monster's Ring**. Illustrated by Katherine Coville. New York: Pantheon Books, 1982. 87 p. Minstrel Books, 1989 (pb). A shy boy gets a magic ring with the power to change him into a terrifying monster so that he can frighten the school bully. Grades: 3-7

Dahl, Roald. **The BFG**. Illustrated by Quentin Blake. New York: Farrar, Straus, & Giroux, 1982. 219 p. Penguin/Puffin, 1985 (pb). Sophie and the BFG (Big Friendly Giant) concoct a plan to save the world from nine human-eating giants. Grades: 4-6

_____. **Charlie and the Chocolate Factory**. Illustrated by Joseph Schindelman. New York: Knopf, 1964. 161 p. Puffin, 1988 (pb). Charlie Buckett gets a golden ticket that makes him one of the select children who get to tour Willy Wonka's chocolate factory. The prize is actually the ownership of Wonka's factory. In this, Charlie has an advantage: The other children are brats. Grades: 3-6

_____. **Charlie and the Great Glass Elevator: The Further Adventures of Charlie Bucket and Willy Wonka, Chocolate-Maker Extraordinary.** Illustrated by Joseph Schindelman. New York: Knopf, 1972. 161 p. Puffin, 1998 (pb.) 159 p. Aboard Mr. Willy Wonka's great glass elevator, Charlie Bucket, his family, and Mr. Wonka are launched into space instead of back into the chocolate factory after an accident occurs. Sequel to *Charlie and the Chocolate Factory.*

_____. **James and the Giant Peach**. Illustrated by Nancy Ekholm Burkert. New York: Alfred A. Knopf, 1961. 118 p. Random, 1996 (pb). When a little man gives James a bag filled with strange green objects, magical things begin to happen that propel James into a series of adventures with the creatures in an oversized peach. Grades: 3-5

_____. ***The Witches***. Illustrated by Quentin Blake. New York: Farrar, Straus, & Giroux, 1983. 201 p. Penguin/Puffin, 1985 (pb). A young boy and his Norwegian grandmother foil the plot of the witches to turn all the world's children into mice. Grades: 4-6

Dalkey, Kara. ***Little Sister***. San Diego: Jane Yolen Books/Harcourt Brace & Co., 1996. 200 p. Puffin, 1998. 208 p. (pb). To find her sister's wandering soul and save her life, 13-year-old Fujiwara no Mitsuko, daughter of a noble family in twelfth century Japan, enlists the help of Goranu, a flying, shape-shifting *tengu*, and other figures from Japanese mythology. Grades: 6-10

_____. ***The Heavenward Path***. San Diego: Harcourt Brace & Co., 1998. 230 p. Mitsuko again seeks the help of her shape-shifting friend Goranu when she is haunted by a broken promise to fix the shrine of a powerful god. Sequel to *Little Sister*. Grades: 6-10

DeFelice, Cynthia C. ***The Ghost of Fossil Glen***. New York: Farrar, Straus and Giroux, 1998. 167 p. Avon, 1999. 160 p. (pb). Allie knows it can't just be her imagination when she starts hearing a voice and sees the face of a long-dead girl who is seeking her help to uncover the sinister plot that lead to the girl's murder. Grades: 6-8

Dickinson, Peter. "Changes Trilogy"
***The Devil's Children***. New York: Delacorte Press, 1986. 187 p. Dell, 1988 (pb). Nicola Gore finds refuge with a band of Sikhs after England suddenly goes mad and rejects the products of the Industrial Revolution. Grades: 6-9
***Heartsease***. Boston: Little, Brown, 1969. 223 p. Dell, 1988 (pb). In a future England in which anyone knowledgeable about machines is severely punished as a witch, four children aid the escape of one such witch who has been left for dead. Grades 6-9
***The Weathermonger***. Boston: Little Brown, 1969. 216 p. Delacorte, 1986. 190 p. Geoffery has the power to control the weather. He is forced to flee England along with Sally, his sister, when it is discovered that he has been using machines. The two eventually return to England and undertake a perilous journey to break the curse. Grades: 6-9

_____. ***Eva***. New York: Delacorte Press, 1988. 219 p. Laureleaf, 1990 (pb). A young girl wakes up one day to discover that she has been given the body of a chimpanzee after she was hurt in a terrible accident. Grades: 6-9

Duane, Diane. "Wizard Quartet"
***So You Want to be a Wizard?*** New York: Delacorte Press, 1983. 226 p. Harcourt Brace, 1996 (pb). In her local library Nita finds a book just for her that teaches her how to be a wizard. She meets another kid wizard named Kit, and together they try to find a book that will help hold the universe together. Grades 5-8
***Deep Wizardry***. New York: Delacorte, 1985. 272 p. Harcourt Brace, 1996 (pb). During their summer vacation to the beach, Nita and her friend Kit assist a whale wizard named S'ree to combat an evil power. Grades: 5-8
***High Wizardry***. New York Delacorte Press, 1990. 269 p. Harcourt Brace, 1997 (pb). When her younger sister uses her computer and some wizard software to travel light years away, it is up to Nita to save her. Grades: 5-8
***Wizard Abroad***. New York: Harcourt Brace, 1997. 352 p. 1998 (pb). While on vacation to Ireland, Nita becomes entangled in a magic battle with ghosts from the past, the outcome of which will determine the fate of the entire country. Grades: 5-8

Duffey, Betsy. ***Alien for Rent***. Illustrated by David Gaadt. New York: Delacorte, 1999. 80 p. J.P. and Lexie answer an ad to rent an alien for two Twinkies an hour. He helps them to fend off the fifth grade bully. Grades: 4-6

Eager, Edward. ***Seven Day Magic***. Illustrated by N.M. Bodecker. New York: Harcourt, Brace & World, 1962. 156 p. 1995 (pb). Five children must learn how to tame and learn the rules of a book of magic. Grades: 4-6

_____. ***The Time Garden***. Illustrated by N.M. Bodecker. San Diego: Harcourt Brace Jovanovich, 1958. 188 p. 1990 (pb). During the summer, four cousins have many exciting adventures as they travel in time using a magic thyme garden. Grades: 3-7

Engdahl, Sylvia Louise. "Elana Books"
***Enchantress from the Stars***. Illustrated by Rodney Shackell. New York: Atheneum, 1970. 275 p. Collier Books, 1989 (pb). A group from a

high-tech culture come to a planet with a primitive culture. The natives see them in terms we would associate with fairy tales. Grades: 7-12

*The Far Side of Evil*. Illustrated by Richard Cuffari. New York: Atheneum, 1971. 292 p. Elana is sent to be an observer on a planet that has not yet learned to control atomic power. Grades: 7-12

Engdahl, Sylvia Louise. *Journey Between Worlds*. Illus. James and Ruth McCrea. New York: Atheneum, 1970. 235 p. Melinda's whole life is changed when she decides to make an impromptu trip to Mars to prove her independence to her boyfriend. Grades: 7-12.

_____. "Star Trilogy"
*This Star Shall Abide*. Illustrated by Richard Cuffari. New York: Atheneum, 1972. 247 p. Macmillan, 1979. Noren is labeled a heretic when he rebels against the tyranny of the ruling class. Grades 7-12

*Beyond the Tomorrow Mountains*. Illustrated by Richard Cuffari. New York: Atheneum, 1973. 257 p. Noren finds despair but also hope when he seeks deliverance for the people of his hostile planet. Grades: 7-12

*The Doors of the Universe*. New York: Athenaeum, 1981. 262 p. When genetic engineering is the only salvation for the people on a hostile planet, Noren must face many problems in order to overcome the taboo on genetic research. Grades: 7-12

Enzensberger, Hans Magnus. *The Number Devil*. Illustrated by Rotraut Susanne Berner. New York : Henry Holt, 1998. 260 p. Twelve year-old Robert learns math tricks and patterns from the number devil in his dreams after he becomes annoyed with his math teacher for assigning the class word problems but not letting them use a calculator. Grades: 5-8

Farmer, Nancy. *The Ear, the Eye and the Arm*. New York: Orchard Books, 1994. 311 p. Puffin, 1995 (pb). When General Matsika's three children are kidnapped and put to work in a plastic mine, three mutant detectives are hired to use their special powers to search for them. Grades: 6-9

_____. *The Warm Place*. New York: Orchard Books, 1995. 152 p. Puffin, 1996 (pb). Ruva, a darling baby giraffe, gets captured and taken from Africa to an American zoo from hell. She's passed off as a rare pygmy giraffe, when she's really just a baby. She escapes with the help of a chameleon named Norman and a rat named Troll. She also meets a rat named Rodentus von Stroheim the Third. They have encounters with gross green seagoing Sargasso snails, and a seagoing group of human demons. Grades: 4-6

Feiffer, Jules. *A Barrel of Laughs, a Vale of Tears*. New York: Harper Collins, 1995. 180 p. 1998 (pb). Prince Roger is sent on a quest to find a way to stop people from laughing uncontrollably in his presence. Feiffer has great fun playing with the conventions of books, especially with a character named Tom, whom he can't control and who keeps coming in and out of the book. The moral: You may not have gone on what you thought was the right quest, but look around and be thankful for all that's happened due to the quest you have achieved. Grades: 3-7

Fleischman, Sid. *The Ghost in the Noonday Sun*. Illustrated by Peter Sis. New York: Greenwillow, 1965, 1989. 131 p. Scholastic, 1995 (pb). Twelve year-old Oliver is taken by pirates to find the ghost and the treasure of Gentleman Jack. Grades: 4-6

_____. *The 13th Floor: A Ghost Story*. Illustrated by Peter Sis. New York: Greenwillow, 1995. 95 p. Dell/Yearling, 1997 (pb). Twelve year-old Buddy Stebbins follows his older sister, who has disappeared, back in time and finds himself aboard a 17th century pirate ship.
Grades: 3 and up

Fleming, Ian. *Chitty Chitty Bang Bang, the Magical Car*. Illustrated by John Burningham. New York: Random House, 1964. 111 p. Bullseye Books, 1994 (pb). Two children find that the car they persuaded their inventor father to buy and restore really has magic powers. Grades: 4-6

Fletcher, Susan. *Shadow Spinner*. New York : Atheneum Books for Young Readers, 1998. 219 p. Marjan, a crippled orphan, becomes a handmaiden to the famous Shahrazad and is sent by the queen to discover new stories she can tell the Sultan in order to save her life. Grades: 6-9

Fry, Rosalie K. *The Secret of Roan Inish*. New York: Dutton, 1959. 89 p. Hyperion, 1995 (pb). When Fiona comes to live with her grandparents on the coast of the island Roan Inish, she hopes to find her baby brother, Jamie, who disappeared several years earlier. Grades: 4-8

Garden, Nancy. *My Sister, the Vampire*. New York: A.A. Knopf, 1992. 186 p. Sarah, Tim, and Jenny Hoskins face great dangers when they discover that the strange new owners of Spool Island are really vampires. Grades: 4-8

Garner, Alan. *Elidor*. New York: Philomel Books, 1965, 1979. 148 p. Dell/Yearling, 1993 (pb). Four children are drawn into another world where they must battle the evil powers that grip the land. Grades: 6-8

_____. *The Owl Service*. New York: Philomel Books, 1979. 156 p. Dell/Yearling, 1992. During a summer in Wales, three young people find themselves compelled to re-enact an old tragedy when mythical spirits haunt them. Grades: 6-9

_____. *Red Shift*. New York: Macmillan, 1973. 197 p. Ballantine, 1981 (pb). When the lives of three young men from different periods of British history converge, they each influence the destiny of the others. Grades: 8 and up

_____. "Tales of Alderley"
*The Weirdstone of Brisingamen a Tale of Alderley*. New York: H. Z. Walck, 1963. 253 p. Harcourt Brace, 1998 (pb). Colin and Susan come to Alderly to stay with a relative named Growther Mossack. Susan soon discovers that she possesses the "firestone" that the forces of evil are trying to obtain. It is stolen, and the quest to get it back takes Colin and Susan into some deep abandoned mines where they meet dwarfs, and on a slow, torturous trek through the English countryside. Grades: 5-8
*The Moon of Gomrath*. New York: Philomel Books, 1963, 1967. 160 p. Harcourt Brace, 1998 (pb). Colin, the wizard Cadellin, and elves battle to save Colin's sister from the evil witch Morrigan. Grades: 5-8

Gilden, Mel. *The Pumpkins of Time*. New York: Harcourt Brace & Co., 1994. 209 p. Browndeer, 1994 (pb). An alien being travels to earth in a pickup truck. A gigantic pumpkin acts like a flying saucer. Zombies are made from pumpkin insides. An evil alien wants weapons from comic books to rule the world. A cat is named H. G. Wells. A weird but imaginative book. Grades: 6 and up

Goodwin, Marie D. *Where the Towers Pierce the Sky*. New York: Four Winds Press, 1989. 185 p. With the help of an apprentice astrologer, Lizzie Patterson travels back in time to France in 1429, where she finds herself working as a double agent to protect Joan of Arc from her enemies. Grades: 6-9

Gormley, Beatrice. "Andrea Books"
*Mail Order Wings*. Illustrated by Emily Arnold McCully. New York: Dutton, 1981. 164 p. Avon, 1984 (pb). Nine-year-old Andrea gets in the mail a set of wings guaranteed to enable her to fly. They work, but unfortunately, they can't be removed. Grades: 4-6
*The Ghastly Glasses*. Illustrated by. Emily Arnold McCully. New York: Dutton, 1985. 117 p. Avon, 1987 (pb). Andrea's new glasses give her the power to control the minds of her family and friends, but her experiments to improve them have distressing results. Grades: 4-6

Gorog, Judith. *In a Messy Messy Room and Other Strange Stories*. New York: Philomel, 1990. Harper Trophy, 1994 (pb). Includes the title story about an evil chameleon who hides in a messy room, and a story about the boy who wanted the smelliest sneakers in the world. Grades: 2-5

Grahame, Kenneth. *The Reluctant Dragon*. Illustrated by Ernest H. Shepard. New York: Holiday House, 1938, 1953. 57 p. Troll, 1997 (pb). A young boy tries to convince the frightened villagers and St. George, the dragon killer, that the dragon who lives in a nearby cave is really kind and harmless. Grades: 4-6

_____. *The Wind in the Willows*. Illustrated by Ernest H. Shepard. New York: Scribner, 1960. 241 p. Dell/Yearling Classics, 1990 (pb). The adventures of Toad, Mole, Rat, and Badger, four animal friends who live along a river in the English countryside. Grades: 4-8

Greer, Gery and Bob Ruddick. *Jason and the Aliens Down the Street*. Illustrated by Blanche L. Sims. New York: HarperCollins, 1991. 94 p. Jason travels with Cooper Vor and Lootna, two aliens living on Earth, to a distant planet with the hope of retrieving the alien's stolen energy crystal. Grades: 2-6

_____. *Let Me Off This Spaceship!* Illustrated by Blanche L. Sims. New York: HarperCollins, 1991. 54 p. When Tod and Billy are kidnapped, they try to force the captain of an alien spaceship to take them back to Earth by making as much trouble aboard the ship as they can. Grades: 2-5

Gurney, James. "Dinotopia Books"
***Dinotopia: A Land Apart From Time***. Atlanta, GA: Turner Publishing, 1992. 159 p. Arthur Dennison and his son, Will, discover a world where humans and dinosaurs peacefully coexist. Grades: 4-8

***Dinotopia: The World Beneath***. Atlanta, GA: Turner Publishing, 1995. 158 p. HarperCollins, 1998. 160 p. Four years after being shipwrecked on the lost island of Dinotopia, 16-year-old Will Denison, now trained Skybax Corps pilot, explores the skies over the island while his father Arthur explores the world beneath the surface. Grades: 4-8

_____. ***Dinotopia Pop-up Book***. Atlanta: Turner Publishing, Inc., 1993 (unpaged). This retelling of the discovery of Dinotopia describes many of the dinosaurs who live there. Grades: 2-6

Haddix, Margaret Peterson. ***Among the Hidden***. Illustrated by Mark Ulriksen. New York: Simon & Schuster, 1998. 160 p. In a world where families may only have two children, Luke breaks the law by becoming the third child. But when his existence is discovered after 12 years of hiding, Luke must face the totalitarian government to become free. Grades: 6-9

Hahn, Mary Downing. ***Time for Andrew: A Ghost Story***. New York: Clarion Books, 1994. 165 p. Avon, 1995 (pb). While spending the summer with his great aunt, 11-year-old Drew travels back in time 80 years and trades places with his great-great-uncle, who is dying of diphtheria. Grades: 5-7

_____. ***The Time of the Witch***. New York: Clarion Books, 1982. 171 p. Avon, 1991 (pb). Without realizing that she is actually talking to a real witch, Laura tells an old woman that she wishes that her parents would get back together. Grades: 5-7

_____. ***Wait Till Helen Comes: A Ghost Story***. New York: Clarion Books, 1986. 184 p. Avon, 1987 (pb). Even though they do not like her, Molly and Michael must try to save their new stepsister when she tries to follow a ghost child, an act that may lead to her doom. Grades: 4-7

Hamilton, Virginia. "Justice Cycle"
***Justice and Her Brothers***. New York: Greenwillow, 1978. 217 p. Scholastic, 1998 (pb). An 11-year-old and her older twin brothers struggle to understand their extraordinary mental powers. Grades: 7 and up

***Dustland***. New York: Greenwillow, 1980. 180 p. Point Pub. 1998 (pb). Four children who posses extraordinary mental powers are thrown far into the future to a bleak region called Dustland. Grades: 7 and up

***The Gathering***. New York: Greenwillow, 1980. 179 p. Scholastic, 1998 (pb). Justice and her brothers return to Dustland to destroy the power that is retarding the advancement of their civilization. Grades: 7 and up

Hass, E. A. ***Incognito Mosquito, Private Insective***. New York: Lothrop Lee & Shepard, 1982. 92 p. Random, 1985 (pb). The mosquito detective recounts to a reporter some of the adventures he has had with such famous insects as Micky Mantis and F. Flea Bailey. Grades: 3-5

Heide, Florence Parry. "Treehorn Books"
***The Shrinking of Treehorn***. Illustrated by Edward Gorey. New York: Holiday House, 1971. 63 p. Dell, 1983 (pb). A boy discovers he is shrinking, but he doesn't know the cause or cure. Grades: 2-4.

***Treehorn's Treasure***. Illus. by Edward Gorey. New York: Holiday House, 1981. 63 p. For one day only, the leaves of the maple tree in Treehorn's backyard turn into dollar bills. Grades: 2-4

***Treehorn's Wish***. New York: Holiday House, 1984. 62 p. On his birthday, Treehorn finds a genie in a bottle who grants him three wishes. Grades: 2-4

Hilgartner, Beth. ***A Necklace of Fallen Stars***. Illustrated by Michael R. Hague. Boston, Mass.: Little, Brown, 1979. 209 p. Fytrian, the wizard, is sent to find and bring home the King of Visin's youngest daughter, who ran away to avoid marriage to the man that her father had chosen. Grades: 6-8

_____. "Zan Scarsdale Books"
***Colors in the Dreamweaver's Loom***. Boston, Mass.: Houghton Mifflin Co., 1989. 241 p. Still grieving after her father's death, a young girl named Zan Scarsdale becomes lost in the woods and finds her way into a fantasy world where she must help the Orathi fight to save their land from invaders. She becomes a hero of the tribe. Grades: 7-12

***The Feast of the Trickster***. Boston, Mass.: Houghton Mifflin, 1991. 230 p. Five of Zan's companions of the Orathi tribe journey to the world we know to rescue Zan, whose memories have been erased. Grades: 7-12

Hite, Sid. ***Answer My Prayer***. New York: H. Holt and Co., 1995. 182 p. Bantam Books, 1997. 192 p. (pb). Finding herself in the middle of a romance and political intrigues, 16-year-old Lydia's prayers for help are answered by the angel Ebol. Grades: 7-10

Hoban, Russell. ***The Mouse and His Child***. Illustrated by Lillian Hoban. New York: HarperCollins, 1967. 181 p. Dell, 1990 (pb). A broken wind-up mouse embarks on an adventure with his son in search of happiness "beyond the last visible dog." An evil rat intent on enslaving the pair provides conflict. Grades: 3-5

Horowitz, Anthony. "Pentagram Chronicles"
***The Devil's Door-Bell***. New York: Holt, Rinehart and Winston, 1983. 158 p. Thirteen year-old Martin is threatened by a great evil soon after he moves in with his new foster mother on a Yorkshire farm. Grades: 6-8
***The Night of the Scorpion***. New York: Pacer Books, 1984. 159 p. (pb). Three companions fight the evil Old Ones who are planning to enter the real world through a secret gate that is located somewhere in Peru. Grades: 6-8

Howe, Deborah and James. "Bunnicula Books" Note: This husband-and-wife team wrote the first book in the series together. James wrote the other titles after his wife's death.
***Bunnicula, a Rabbit Tale of Mystery***. Illustrated by Alan Daniel. New York: Atheneum, 1979. 98 p. Aladdin Paperbacks, 1996 (pb). Chester the cat tries to warn his masters that the baby bunny who has come to live with them is really a vampire. Grades: 3-5
***The Celery Stalks at Midnight***. Illustrated by Leslie Morrill. New York: Atheneum, 1983. 111 p. Avon, 1985 (pb). When his masters harvest white vegetables the morning after Bunnicula was out wandering the town, Chester the cat is even more convinced that the bunny is a vampire. Grades: 3-5
Other books featuring these characters are:
***Howliday Inn***
***Nighty-Nightmare***
***Harold and Chester in the Fright Before Christmas***
***Scared Silly: A Halloween Treat***
***Harold and Chester in Hot Fudge***
***Return to Howliday Inn***
***Rabbit-Cadabara!***

Hughes, Monica. ***The Dream Catcher***. New York: Atheneum, 1986. 171 p. Frightened that she has no talent and will not find a profession, Ruth joins a small band of adventurers who are led out of the protective dome of their world, Ark Three, on a dangerous mission to rescue Ark One, where a giant computer has taken control of the people's minds. Grades: 6-8

_____. ***Invitation to the Game***. New York: Simon & Schuster, 1990. 183 p. Aladdin Paperbacks, 1993 (pb). Unemployed and bored after high school, Lisse and her friends resign themselves to an uninteresting life in the robotic society of 2154—that is, until they are invited by the government to play the Game. Grades: 5-9

_____. "Isis Planet Books"
***Keeper of the Isis Light***. New York: Atheneum, 1980. 136 p. Along with a robot named Guardian, Olwen Pendennis enjoys the freedom of the planet Isis as she tends the Isis light, a lighthouse in space used to guide settlers from earth. Olwen's peaceful life is changed when the first settlers finally arrive from Earth, and she must learn to love and accept them as they try to adapt to their strange new home. Grades: 6-8
***The Guardian of Isis***. New York: Atheneum, 1982. 140 p. Four generations have passed since the first Isis settlers, and the Isis community has evolved into one governed by strong taboos. Jody N'Kumo, who questions and finally breaks these taboos, is sentenced to leave the community and go out beyond the valley, where he will probably find only death. But Jody's courage and conviction help him to survive and to accomplish more than anyone thought possible. Grades: 6-8
***The Isis Pedlar***. New York: Atheneum, 1982. 121 p. When their ship breaks down, Michael Joseph Flynn, a scoundrel who tricks people out of their valuables, and his 15-year-old daughter, Moire, land on the planet Isis. As always, Mike upsets the whole colony, but with the help of a boy who comes to love her and the robot Gardian, Moira sets things right. Grades: 6-8

Hunter, Mollie. ***The Mermaid Summer***. New York: HarperCollins, 1988. 118 p. HarperTrophy, 1990 (pb). Jon and Anna try to undo the curse placed on their grandfather by a mermaid many years ago. Grades: 3-7

_____. ***The Wicked One: A Story of Suspense***. New York: HarperCollins, 1977. 136 p. 1980 (pb). Tormented by a Grollican, a creature from the Otherworld, Coling Grant and his family flee from their home in the Scottish highlands to America. Grades: 5-8

Ibbotson, Eva. ***The Secret of Platform 13***. New York: Dutton, 1994. 231 p. Platform 13 is a station in the London "tube" that is also a gateway to an "other world" known as the Island. The passageway between our world and the Island is open for only nine days every nine years. During one of these periods, the prince of the Island is stolen by a woman from our world who wants to pass him off as her own. The story relates how the king and queen of the Island send out a motley crew to rescue the prince. Grades 5-8

Jacques, Brian. ***The Great Redwall Feast***. Illustrated by Christopher Denise. New York: Philomel Books, 1996. 64 p. A story told in rhyme details preparations for a surprise feast given in honor of the abbot of Redwall Abbey. Grades: 5-9

_____. "Redwall Series"
Note: These books were not published in chronological order. However, the author suggests reading the books in the order in which they were published. See the Redwall Website listed in the appendix for a list of the books in chronological order.

***Redwall***. Illustrated by Gary Chalk. New York: Philomel Books, 1986, 1997. 351 p. Ace Books, 1998 (pb). The peaceful life of Redwall Abbey is shattered by the arrival of Cluny, the evil rat, and his villainous hordes. With hopes of destroying the enemy, Matthias, a young mouse, resolves to find the legendary sword of Martin the Warrior. Grades: 5-9

***Mossflower***. Illustrated by Gary Chalk. New York: Philomel Books, 1988. 431 p. Avon 1990, (pb). While the animal inhabitants of the woodland prepare a rebellion against the evil wildcat who has seized power, Martin, the warrior mouse, and Gonff, the mouse thief, set out to find their missing ruler. Grades: 5-9

***Mattimeo***. Illustrated by Gary Chalk. New York: Philomel Books, 1990. 446 p. AvoNova, 1991 (pb). Mattimeo, the son of Matthias, takes up his sword and joins the animal inhabitants of Redwall Abbey in fighting Slagar Fox and his marauders. Grades: 5-9

***Mariel of Redwall***. Illustrated by Gary Chalk. New York: Philomel Books, 1992. 387 p. AvoNova, 1993 (pb). The animals of Redwall Abbey gain a victory when the mousemaid Mariel defeats the savage pirate rat, Gabool the Wild, at sea. Grades: 5-9

***Salamandastron***. Illustrated by Gary Chalk. New York: Philomel Books, 1993. 391 p. Ace Books, 1994 (pb). A wise old badger, Urthstripe the Strong, leads the animals of the fortress of Salamandastron and Redwall Abbey against the weasel, Ferahgo the Assassin, and his band of vermin. Grades: 5-9

***Martin the Warrior***. Illustrated by Gary Chalk. New York: Philomel Books, 1994. 376 p. Ace Books, 1996 (pb). The young warrior mouse Martin, captured and enslaved by the pirate Bodrang, vows to see an end to the pirate's senseless plundering and killing. Grades: 5-9

***The Bellmaker***. Illustrated by Allan Curless. New York: Philomel Books, 1994, 1995. 336 p. Ace Books, 1996 (pb). Joseph the Bellmaker is concerned about his daughter Mariel. A dream leads him to travel from Redwall Abbey to Southsward, where he finds himself involved in a battle between Squirrelking Gael and Nagru the Foxwolf. Grades: 5-9

***Outcast of Redwall***. Illustrated by Allan Curless. New York: Philomel Books, 1996. 360 p. Ace Books, 1997 (pb). Sunflash the Badger Lord and the ferret warlord Swartt Sixclaw are are mortal enemies. Their fates become entwined with those of many creatures, particularly the inhabitants of Redwall. Grades: 5-9

***Pearls of Lutra***. Illustrated by Allan Curless. New York: Philomel Books, 1997. 408 p. Ace Books, 1998 (pb). Tansy, a young hedgehog living at Redwall Abbey, tries to solve the riddle of the missing pearls, while the evil marten, Mad Eyes, wants them for himself. Grades: 5-9

***The Long Patrol***. Illustrated by Allan Curless. New York: Philomel Books, 1998. 358 p. Ace Books, 1999 (pb). Tammello De Fformelo Tussock is a young hare who wants to join the legendary Long Patrol. His father opposes this, but his mother finds a way for him to fulfill this wish. Meanwhile, the leadership of the Rapscallion army of rats is up for grabs, and the Southern Wall of Redwall Abbey is sinking into the ground. Grades: 5-9

*Marlfox*. Illustrated by Fangorn. New York: Philomel Books, 1999. 386 p. The quest in this installment is to reclaim a lost tapestry stolen by the Marlfoxes. Three brave inhabitants of Redwall break a curse placed on these animals. Grades: 5-9

Jones, Diana Wynne. *Archer's Goon*. New York: Greenwillow, 1984. 241 p. Berkley, 1987 (pb). Thirteen year-old Howard learns that he is adopted, that his father is in league with the seven wizards who run the town, and some other shocking information about his family, when a Goon moves into his family's house and will not leave. Grades: 6-9

_____. *Castle in the Air*. New York: Greenwillow, 1991. 199 p. Abdullah, a lowly carpet merchant, purchases a magic carpet that makes his daydreams of having dangerous adventures come true. Grades: 6 and up

_____. "Chrestomanci Series"
*The Lives of Christopher Chant*. New York: Greenwillow, 1988. 230 p. Because he has nine lives, the next Chrestomanci, or head controller of magic, is required to do battle with a group of renegade sorcerers in training. Grades: 5-9
*Charmed Life*. New York: Greenwillow, 1977, 1978. 218 p. Gwendolen Chant and her brother Cat quickly find out that the powerful family of the Chrestomanci Castle are no match for the Coven Street witches. Grades: 5-9
*The Magicians of Caprona*. New York: Greenwillow, 1980. 223 p. It is up to the youngest members of the two families of magicians in Caprona to stop a war when their parents become too weak to fight after two centuries of feuding. Grades: 5-9
*Witch Week*. New York: Greenwillow, 1982, 1993. 213 p. An Inquisitor must be summoned when a teacher in an English boarding school finds a note on his desk that accuses someone in his class of being a witch. Grades: 5-9

_____. "Dalemark Quartet"
*Cart and Cwidder*. New York: Atheneum, 1977. 193 p. Greenwillow, 1995 (pb). Three children become involved in rebellion and intrigue when they inherit from their father, a traveling minstrel, a lute-like cwidder that has more than musical powers. Grades: 6-9
*Drowned Ammet*. New York: Greenwillow, 1995. 225 p. Beach Tree Books, 1995 (pb). A young boy and two other children escape to the Holy Islands, where they learn the true identity of some of their folk heroes. Grades: 6-9
*The Spellcoats*. New York: Atheneum, 1979. 249 p. Greenwillow, 1995 (pb). Tanqui is the only one who can defeat the evil Kankredin who has been threatening her people as well as the Heathens who originally invaded prehistoric Dalemark. Grades: 6-9
*The Crown of Dalemark*. New York: Greenwillow, 1995. 471 p. 1996 (pb). Mitt is sent to kill a young woman by the name of Noreth Onesdaughter because she claims to know where the lost crown is hidden. Grades: 6-9

_____. *Howl's Moving Castle*. New York: Greenwillow, 1986. 212 p. The unfortunate Sophie resigns herself to her destiny, making hats, until she is turned into an old woman by a nasty witch and seeks refuge in the flying castle of the feared wizard Howl. Grades: 7-12

Jones, Terry. *Fantastic Stories*. Illustrated by Michael Foreman. New York: Viking, 1992. 128 p. This collection includes the delightful read-aloud, "The Slow Ogre." Grades: 3-6

_____. *Fairy Tales*. Illustrated by Michael Foreman. New York: Schocken, 1981. 127 p. Puffin, 1993 (pb). Wonderful fairy tales that read like classics and have the depth of Aesop and Grimm, written by a former member of Monty Python. Among the memorable stories are "Jack One-Step," in which Jack is granted one step by a fairy, but finds the step will only take him one way. "The Glass Cupboard" is an object from which anything may be taken only if you put something back in. "Simple Peter's Mirror" allows you to see yourself as others see you. "Brave Molly" meets a monster at night but finds it's nothing to be afraid of. In "The Witch and the Rainbow Cat," a girl stumbles into a mirror that allows her to see the future. A boy tames "The Beast With a Thousand Teeth" with tarts with pink icing. In "The Boat That Went Nowhere," a boy goes off to seek his fortune and returns with nothing. His mother tells him, "I shall make soup from your stories, and we'll have our hopes for bread." Grades: 3-6

_____. *Nicobobinus*. Illus. Michael Foreman. New York: Bedrick, 1986. 175 p. This is really delightful stuff, with a feeling a lot like the Oz books. Nicobobinus accidentally gets parts of his body changed into gold. He is suddenly valuable, so, along with his friend Ruthie, Nicobobinus searches for the land of the Dragons. They have been led to believe that dragon's blood will cure Nicobobinus. They have incredible adventures in places such as the City of Cries and the Sea of Mountains. Grades: 5-7

Jordan, Sherryl. **Winter of Fire**. New York: Scholastic, 1992. 321 p. A young woman with extraordinary powers saves her world from destruction. Grades: 7-9.

Juster, Norton. **The Phantom Tollbooth**. Illustrated by Jules Feiffer. New York: Random House, 1961. 255 p. Bullseye, 1993 (pb). Milo is bored stiff until he finds a tollbooth in his room. He drives through it into the Lands Beyond and gets caught up with extraordinary characters in a search for the missing princesses, Rhyme and Reason. Grades: 5-7

Kaye, M. M. **The Ordinary Princess**. Illustrated by Faith Jaques. Garden City, New York: Doubleday, 1984. Dell, 1993 (pb). A young princess, given the gift of "ordinariness" by a fairy at her christening, runs away from home to become a fourteenth assistant kitchen maid. Grades: 3-6

Kendall, Carol. **The Gammage Cup**. Illustrated by Erik Blegvad. New York: Harcourt, Brace, 1959. 221 p. 1990 (pb). The peaceful life of a land inhabited by Little People changes when an enemy enters from the outside. Grades: 4-7

Kennedy, Richard. **Amy's Eyes**. Illustrated by Richard Egielski. New York: HarperCollins, 1985. 437 p. Young Amy, a girl who has changed into a doll, sails the high seas in search of gold treasure with her sea captain doll who has changed into a man and a crew of stuffed animals brought to life. She loses her button eyes that are the only way a sunken treasure can be found. Grades: 5-7

Key, Alexander. **Escape to Witch Mountain**. Illustrated by Leon B. Wisdom, Jr. Philadelphia: Westminster Press, 1968. 172 p. Tia and Tony realize that they are not of this world. They have recurring visions and special powers. They finally find their way back to Witch Mountain, where their people are. Grades: 4-7

_____. **The Forgotten Door**. Philadelphia: Westminster Press, 1965. 126 p. Scholastic, 1989 (pb). When a boy from outer space falls to earth, he loses his memory but still has telepathic powers and can understand animals. Grades: 5-7

King-Smith, Dick. **Babe: The Gallant Pig**. Illustrated by Mary Rayner. New York: Crown, 1983. 118 p. Knopf, 1997 (pb). A piglet is adopted by an old sheep dog and soon discovers that the secret to staying alive is to learn how to herd the sheep as the dogs do. Grades: 4-6

_____. **Harriet's Hare**. Illustrated by Roger Roth. New York: Crown Publishers, 1995. 104 p. Knopf, 1997 (pb). When a young girl makes friends with a talking hare that turns out to be a shape-changing alien, her life is changed forever. Grades: 3-6

_____. **Paddy's Pot of Gold**. Illustrated by David Parkins. New York: Crown, 1992. 114 p. After making friends with Paddy, the leprechaun, Brigid wonders if he has a pot of gold. Grades: 3-6

_____. **Three Terrible Trins**. Illustrated by Mark Teague. New York: Crown Pub., 1994. 105 p. Knopf, 1997 (pb). Ignoring the class system separating the rodents in the farmhouse, three mice brothers befriend a mouse from a lower class and form a team to fight the cats. Grades: 2-7

Klause, Annette Curtis. **Alien Secrets**. New York: Delacorte Press, 1993. 227 p. Dell, 1995 (pb). Terrific sci-fi mystery about a girl named Robin Goodfellow (Puck) who finds herself on a starship on the way home after getting kicked out of school. She befriends an alien, Hush, who is distraught because he has lost the Soo, a symbol of freedom for his people, who have been cruelly enslaved by the evil Grakk. They must find and protect the Soo, and the people on the ship are not all that they seem. Grades: 4-7

_____. **The Silver Kiss**. New York: Delacorte Press, 1990. 198 p. Laurel Leaf, 1992 (pb). Touchstone YA novel about a girl whose mother is dying of cancer, who just happens to meet a charming young vampire who is out for revenge against his brother, forever doomed to the shape of a child who is a serial killer. Grades: 7 and up

Koller, Jackie French. **The Dragonling**. Illustrated by Judith Mitchell. Boston: Little, Brown, 1990. 60 p. Minstrel Books, 1995 (pb). Hoping to be just like his heroic older brother, Darek dreams of going on his own Dragonquest, but when he accidentally finds a baby dragon he must risk death and the anger of his people to return it to the Valley of the Dragons. Grades: 3-5

Krensky, Stephen. "Dragon Books"
**The Dragon Circle**. Illustrated by A. Delaney. New York: Atheneum, 1977. 116 p. When his four children are kidnapped by five dragons greedily seeking lost gold, Professor Wynd is forced to use his magical power to retrieve the treasure, outwit the dragons, and rescue the children. Grades: 4-6

**The Witching Hour**. Illustrated by A. Delaney. New York: Atheneum, 1981. 155 p. Alison Wynd of the magical Wynd family is excited about her new job at the Westbridge Inn running errands for a big conference. But when the delegates arrive with cats that don't act like cats and strange spells affect the Wynd children and the neighborhood, it is up to Alison and her family to save their town, and the world, from disaster. Grades: 4-6

**A Ghostly Business**. New York: Aladdin Books, 1984, 1990. 144 p. This time the Wynd family have to keep ghosts from allowing a sleazy real-estate developer get his hands on some valuable property. Grades 4-6

_____. **The Perils of Putney**. Illustrated by Jurg Obrist. New York: Atheneum, 1978. 116 p. A giant with no experience at being a hero goes on a quest in search of the world's only Fair Damsel after she disappears. Grades: 4-6

LeGuin, Ursula K. "Earthsea Series"
**A Wizard of Earthsea**. Illustrated by Ruth Robbins. Berkeley, California: Parnassus, 1968. 205 p. Bantam, 1975 (pb). After releasing an evil creature into the world, young Sparrowhawk must conquer it and master his powers at the same time. Ged discovers that there is a dark half inside of him that he must embrace. Grades: 6 and up

**The Tombs of Atuan**. Illustrated by Gail Garraty. New York: Atheneum, 1971 163 p. Bantam, 1984 (pb). Ged has now become a wizard. When he comes seeking a special treasure, Tenar, the high priestess in the tombs of Atuan, has to make a choice to remain in her place or escape. Grades: 6 and up

**The Farthest Shore**. Illustrated by Gail Garraty. New York: Atheneum, 1972. 223 p. Bantam, 1984 (pb). Ged and Prince Arren join forces and make a journey to the Shadow Kingdom to find what is causing Earthsea to lose all its magic. They discover the cause to be an evil mage. Grades: 6 and up

**Tehanu: The Last Book of Earthsea**. New York: Atheneum, 1990. 226 p. Returning from the dark lands and having lost his magic powers in battle, Ged, Archmage of Earthsea, Sparrowhawk, takes shelter with the widow Tenar and a crippled girl with a great destiny. Grades: 6 and up

L'Engle, Madeleine. "Time Quartet"
**A Wrinkle in Time**. New York: Farrar, Straus, & Giroux, 1962. 211 p. Dell/Yearling Books, 1973 (pb). Meg, her brother Charles Wallace, and her boyfriend Calvin search for Meg and Charles' father, who has disappeared while performing a government experiment. They rescue him from a planet that has been totally taken over by evil. On it, all houses and people are the same. Boys and girls emerge from look-alike houses and bounce balls and skip ropes in perfect unison. Grades: 6-10

**A Wind in the Door**. New York: Farrar, Straus & Giroux, 1973. 211 p. Dell/Yearling Books, 1974 (pb). Meg Murry and a dragon-like creature travel into galactic space and finally into the microscopic world of the mitochondrion in an effort to save Meg's brother Charles Wallace and the universe. Grades: 6-10

**A Swiftly Tilting Planet**. New York: Farrar, Straus and Giroux, 1978. 278 p. Dell/Yearling Books, 1981 (pb). The youngest Murry child, Charles Wallace, travels through time on a quest to vanquish an evil dictator who could destroy the entire universe. Grades: 6-10

**Many Waters**. New York: Farrar, Straus, & Giroux, 1986. 310 p. 1987 (pb). Dell/Yearling Books, 1987 (pb). Sandy and Dennys, the Murray twins, get blasted back in time to a pre-Flood earth, and meet Noah, who has been told by El to build an ark. They fall in love with Yalith, Noah's daughter, and wonder how she'll survive the flood. Grades: 6-10

Levine, Gail Carson. **Ella Enchanted**. New York: HarperCollins, 1997. 232 p. A wry take on the Cinderella story. Ella is enchanted at birth by the fairy Lucinda with a curse that she must always obey any command given her. She finds her way out of the curse and out of the clutches of ogres and her stepfamily, into the arms of her prince. Grades: 5-7

_____. "Princess Tales"
***The Fairy's Mistake***. Illustrated by Mark Elliott. New York: HarperCollins, 1999. 87 p. Based on the Grimm fairy tale, "Toads and Diamonds." The fairy Ethelinda thanks Rosella for helping her by giving her the gift of diamonds, which come out of her mouth whenever she talks. Rosella's greedy sister, Myrtle, seeks a gift as well and is cursed to have bugs, snakes, and other disgusting creatures emerge from her mouth when she speaks. Rosella's gift turns out to be a curse when she marries a prince who is interested only in how her diamonds can help remodel the castle. Myrtle, on the other hand, is having great fun tormenting people with her gift. Ethelinda must persuade Myrtle to set things right. Grades: 3-6

***The Princess Test***. Illustrated by Mark Elliott. New York: HarperCollins, 1999. 91 p. Based on Hans Christian Andersen's story "The Princess and the Pea." Lorelei inadvertently stumbles into a castle where the King and Queen are in the process of administering a number of tests to prospective princesses to find a true princess. Grades: 3-6

Lewis, C. S. "Chronicles of Narnia"
***The Magician's Nephew***. Illustrated by Pauline Baynes. New York: Macmillan, 1955, 1970. 202 p. Harper Collins, 1994 (hb and pb). While returning the wicked witch Jadis to her own world, Digory and Polly accidentally land in Narnia and witness Aslan giving the animals human speech. Grades: 4-7

***The Lion, the Witch, and the Wardrobe***. Illustrated by Pauline Baynes. New York: Macmillan, 1950, 1983. 189 p. Harper Collins, 1994 (hb and pb). Peter, Edward, and Lucy find their way separately through a wardrobe in an English country home into the land of Narnia, where at first everything is in a state of perpetual winter, because of the evil rule of the White Witch. They meet the kindly Lion, Aslan, who is the true ruler. Grades: 4-7

***The Horse and His Boy***. Illustrated by Pauline Baynes. New York: Macmillan, 1954. 224 p. HarperCollins, 1994 (hb and pb). A boy and a talking horse try to warn the people of Narnia of an impending invasion by barbarians. Grades: 4-7

***Prince Caspian***. Illustrated by Pauline Baynes. New York: Macmillan, 1951, 1970. 223 p. Harper Collins, 1994 (hb. and pb). Four children, Prince Caspian, and an army of talking animals free Narnia from evil. Grades: 4-7

***Voyage of the Dawn Treader***. Illustrated by Pauline Baynes. New York: Macmillan, 1952. 248 p. Harper Collins, 1994 (hb and pb). Lucy, Edmund, and Eustace sail on the Dawn Treader around Narnia and have many great adventures. Grades: 4-7

***The Silver Chair***. Illustrated by Pauline Baynes. New York: Macmillan, 1953. 243 p. Harper Collins, 1994 (hb and pb). Four children embark on a quest to find Prince Rilian and return him to Narnia. Grades: 4-7

***The Last Battle***. Illustrated by Pauline Baynes. New York: Macmillan, 1956. 211 p. Harper Collins, 1994 (hb. and pb). Jill and Eustace help fight the great last battle against evil in Narnia. Grades: 4-7

Lindbergh, Anne. ***Travel Far, Pay No Fare***. New York: HarperCollins, 1992. 199 p. Owen and his cousin use a magic bookmark to travel into different stories on a quest to prevent their parents from marrying. Grades: 5-8

Lisle, Janet Taylor. ***The Lampfish of Twill***. Illustrated by Wendy Anderson Halperin. New York: Orchard Books, 1991. 161 p. Apple, 1995 (pb). An old fisherman and a boy named Eric travel down a whirlpool to a beautiful world that is at the center of the Earth. Grades: 5 and up

Lively, Penelope. ***The Wild Hunt of the Ghost Hounds***. New York: Dutton, 1972. 141 p. Ace Books, 1986 (pb). Invisible evil spirits threaten a young girl and her friend after they are awakened by the revival of an ancient dance and become involved in an ancient myth of Herne the Hunter and his hounds. Grades: 5-8

Lofting, Hugh. ***The Story of Doctor Doolittle: Being the History of His Peculiar Life at Home and Astonishing Adventures in Foreign Parts***. Philadelphia: J. B. Lippincott, 1920. 172 p. Dell/Yearling, 1997 (pb). The tale of the adventures of Doctor Doolittle, a man who can talk with animals. Grades: 3-6

_____. ***The Voyages of Doctor Doolittle***. Philadelphia: J.B. Lippincott, 1922. 364 p. Dell/Yearling, 1998 (pb). The further adventures of Doctor Doolittle, a man who can talk with animals. Grades: 4-7

Lowry, Lois. ***The Giver***. Boston: Houghton Mifflin, 1993. 180 p. Dell, 1997 (pb). A science fiction novel about a community of the future where everything is kept in harmony through everyone's being the same. It is a world without colors or memories. Jonas is chosen to be the new receiver of memory for the community, and in the process of his training from the Giver learns how to feel. Grades: 7-9

Lunn, Janet Louise. ***The Root Cellar***. New York: Scribner, 1983. 229 p. Penguin/Puffin, 1996 (pb). Twelve year-old Rose makes friends with people who lived more than a century earlier, when she travels to their time through her aunt's root cellar. Grades: 5-7

MacDonald, George. ***The Light Princess***. Illustrated by Maurice Sendak. New York: Farrar, Straus & Giroux, 1969. Sunburst, 1992 (pb). Seeking her revenge because she was not invited to the christening, the King's sister curses the young princess to a life without gravity or the ability to cry. Grades 3-6

_____. ***The Princess and the Goblin***. Illustrated by Arthur Hughes. New York: Grosset & Dunlap, 1907. 304 p. Dell/Yearling, 1985 (pb). When the goblin miners who live below the castle threaten the life of the young princess, she is protected by her friend Curdie. Grades: 5-7

Mahy, Margaret. ***The Changeover: A Supernatural Romance***. New York: Atheneum, 1984. 214 p. Puffin, 1994 (pb). When her younger brother is possessed by an evil spirit, Laura seeks the help of a boy with supernatural powers. Grades: 6-10

_____. ***The Haunting***. New York: Macmillan, 1982. 135 p. 1984 (pb). A boy is haunted by a ghost who turns out to be his very real great uncle Cole. Cole is seeking him out because he thinks the boy is the next in a line of Scholar Magicians, members of the family who have special magical powers. The real magician turns out to be his sister Troy. Grades: 5-8

Masefield, John. ***The Midnight Folk***. Illustrated by Rowland Hilder. New York: Macmillan. 224 p. Dell, 1985 (pb). Kay goes in and out of the past in his attempts to outwit the witches and find his great-grandfather's buried treasure with the help of talking paintings and animals. Grades: 5-7

Massie, Diane Redfield. ***Chameleon Was a Spy***. New York: Crowell, 1979. 40 p. A clever spoof about a chameleon hired on by a pickle company to steal back their secret recipe from a rival company. Chameleon, of course, can change himself to be the same color as whatever he is on, even to the point of concealing himself on a piece of paper. The word he is covering up forms on his body. Grades: 3-6

Matas, Carol and Perry Nodelman. ***Of Two Minds***. Canada: Bain & Cox, 1994. New York : Simon & Schuster Books for Young Readers, 1995. 200 p. Scholastic Paperbacks, 1998 (pb). While running away from her parent's strict rules, Princess Lenora and her fiancé Prince Coren are caught in a world that holds them hostage and robs them of their special mental powers. Grades: 7-10

Marsden, John. ***Tomorrow, When the War Began***. Boston: Houghton Mifflin Co., 1995. 286 p. Laureleaf, 1996 (pb). Returning from a camping trip in the Australian bush, seven teenagers find that their country has been invaded. They must struggle to stay alive and defend what little they have left. Grades: 10-12

Mayne, William. ***Antar and the Eagles***. New York: Delacorte Press, 1989. 166 p. A young boy who was abducted and raised by eagles is sent on a quest to rescue a lost egg and save the race of eagles. Grades: 5-9

McGowen, Tom. "Magician Trilogy"
***The Magician's Apprentice***. New York: Dutton, 1987. 119 p. Together a young pickpocket turned magician's apprentice and an old magician search for the knowledge that has been lost for thousands of years since the Age of Magic. Grades: 5-7
***The Magician's Company***. New York: Lodestar Books, 1988. 119 p. While the Reen, intelligent ratlike creatures, hide in the city, ready to destroy all human beings, the magician Armindor and his young apprentice Tigg try to warn the rest of the world of their presence. Grades: 5-7
***The Magician's Challenge***. New York: Lodestar Books, 1989. 138 p. As the Reen, intelligent ratlike creatures, plan a bloody takeover, the magician Armindor and his young apprentice Tigg continue their battle against them. Grades: 5-7

McGraw, Eloise Jarvis. ***The Moorchild***. New York: Margaret K. McElderry Books, 1996. 241 p. The changeling child Saaski was given at birth to a human family by the Folk, a race of people who live underground. Saaski learns her true identity and attempts to find the child who was taken by her people. Grades: 5-7.

McKenzie, Ellen Kindt. ***The Golden Band of Eddris***. New York: H. Holt and Co., 1998. 293 p. It is up to Keld and Elylden to save the village of Adnor from the evil witch Eddris with the help of a wizard and the special powers their mother gave them. Grades: 6-10

McKillip, Patricia A. ***The Forgotten Beasts of Eld***. New York: Atheneum, 1974. 217 p. Harcourt Brace, 1996 (pb). Sybel is a wizard who has at her command a bevy of magical beasts. She learns about the human world when a baby is thrust into her care. Grades: 6-9

_____. "Star-Bearer Trilogy"
***The Riddle-Master of Hed***. New York: Atheneum, 1976. 228 p. Ballantine, 1978 (pb). Morgon, a simple farmer well-versed in riddles, journeys to seek the High One in the Erlenstar Mountains to try to unravel the riddle of the three stars on his forehead and on his enchanted harp. Grades: 6-9
***Heir of Sea and Fire***. New York: Atheneum, 1977. 204 p. 1978 (pb). The fiancée and the sister of the Prince of Hed set out on a quest to find him when he does not return from his journey to the High One. Grades: 6-9
***Harpist in the Wind***. New York: Atheneum, 1979. 256 p. 1980 (pb). Dell Rey, 1989 (pb). Despite the conflict that rages around him, the Prince of Hed finds his destiny when he learns to harp and wind, to understand himself better, and when he uncovers some important secrets. Grades: 6-9

McKinley, Robin. ***Beauty: A Retelling of the Story of Beauty and the Beast***. New York: HarperCollins, 1978, 1985. 247 p. 1993 (pb). McKinley tells the story of Beauty from her point of view, expanding greatly on the traditional fairy tale. McKinley makes it real and gives the story heart-thumping suspense. There are many literary allusions. McKinley also does something that no other reteller of this story has ever done: She makes the sisters sympathetic. Grades: 5-9

_____. ***The Blue Sword***. New York: Greenwillow, 1982. 272 p. Ace Books, 1991 (pb). When a king with mysterious powers kidnaps Harry, she discovers that she has magic within herself. Sequel to *The Hero and the Crown*. Grades: 6-12

_____. ***The Hero and the Crown***. New York: Greenwillow, 1984. 246 p. Ace Books, 1998 (pb). Aerin, guided by the wizard Luthe and helped by the blue sword, regains her birthright as the daughter of the Damarian king and as a witchwoman of the North. Grades: 6-12

_____. ***The Outlaws of Sherwood***. New York: Greenwillow, 1988. 282 p. Ace Books, 1989 (pb). A retelling of the adventures of Robin Hood and his band of outlaws who live in Sherwood Forest in twelfth century England. Grades: 7 and up

_____. ***Rose Daughter***. New York: Greenwillow, 1997. 320 p. A different retelling of "Beauty and the Beast" with a new sensibility. Grades: 8 and up

Milne, A. A. ***The House at Pooh Corner***. Illustrated by Ernest H. Shepard. New York: Dutton, 1928, 1961. 178 p. 1998 (pb). Ten stories about the adventures of Pooh, Eeyore, Tigger, Piglet, Owl, and the other friends of Christopher Robin. Grades: 2-4

_____. ***Winnie the Pooh***. Illustrated by Ernest H. Shepard. New York: Dutton, 1926, 1954. 161 p. Puffin, 1992 (pb). The adventures of the stuffed bear Winnie the Pooh and his friends Eeyore, Tigger, Piglet, Owl, Kanga, and Roo. Pooh gets in many scrapes, including getting his head stuck in Rabbit's burrow. Grades: 2-4

Napoli, Donna Jo. ***Jimmy: The Pickpocket of the Palace***. Illustrated by Judith Byron Schachner. New York : Dutton Children's Books, 1995. 166 p. Puffin, 1997. (pb). Jimmy, the froglet son of an enchanted frog-prince, is transformed into a human boy when he tries to save his pond from the evil hag by finding a magic ring. Grades: 3-6

_____. ***The Magic Circle***. New York: Dutton Children's Books, 1993 (hb. and pb). 118 p. Evil spirits turn a good-hearted woman into a witch. She fights their power until she encounters Hansel and Gretel years later. Grades: 7 and up

_____. ***The Prince of the Pond: Otherwise Known as De Fawg Pin***. Illustrated by Judith Byron Schachner. New York: E.P. Dutton, 1992. 151 p. Puffin, 1994 (pb). When a hag turns a prince into a frog, he learns the ways of frogs, raises a family, and teaches the frogs a new kind of thinking. Grades: 3-6.

_____. ***Zel***. New York: Dutton Children's Books, 1996. 227 p. A retelling of the fairy tale Rapunzel, that delves into the psychological motivations of the characters. Grades: 7-12.

Naylor, Phyllis Reynolds. The **Grand Escape**. Illus. Alan Daniel. New York: Atheneum, 1993. 148 p. Bantam, 1998 (pb). Marco and Polo, two house kittens, escape and join up with a group of street cats. They have to solve three great mysteries before they can be members of the club. Grades: 3-7.

_____. "Witch Books"
***Witch's Sister***. Illustrated by Gail Owens. New York: Atheneum, 1975. 150 p. Dell/Yearling, 1993 (pb). Lynn's suspicion that her sister is learning witchcraft from their neighbor Mrs. Tuggle is confirmed when she and her two siblings must stay with her for one weekend. Grades: 4-8.
***Witch Water***. Illustrated by Gail Owens. New York: Atheneum, 1977. 179 p. Dell/Yearling, 1988 (pb). Lynn cannot convince her family that their neighbor Mrs. Tuggle is really a witch. Grades: 4-8.
***The Witch Herself***. Illustrated by Gail Owens. New York: Atheneum, 1978. 164 p. Dell, 1988 (pb). Lynn and Mouse struggle to try to find a way to stop the witch Mrs. Tuggle from gaining power over more people. Grades: 4-8.

Nesbit, E. **Five Children and It**. Illus. J.S. Goodall. New York: Looking Glass Library, 1948, 1959. 255 p. Puffin, 1996 (pb). Five children become friends with a strange little sand creature known as the Pssamead. Grades: 5-7.

_____. ***Melisande***. Illustrated by P.J. Lynch. New York: Harcourt Brace Jovanovich, 1989. 42 p. Cursed to be bald, Princess Melisande gets a whole set of problems when her wish for golden hair is granted. Grades: 5-7.

Nix, Garth. **Sabriel**. New York: HarperCollins, 1996. 292 p. HarperTrophy, 1997. 496 p. (pb). When her father, the necromancer Abhorsen, disappears, Sabriel must journey into the magical Old Kingdom and with the help of Mogget, a Free Magic elemental, and Touchstone, a young man with a terrible secret, save him from the evil Kerrigor. Grades 7-10

_____. ***Shade's Children***. New York: HarperCollins, 1997. 310 p. HarperTrophy, 1998. 345 p. (pb). Led by the mysterious Shade, a man whose personality has been saved and is projected by a computer, a group of youngsters struggle to save themselves and their world from the bloodthirsty Overlords. Grades 7-10

Norton, Andre. **Red Hart Magic**. Illustrated by Donna Diamond. New York: Crowell, 1976. 179 p. A brother and sister travel back to the time of King James I in England, where they find solutions that help them to better deal with some serious peer problems in their own time. Grades: 5-7

Norton, Mary. **Bed-Knob and Broomstick**. Illustrated by Erik Blegvad. San Diego: Harcourt Brace Jovanovich, 1957. 189 p. 1975 (pb). A spinster who is studying to be a witch and three children go on some exciting and frightening adventures. Grades: 4-6

_____. ***The Borrowers***. Illustrated by Beth and Joe Krush. New York: Harcourt, Brace, 1953. 180 p. 1998 (pb). By borrowing things from the humans who live above them, miniature people are able to live in an old country house until they are forced to move. They are discovered first by a boy who helps them and then by adults who want to exterminate them. Grades: 4-7

O'Brien, Robert C. "Rats of NIMH Series"
Note: After O'Brien's death, his daughter, Jane Leslie Conly, continued this series by writing *Racso and the Rats of NIMH* and *R-T, Margaret, and the Rats of NIMH*.
***Mrs. Frisby and the Rats of NIMH***. Illustrated by Zena Bernstein. New York: Atheneum, 1971. 233 p. 1998 (pb). A group of rats who become extraordinarily intelligent when they are imprisoned in a laboratory help a young widowed mouse save her home. Grades: 4-7

_____. ***Z for Zachariah***. New York: Atheneum, 1975. 249 p. Aladdin, 1987 (pb). After a nuclear holocaust, Ann Borden thinks she may be the only one left alive. Somehow her valley has escaped the devastation. Then Mr. Loomis enters the valley wearing what he says is the world's only "safe suit." Ann finally makes her presence known when Mr. Loomis gets ill from swimming in a radiated stream. She has dreamed about repopulating the valley with him, perpetuating the race. But in his delirium, Mr. Loomis inadvertently reveals that he killed someone to gain possession of his "safe suit." And as he gets well, his behavior becomes increasingly obsessive, to the point of trying to rape Ann. To escape his control and demands, Ann steals the safe suit and sets off into the "deadness," propelled by a dream she has of a classroom of students waiting for a teacher. A chilling tale, especially as Ann thinks she might be the last person on earth, and that Mr. Loomis' voice might be the last one she would ever hear. Grades: 7 and up

Oppel, Kenneth. **Silverwing**. New York: Simon & Schuster, 1997. 217 p. Aladdin Paperbacks, 1999. 224 p. (pb). By satisfying his desire to catch a glimpse of the sun, a newborn bat named Shade touches off a war of extermination against all of his kind. Grades: 5-8

Osborne, Mary Pope. "Magic Tree House Series" (selected titles)

**Dinosaurs Before Dark**. Illustrated by Sal Murdocca. New York: Random House, 1992 (hb and pb). Jack and his sister Annie find a magic tree house that takes them back to the time when dinosaurs roamed the earth. Grades: 1-4

**The Knight at Dawn**. Illustrated by Sal Murdocca. New York: Random House, 1993 (hb and pb). 65 p. Jack and Annie use their magic tree house to travel back to the Middle Ages, where they explore a castle and are helped by a mysterious knight. Grades: 1-4

**Mummies in the Morning**. Illustrated by Sal Murdocca. New York: Random House, 1993 (hb and pb). 64 p. Jack and Annie journey in their magic tree house back to ancient Egypt, where they help a queen's mummy continue her voyage to the next life. Grades: 1-4.

**Pirates Past Noon**. Illustrated by Sal Murdocca. New York: Random House, 1994 (hb and pb). 67 p. Jack and Annie with the aid of their magic tree house travel back to the age of pirates and treasure maps. Grades: 1-4

**Night of the Ninjas**. Illustrated by Sal Murdocca. New York: Random House, 1995 (hb and pb). 68 p. Jack and Annie travel in their magic tree house back in time to feudal Japan where they learn about the ways of the Ninja. Grades: 1-4

**Afternoon on the Amazon**. Illustrated by Sal Murdocca. New York: Random House, 1995 (hb and pb). 67 p. Eight-year-old Jack, his seven-year-old sister, Annie, and Peanut the mouse ride in their tree house to the Amazon rain forests, where they find giant ants, flesh-eating piranhas, hungry crocodiles, and wild jaguars. Grades: 1-4

**Sunset of the Sabertooth**. Illustrated by Sal Murdocca. New York: Random House, 1996 (hb and pb). 66 p. The magic tree house transports Jack and Annie on a mission to the Ice Age where they encounter Cro-Magnons, cave bears, sabertooth tigers, and woolly mammoths. Grades: 1-4

O'Shea, Pat. **The Hounds of the Morrigan**. New York: Holiday, 1986. 469 p. A 10-year-old boy is caught between the forces of good and evil when he finds an old book of magic in a book shop that both sides want. Grades: 6-9

Paton Walsh, Jill. **A Chance Child**. New York: Farrar, Straus and Giroux, 1978. 185 p. Sunburst, 1991 (pb). Although some people believe he does not exist, Christopher feels compelled to search for his half-brother, Creep, and is led to some papers that contain the personal narrative of Nathaniel Creep discussing the working conditions of the Industrial Revolution 100 years earlier. Grades: 6-9

Paulsen, Gary. **Transall Saga**. New York: Delacorte, 1998. 248 p. Thirteen year-old Mark is forced to make a new life for himself in a strange and terrifying world after a mysterious light transports him to a new dimension while he is on a solo camping trip. Grades: 6-8

Pattou, Edith. **Hero's Song**. San Diego: Harcourt Brace Jovanovich, 1991. 290 p. 1998. 368 p. (pb). Collun sets out on a quest to rescue his kidnapped sister, but he and his companions soon find that they are part of a greater quest to save the kingdom of Eirren from enslavement by the Queen of Ghosts. Grades: 6-10

_____. **Fire Arrow: The Second Song of Eirren**. San Diego: Harcourt Brace & Co., 1998. 332 p. Brie, a warrior maiden, learns of her birthright, a magical arrow, from her nursemaid on her deathbed. Setting out on a quest of revenge for her father's murderers, she discovers the sinister plot of an evil sorcerer. Companion to *Hero's Song*. Grades: 6-10

Pearce, Philippa. ***Tom's Midnight Garden***. Illustrated by Susan Einzig. New York: Lippincott, 1959. 229 p. Dell, 1986 (pb). Daytime life is dull for Tom in his aunt's and uncle's apartment. However, when Tom hears the clock strike 13, it creates a time slip, enabling Tom to travel to an enchanted garden where he plays with Hatty, a girl from the past. He finds himself transported into the lives of the previous inhabitants of the house where he's staying and sees Hatty at many different stages of her life. She turns out to be the same person as an old lady who lives next door. Grades: 5-8

_____. ***The Way to Sattin Shore***. Illustrated by Charlotte Voake. New York: Greenwillow, 1983. 182 p. When his tombstone mysteriously disappears from the graveyard, a young schoolgirl starts to solve the mystery of her father's death. Grades: 5-8

Peck, Richard. ***The Ghost Belonged to Me***. New York: Viking Press, 1975. 183 p. Dell/Yearling, 1987 (pb). Alexander sees the ghost of Meg Dwaine, who warns him of an impending trolley car tragedy that he averts. This exciting adventure includes such things as exploding steamboats and ghosts. Grades: 6-9

_____. "Blossom Culp Books"
***Ghosts I Have Been***. New York: Viking Press, 1977. 253 p. Bantam Doubleday, 1987 (pb). A girl with the gift of second sight named Blossom Culp is led on some unusual adventures. Grades: 6-9

***Blossom Culp and the Sleep of Death***. New York: Delacorte Press, 1986. 185 p. Bantam Doubleday, 1994 (pb). High-school freshman and possessor of second sight, Blossom Culp helps an Egyptian princess recover her tomb and saves a suffragette teacher from losing her job in 1914. Grades: 6-9

***The Dreadful Future of Blossom Culp***. New York: Delacorte Press, 1983. 183 p. Bantam Doubleday, 1994 (pb). From 1914, Blossom Culp travels ahead 70 years so she can make Halloween night unforgettable for her classmates and teachers. Grades: 6-9

_____. ***The Great Interactive Dream Machine: Another Adventure in Cyberspace***. New York: Dial Press. 1996. 160 p. Josh Lewis is unwillingly drawn into his friend Aaron's computer experiments and the two find themselves uncontrollably transported through space and time. Companion to: *Lost in Cyberspace*. Grades: 5 and up

_____. ***Lost in Cyberspace***. New York: Dial Press, 1995 (hb and pb). 151 p. Josh and his friend Aaron use the computer at their school to travel through time where they learn secrets about the school's past and find help to improve their home situations. Grades: 5 and up

_____. "Darkangel Trilogy"
***The Darkangel***. Boston: Little Brown, 1982. 292 p. Harcourt Brace, 1998 (pb). A maiden redeems a vampire who takes wives to his lair and sucks out their souls, which he keeps in vials around his neck. Grades: 6-10

***A Gathering of Gargoyles***. Boston: Little, Brown, 1984. 263 p. Harcourt Brace, 1998 (pb). Painfully aware that her husband Irrylath is still not free of the White Witch's spell, Aeriel sets out on a quest to gather the winged steeds that Irrylath and his brothers need to do battle against the powerful witch. Grades: 6-10

***The Pearl of the Soul of the World***. Boston: Joy Street, 1990. Harcourt Brace, 1999 (pb). With the aid of a shimmering pearl, Ariel battles the White Witch to free her husband Irrylath from the witch's power. Wonderful up to the denouement, in which Ariel is forced to reject her husband and go off to the Crystalglass city to gather the world's shattered soul. Grades: 6-10

Pierce, Meredith Ann. "Firebringer Trilogy"
***Birth of the Firebringer***. New York: Four Winds Press, 1985. 234 p. The son of the prince of the unicorns discovers that he has a great destiny to help his people in their struggle against the giant dragons that are taking their land. Grades: 7-10

***Dark Moon***. Boston: Joy Street Books, 1992. 237 p. The prince of the unicorns goes on a quest to the distant land of two-footed creatures to find fire, the only thing that will destroy his enemies. Grades: 7-10.

***The Son of Summer Stars***. Boston: Little, Brown, 1996. 250 p. The prince of the unicorns uses his knowledge of fire to forge an alliance between his people and their enemies and returns the unicorns to their homeland. Grades: 7-10

Pierce, Tamora. "Song of the Lioness Series"
***Alanna: The First Adventure***. New York: Atheneum, 1983. 241 p. Knopf, 1997 (pb). Eleven-

year-old Alanna wants to be a knight, so she disguises herself as a boy in order to become a royal page. Grades: 5-10

*In the Hand of the Goddess*. New York: Atheneum, 1984. 232 p. Knopf, 1997 (pb). Alanna, acting as the squire to Prince Jonathan, learns many new things as she pursues her wish to become a knight. Grades: 5-10

*The Woman Who Rides Like a Man*. New York: Atheneum, 1986. 253 p. Knopf, 1997 (pb). Now a knight errant, Alanna takes a position of authority in a desert tribe and helps to make some changes in the role of women in that society. Grades: 5-10

*Lioness Rampant*. New York: Atheneum, 1988. 320 p. Knopf, 1997 (pb). Alanna, the female warrior, and her new companions go on a quest to the Roof of the World to find the Dominion Jewel with the hope that the jewel will be able to save their country from hostile magic. Grades: 5-10

Pinkwater, Daniel Manus. *Alan Mendelsohn, the Boy From Mars*. New York: Dutton, 1979. 248 p. Life at Leonard's new junior high is unbearable until he meets Alan Mendelsohn, a boy who claims he is from Mars. Grades: 5-9

_____. *Fat Men From Space*. New York: Dodd, Mead, 1977. 57 p. Bantam Doubleday, 1980 (pb). To his great dismay, William learns of an impending invasion by aliens who are planning to take all of earth's junk food. Grades: 4-6

Prelutsky, Jack. *Nightmares: Poems to Trouble Your Sleep*. Illustrated by Arnold Lobel. New York: Greenwillow, 1976. 38 p. Gruesome, scary poems enhanced with equally scary b&w illustrations. Grades: 3 and up
A sequel is *The Headless Horseman Rides Tonight: More Poems to Trouble Your Sleep*.

Pullman, Phillip. *Count Karlstein*. Illustrated by Diana Bryan. New York: Knopf, 1998. 243 p. When the despicable Count Karlstein plans to sacrifice his two young nieces to the Demon Huntsman, it is up to Hildi Kelmar, a servant, and a bumbling cast of characters to save them. Grades: 5-8

_____. "His Dark Materials Trilogy"
*The Golden Compass*. New York: Alfred A. Knopf, 1995, 1996. 397 p. Del Rey, 1997 (pb). 420 p. Lyra Belaqua is a child fated to perform a great quest. She and her daemon set out on a quest to find out the fate of her best friend and other children who have been kidnapped for gruesome experiments. One of the most compelling things about the world Pullman creates is that each human in it has a personal demon, an inseparable companion. He creates the rules of this world perfectly. Except in rare cases, the demon is the opposite sex of its human. It is taboo to touch another person's demon. Demons can change shape until their human reaches puberty; then they settle on one particular shape. Grades: 6 and up

*The Subtle Knife*. New York: Alfred A. Knopf, 1997. Dell Rey, 1998 (pb). Lyra meets a boy from our world, and together they discover a knife with the power to cut through the boundaries between worlds. Grades: 6 and up

*The Amber Spyglass*. Yet to be published.

Pyle, Howard. *The Merry Adventures of Robinhood: Of Great Renown in Nottinghamshire*. New York: C. Scribner's Sons, 1911. 296 p. Troll, 1992 (pb). A retelling of the legendary adventures of Robin Hood and his band of outlaws in Sherwood Forest. Grades: 5-12

_____. *The Story of King Arthur and His Knights*. New York: C. Scribner's Sons, 1903. 312 p. New American Library, 1994 (pb). A retelling of the legendary adventures of King Arthur and the Knights of the Round Table. Grades: 5-12

Reid Banks, Lynne. *The Adventures of King Midas*. Illustrated by Joseph A. Smith. New York: Morrow Junior Books, 1992. 153 p. Camelot, 1993 (pb). King Midas must deal with a magician, a witch, and a dragon as he tries to undo the magic spell that causes all he touches to turn into gold. Grades: 3-6

_____. *The Fairy Rebel*. Illustrated by William Geldart. Santa Barbara, Calif.: Cornerstone Books, 1985. 154 p. Camelot, 1989 (pb). Even though she is already in trouble for wearing jeans, a fairy named Tiki risks further punishment from the queen of the fairies by helping the human couple, Jan and Charles, fulfill their deepest wish to have a baby. The little girl born to the couple has some hidden blue hairs through which she can work fairy magic, and she uses one to cure her mother's foot. Grades: 3-6

_____. "Indian in the Cupboard Series"
**The Indian in the Cupboard**. Illustrated by Brock Cole. Garden City, New York: Doubleday, 1980. 181 p. Avon, 1982 (pb). A nine year-old boy's plastic Indian magically comes to life when he places him in a cupboard and locks it with a special key. The same thing happens with other plastic figures as well. The little people are treated with respect and they emerge as thinking, feeling human beings. Being alive as small figures is not a natural state for them, but an adventure. In the end they have to be sent "home." The ending is very moving. Grades: 4-6

**The Return of the Indian**. Illustrated by William Geldart. Garden City, New York: Doubleday, 1986. 189 p. Avon, 1995 (pb). Omri decides to use his magic cupboard again to brink back his friend Little Bear, only to find that the Indian is in desperate need of help. Grades: 4-6

**The Secret of the Indian**. Illustrated by Ted Lewin. New York: Doubleday, 1989. 147 p. Avon, 1995 (pb). When Omri and Patrick enter the Old West through their magic cupboard, they find themselves in need of plastic toy doctors to save some wounded men. Grades: 4-6

**The Mystery of the Cupboard**. Illustrated by Tom Newsom. New York: Morrow, 1993. 246 p. Avon, 1994 (pb). Omri and his family move to a thatch-roofed country house inherited by his mother. Omri soon discovers a link between the house and his magic cupboard. Grades: 4-6

**The Key to the Indian**. Illustrated by James Watling. New York: Avon Camelot, 1998. 228 p. Omri and his father travel to Little Bear's time to use their knowledge of the future to save Little Bear's people. Grades: 4-6

Roberts, Willo Davis. **The Girl With the Silver Eyes**. New York: Atheneum, 1980. 181 p. Scholastic, 1991 (pb). A 10-year-old girl with silver eyes and strange powers finds out that she is not the only one of her kind. Grades: 4-6

Rodgers, Mary. **Freaky Friday**. New York: HarperCollins, 1972. 145 p. 1991 (pb). Annabel and her mother really don't understand each other. The situation is remedied when they magically switch places for a day. Grades: 5-7

_____. **A Billion for Boris**. New York: HarperCollins, 1974. 211 p. 1991 (pb). To earn money and help humanity, Annabel and Boris use an old TV that plays only programs that won't show until the next day. Grades 5-7

_____. **Summer Switch**. New York: HarperCollins, 1982. 185 p. 1991 (pb). Boris and his father magically switch places for a summer. Grades: 5-7

Rowling, J. K. "Harry Potter Books"
**Harry Potter and the Sorcerer's Stone**. Illustrated by Mary Grandpré. New York: A.A. Levine Books/Scholastic Press, 1998. 309 p. Harry Potter thinks he is an ordinary boy until he is rescued from his hideous aunt and uncle and taken to Hogwarts School for Witchcraft and Wizardry, where he learns the truth about his parents and faces the evil master wizard that destroyed them. Grades: 5-12

**Harry Potter and the Chamber of Secrets**. A. A. Levine Books/Scholastic Press, 1999. 251 p. Harry Potter's second year at Hogwarts School for Witchcraft and Wizardry starts out normally, but when Harry starts hearing evil voices and menacing messages appear on the walls, it is up to Harry and his friends to discover who or what is threatening the school. Grades: 5-12

**Harry Potter and the Prisoner of Azkaban.** New York: Scholastic, 1999. 431 p. In this third installment, Harry becomes involved in a search for Sirius Black, an infamous murderer escaped from the Azkaban prison fortress, who may be, himself, searching for Harry. Grades 5-12

Sauer, Julia L. **Fog Magic**. New York: Viking, 1943. 107 p. Penguin/Puffin, 1986 (pb). Whenever the fog comes, a young girl is transported into a secret world of her own. Grades: 4-6

Scieszka, Jon. **Squids Will Be Squids**. Illustrated by Lane Smith. New York: Scholastic, 1998. 48 p. 18 contemporary fables that use animals and even foodstuffs to comment on issues to which modern kids will relate, such as television advertising and curfews. Grades 2-5

_____. "Time Warp Trio Series"
**Knights of the Kitchen Table**. Illustrated by Lane Smith. New York: Viking, 1991. 55 p. Puffin, 1993 (pb). For his birthday, Joe gets a mysterious book that grants wishes. It transports Joe and his friends into the time of King Arthur, where they outwit a black knight and a goofy giant named Bleob, whom they persuade to kill a menacing dragon. Grades: 2-6

***The Not-So-Jolly Roger***. Illustrated by Lane Smith. New York: Puffin, 1993 (hb. and pb). 57 p. The Time Warp Trio are taken prisoner by the evil pirate Blackbeard. The story begins *in media res*, then backs up in Chapter 2 to tell the reader how the kids got in a predicament with the pirates. "While the pirates drop anchor and load their rowboat, maybe I should back up and explain." An epilogue in which what happened to all the main characters is related a la American Grafitti. The tone is just right for cool kids. Grades: 2-6

***The Good, the Bad and the Goofy***. Illustrated by Lane Smith. New York: Viking, 1992. 70 p. Puffin, 1993 (pb). The Time Warp Trio are transported into the wild, wild west. Notable for attacking stereotypes, such as including Black cowboys. Grades: 2-6

***Your Mother Was a Neanderthal***. Illustrated by Lane Smith. New York: Viking, 1993. 78 p. Puffin, 1995 (pb). When the Time Warp Trio find themselves in the middle of prehistoric times, they find new ways of looking at cave paintings and rock music. Grades: 2-6

***2095***. Illustrated by Lane Smith. New York: Viking, 1995. 72 p. Puffin, 1997 (pb). Our heroes use "The Book" to jet to the future where they encounter a "SellBot," an advertising robot that accosts people with "What's your number, buddy?" The trio thinks it is going to fry them with its laser beams, but it just wants their credit card number so it can show them 3D ads. When the boys take to the streets of New York, they see a 3D monster advertising the movie "Slayer 3000, now playing at brain stem theaters everywhere." They encounter a gigantic roll of toilet tissue, and meet their great granddaughters. Grades: 2-6

***Tut Tut***. Illustrated by Lane Smith. New York: Viking, 1996. 74 p. Puffin, 1998 (pb). The Time Warp Trio travel back to ancient Egypt. Grades: 2-6

***Summer Reading is Killing Me***. Illustrated by Lane Smith. New York: Viking, 1998. 64 p. Fred puts the trio's summer reading list inside "The Book," and they are transported into the stories they were supposed only to read. Grades: 2-6

Seidler, Tor. ***Mean Margaret***. Illustrated by Jon Agee. New York: HarperCollins Publishers, 1997. 165 p. A pair of newlywed woodchucks find their tidy life disrupted when they take in an abandoned, demanding, ungrateful human toddler. Grades: 3-6

_____. ***A Rat's Tale***. Illustrated by Fred Marcellino. New York: Farrar, Straus, & Giroux, 1986. 185 p. A young rat named Montague, who lives in the sewers of New York, is shunned by the more sophisticated wharf rats but becomes a hero who he tries to save his friends from extermination. Grades: 4-6

_____. ***The Tar Pit***. New York: Farrar, Straus, Giroux, 1987. 153 p. 1991 (pb). Edward Small and his dinosaur friend have numerous adventures at the edge of a pond filled with dark oily liquid. Grades: 4-6

_____. ***The Wainscott Weasel***. Illustrated by Fred Marcellino. New York: Harper Collins, 1993. 193 p. 1996 (pb). The story of a weasel and his unusual love for a fish. Grades: 2-6

Selden, George. "Chester Cricket Books"
***The Cricket in Times Square***. Illustrated by Garth Williams. New York: Farrar, Straus & Giroux, 1960, 1983. 151 p. Dell, 1996 (pb). A young boy who sells newspapers with his family in Times Square finds a cricket who can truly sing. In a moving scene, Chester Cricket brings all New York to a standstill with his music. There is also a funny scene with a Chinese shopkeeper who sells the boy a cricket cage. Grades: 3-6

***Tucker's Countryside***. Illustrated by Garth Williams. New York: Farrar, Straus and Giroux, 1969. 166 p. Dell/Yearling, 1989 (pb). Adventures of a cat and mouse when they leave the city to go to the country to visit their friend Chester Cricket. Grades: 3-6

***Harry Cat's Pet Puppy***. Illustrated by Garth Williams. New York: Farrar, Straus & Giroux, 1974. 167 p. Dell/Yearling, 1975 (pb). Harry Cat and Tucker Mouse search for a home for a stray puppy. Grades: 3-6

_____. ***The Genie of Sutton Place***. New York: Farrar, Straus and Giroux, 1973. 175 p. Sunburst, 1994 (pb). The summer adventures of a young boy who releases an Arabian genie from a carpet. Grades: 5-7

Senn, Steve. ***A Circle in the Sea***. New York: Atheneum, 1981. 256 p. Through the power of a ring, a 13-year-old girl enters an undersea world where she becomes a dolphin and helps some whales retaliate against their slaughter by hunters. Grades: 5-7

Service, Pamela F. ***Winter of Magic's Return***. New York: Atheneum, 1985. 192 p. Ballantine/Fawcett, 1986 (pb). In the aftermath of the nuclear holocaust, a young resurrected Merlin and two friends, convinced that a new age of magic is about to begin, set out to bring back King Arthur. Grades: 5-8.

_____. ***Tomorrow's Magic***. New York: Atheneum, 1987. 191 p. After successfully bringing back King Arthur to Britain, Merlin and his two young friends try to build a new society while the evil Morgan Le Fay plots against them. Sequel to *Winter of Magic's Return*. Grades: 5-8

Shannon, Mark. ***Sir Gawain and the Green Knight***. Illustrated by Mark Shannon. New York: Putnam, 1994. 32 p. A strange man visits King Arthur's court and offers a challenge which Sir Gawain accepts. In meeting the challenge, Sir Gawain becomes a true knight. Grades: 4-7

Sherman, Josepha. ***Child of Faerie, Child of Earth***. Illustrated by Rick Farley. New York: Walker Pub., 1992. 159 p. Percinet, the half-human son of a queen of Faerie, falls in love with the daughter of a mortal medieval count, leaving his realm to profess his love to her and defend her against her cruel stepmother. Grades: 7 and up

_____. ***Windleaf***. New York: Walker, 1993. 121 p. Eighteen year-old Thierry goes on a quest to free the half-human, half-fairy girl whom he loves from the clutches of her heartless father, the Lord of Faerie. Grades: 7 and up

Silverstein, Shel. ***Where the Sidewalk Ends***. New York: Harper and Row, 1974. 176 p. This classic collection of poetry for children is one of the best-selling books for children of all time. Many of the poems are fantasy. Grades: 4 and up

Sleator, William. ***The Boy Who Reversed Himself***. New York: E.P. Dutton, 1986. 167 p. Puffin, 1998 (pb). Laura takes a dangerous journey when she accompanies the boy next door into the fourth dimension. Grades: 4-8

_____. ***Dangerous Wishes***. New York: Dutton Children's Books, 1995. 182 p. Puffin, 1997 (pb). Fifteen-year-old Dom and his friend Lek search for a jade carving that must be returned to appease a Thai spirit with the hope it will end the bad luck Dom and his parents have been having since their arrival in Thailand. Grades: 4-6

_____. ***The Duplicate***. New York: Dutton, 1988. 154 p. Bantam Starfire, 1990 (pb). After replicating himself with a machine that can make duplicates of living organisms, 16-year-old David must face horrible consequences when his duplicate turns against him. Grades: 5 and up

_____. ***House of Stairs***. New York: Dutton, 1974. 166 p. Puffin, 1991 (pb). Five 15-year-old orphans are placed in a house of endless stairs as subjects for a psychological experiment on conditioned human response. Grades: 7 and up

_____. ***Strange Attractors***. New York: E.P. Dutton, 1990. 169 p. Puffin, 1991 (pb). Max is hunted by two men, a scientist, and the scientist's alter ego from a different timeline, when he suddenly finds himself in possession of a time-travel device. Grades: 5-11

Smith, Dodie. ***The Hundred and One Dalmatians***. Illustrated by Janet and Anne Grahame-Johnstone. New York: Viking Press, 1957. 199 p. Viking, 1989 (pb). The classic tale of Pongo and Missis, two Dalmatians who go on a quest to rescue their puppies from the evil Cruella de Ville. Grades: 2 and up

Smith, Sherwood. "Crown and Court Duet"
***Crown Duel***. San Diego: Harcourt, Brace & Company, 1997. 214 p. Countess Meliara and her brother enter into a war for which they and their people are not prepared. Captured by the enemy, Meliara struggles to find her way home. Grades: 7 and up

***Court Duel***. San Diego: Harcourt, Brace & Company, 1997. 245 p. Now the war is over, but Meliara is swept into political duels in the royal palace. Sequel to ***Crown Duel***. Grades: 7 and up

_____. "Wren Trilogy"
***Wren to the Rescue***. San Diego: Harcourt Brace Jovanovich, 1990. 216 p. Wren, a prince, and an apprentice wizard try to rescue Princess Tess from the castle of a wicked king. Grades: 6 and up

***Wren's Quest***. San Diego: Harcourt Brace Jovanovich, 1993. 199 p. An evil wizard wreaks havoc in Cantimoor and threatens Princess Teressa while Wren and Prince Connor are on a quest to discover the truth about Wren's parentage. Grades: 6 and up

***Wren's War***. San Diego: Harcourt Brace & Co., 1995. 210 p. Wren, Princess Teressa, Prince Connor, and the chief magic-maker Tyron join forces to defeat the evil King Andreus, who has declared war on the royal families of Meldrith. Grades: 6 and up

Snyder, Zilpha Keatley. ***Black and Blue Magic***. Illustrated by Gene Holtan. New York: Atheneum, 1966. 186 p. Aladdin, 1994 (pb). Harry Houdini Marco, named after the famous magician, is awkward and clumsy until he learns how to fly. Grades: 5-7

_____. "Green-sky Books"
***Below the Root***. Illustrated by Alton Raible. New York: Atheneum, 1975. 231 p. Tor, 1985 (pb). Selected to become one of the Chosen, 13-year-old Raamo finds that what really lies below the tree roots of his world of Green-sky is contrary to what the leaders have always passed off as the truth. Grades: 5-8

***And All Between***. Illustrated by Alton Raible. New York: Atheneum, 1976. 216 p. Tor, 1985 (pb). Two youngsters, one a Kindar and one an Erdling, help to unite both those who are working for and those against the reunion of their two peoples. Grades: 5-8

***Until the Celebration***. Illustrated by Alton Raible. New York: Atheneum, 1977. 214 p. Tor, 1985 (pb). Two children become symbols for the unification and help to ease tensions created when the Erdlings start to re-enter Green-sky. Grades: 5-8

_____. ***The Witches of Worm***. Illustrated by Alton Raible. New York: Atheneum, 1972. 183 p. Dell/Yearling, 1986 (pb). A lonely 12-year-old girl blames a cat she believes is really a witch for her own unusual behavior. Grades: 4-8

Springer, Nancy. ***I Am Mordred: A Tale from Camelot***. New York: Philomel Books, 1998. 184 p; 24 cm. Mordred, the son of King Arthur, struggles against his destined killing of the king and father he both loves and hates, and sets out on a quest to save Arthur's life and his own soul. Grades: 6-10

Stevenson, James. ***The Night After Christmas***. New York: Greenwillow, 1981. 32 p. Mulberry, 1993. (pb). A teddy bear and a doll are befriended by a stray dog after they are thrown in the garbage by children who have received new toys for Christmas. They both find new homes. Grades Pre-K-3

Stewart, Mary. ***The Little Broomstick***. Illustrated by Shirley Hughes. New York: Morrow, 1971, 1972. 192 p. Mary Smith and a black cat rescue the cat's brother from a witch's evil spell. Grades: 3-5

_____. ***A Walk in Wolf Wood: A Tale of Fantasy and Magic***. Illustrated by Emanuel Schongut. New York: Morrow, 1980. 148 p. Fawcett, 1989 (pb). A strangely dressed man who is crying goes into the woods. Following him there, a brother and sister become involved in rescuing a werewolf in the 14th century. Grades: 5-8

Stolz, Mary. ***Quentin Corn***. Illustrated by Pamela Johnson. Boston: Godine, 1985 (hb. and pb). 121 p. Godine, 1995 (pb). A pig who has disguised himself as a boy to escape his fate on the farm gets a job and makes friends with a little girl. Grades: 4-6

Sutcliff, Rosemary. ***The Chronicles of Robin Hood***. Illustrated by C. Walter Hodges. Oxford: Oxford University Press, 1950. The life and adventures of the legendary Robin Hood and his followers, who live as outlaws in Sherwood Forest. Grades: 7 and up

_____. "King Arthur Trilogy"
***The Sword and the Circle: King Arthur and the Knights of the Round Table***. New York: Dutton, 1981. 260 p. Puffin, 1994 (pb). A retelling of the adventures of King Arthur, Queen Guenevere, Sir Lancelot, and the knights of the Round Table. Grades: 7 and up

***The Light Beyond the Forest: The Quest for the Holy Grail***. Illustrated by Shirley Felts. New York: Dutton, 1979. 143 p. Puffin, 1994 (pb). A retelling of the adventures of King Arthur and his knights—Sir Lancelot, Sir Galahad, Sir Bors, and Sir Percival—in their search for the Holy Grail. Grades: 7 and up

***The Road to Camlann***. Illustrated by Shirle Felts. New York: Dutton, 1982. 142 p. Puffin, 1994 (pb). Mordred demolishes Camelot, the Round Table, and his father King Arthur when he accuses Queen Guenevere and Sir Lancelot of treachery. Grades: 7 and up

_____. ***Tristan and Iseult***. New York: Dutton, 1971. 150 p. Farrar, Straus, & Giroux, 1991 (pb). A retelling of the Celtic legend about the disastrous love of the warrior Tristan and Iseult, the wife of King Marc of Cornwall. Grades: 7 and up

Tannen, Mary. "Finn Books"
**The Wizard Children of Finn**. Illustrated by John Burgoyne. New York: Knopf, 1981. 214 p. Avon, 1983 (pb). Ten year-old Fiona and her younger brother are the children of a movie star. When they travel back in time to ancient Ireland, they have exciting adventures with a boy who claims to be the leader of the Fianna. Grades: 5-7
**The Lost Legend of Finn**. New York: Knopf, 1982. 144 p. Fiona and Bran use their uncle's magic book to travel back to ninth century Ireland to find out the truth about their father. Grades: 5-7

Tolkien, J. R. R. **The Hobbit, or There and Back Again**. Boston: Houghton Mifflin, 1966. 315 p. Ballantine, 1992 (pb). The adventures of the hobbit, Bilbo Baggins, who lives happily in his comfortable home smoking his pipe until Gandalf the wizard starts him on a quest to help trolls rescue their treasure from the dragon Smaug. A "prequel" to "The Lord of the Rings" series. Grades: 6 and up

_____. "Lord of the Rings Series"
**The Fellowship of the Ring**. Boston: Houghton Mifflin, 1967. 527 p. Ballantine, 1989 (pb). Frodo Baggins, now guardian of the Ring, travels with his faithful servant Sam and a small band of companions to carry the Ring to Mount Doom, where it can be destroyed. This book contains some of the most memorable scenes in fantasy, including a sequence in the mines of Moria, in which the adventurers discover the fate of those who lived there. There is tremendous suspense while the company stays at the inn in Bree with the Dark riders always on their tail. Finally there is the council of Elrond, at which a plan to destroy the ring is decided upon. Grades: 8 and up
**The Two Towers**. Boston: Houghton Mifflin, 1967. 447 p. Ballantine, 1986 (pb). With the Fellowship scattered, Frodo and Sam make the dangerous journey to Mordor to destroy the Ring, while the others brace for war and contend with the evil wizard Sauron. Memorable scenes include the reappearance of Gandalf the wizard; an encounter with Ents; the reappearance of the underground creature Gollum; and a fight with the giant spider Shelob. Grades: 8 and up

**The Return of the King**. Boston: Houghton Mifflin, 1967. 507 p. Ballantine, 1993 (pb). Frodo and Sam struggle deep into Mordor to destroy the Ring, while the Dark Lord Sauron swarms out from his stronghold to conquer all of Middle-earth. After the successful end to their quest, Sam, who has dreamed of having songs sung of their adventures, stands before a gathering of men singing "Praise to the halflings." Then Aragorn, the new king of Gondor, sings the lay of "Frodo of the Nine Fingers and the Ring of Doom." Tolkien relates that "When Sam heard that, he laughed aloud for sheer delight, and he stood up and cried: 'Oh great glory and splendour! All my wishes have come true!' And then he wept." The saga is brought to a close with Frodo's tremendous anticlimactic final line: "Well, I'm back." Grades: 8 and up

_____. **Roverandom**. Edited by Christina Scull and Wayne G. Hammond. Boston: Houghton Mifflin, 1998. 223 p. A recently discovered manuscript of a well-loved tale Tolkien told his children. Roverandom is a real dog who is turned into a toy and has adventures on the moon with a wizard. Eventually he is returned to his proper form and his young owner. Grades: 5-8

Travers, P. L. **Mary Poppins**. Illustrated by Mary Shepard. New York: Harcourt, Brace, 1934, 1997 (pb). 206 p. The well-known tale of the nanny Mary Poppins who takes her charges on magical adventures. Grades: 3-6

Turner, Megan Whalen. **The Thief**. New York: Greenwillow Books, 1996. 219 p. Puffin, 1998. (pb). For a chance to win his freedom from prison, Gen, an ingenious thief, goes on an adventure to a remote temple of the gods to steal a precious stone. Grades: 5-9

Vande Velde, Vivian. **Companions of the Night**. San Diego: Harcourt Brace & Co., 1995. 212 p. Dell, 1996 (pb). Sixteen-year-old Kerry Nowicki confronts some perilous choices when she helps a young man escape from people who insist he is a vampire. Grades: 6-10

_____. **Curses, Inc**. San Diego: Harcourt Brace & Co., 1997. 226 p. A collection of stories all having to do with a spell, enchantment, or curse. Especially delightful is the title story, in which a boy uses the Internet to try to place a curse on a girl who has embarrassed him. Grades: 4-9

_____. ***Dragon's Bait***. San Diego: Harcourt Brace Jovanovich, 1992. 131 p. Bantam Doubleday, 1997 (pb). Fifteen-year-old Alys, wrongly condemned of witchcraft, finds an ally in the dragon to which she has been sacrificed when she is tempted to take revenge on her accusers. Grades: 6-9

_____. ***A Hidden Magic***. Illustrated by Trina Schart Hyman. New York: Crown, 1985. 117 p. Harcourt Brace, 1997. When Princess Jennifer, separated from her prince, gets lost in a magic forest, she gains the assistance of a kind sorcerer to battle an evil witch. Grades: 4-8

_____. ***Never Trust A Dead Man***. San Diego: Harcourt Brace, 1999. 192 p. Seventeen year-old Selwyn, wrongly convicted of murder, is punished by being sealed in a tomb with a dead man. But when Selwyn is rescued by the witch Elswyth, who resurrects the dead man's spirit, Selwyn gets one week to solve the crime. Grades: 6-10

_____. ***Tales From the Brothers Grimm and the Sisters Weird***. San Diego: Harcourt Brace, 1995. 128 p. Bantam, 1997 (pb). Distorted retellings of the classic fairy tales Red Riding Hood, Jack and the Beanstalk, Hansel and Gretel, and The Three Billy Goats Gruff. Grades: 5 and up

_____. ***User Unfriendly***. San Diego: Harcourt Brace Jovanovich, 1991. 244 p. Fourteen-year-old Arvin and his friends use a computer-controlled role-playing game to simulate a magical world in which they become fantasy characters, even though the computer program contains unpredictable errors. Grades: 5 and up

_____. ***A Well-Timed Enchantment***. New York: Crown Pub., 1990. 184 p. Harcourt Brace, 1998 (pb). A girl and her cat travel back in time to retrieve a lost watch. Grades: 4-7

Van de Wetering, Janwillem. ***Hugh Pine***. Illustrated by Lynn Munsinger. Boston: Houghton Mifflin, 1980. 82 p. A porcupine genius named Hugh Pine works with his human friends to save his fellow porcupines from the deadly dangers of the road. Grades: 2-4

Vick, H. H. "Walker Books"
***Walker of Time***. Tucson, Ariz.: Harbinger House 1993, (pb). 205 p. A 15-year-old Hopi boy and his friend travel back 800 years to the world of the Sinagua, a group of people beset by drought and illness and in need of a leader. Grades: 6-12

***Walker's Journey Home***. Tucson, Ariz.: Harbinger House, 1995 (pb). 182 p. Trapped in ancient times, 15-year-old Walker accepts the responsibility of leading a group of Indians on a dangerous journey across the high desert country of northern Arizona to their new home on the Hopi mesas. Grades: 6-12

***Tag Against Time***. Tucson, Ariz.: Harbinger House1996, (pb). 195 p. Twelve-year-old Tag encounters historic figures and events as he time-travels from the ancient cliff-dwellers' period to the present. Grades: 6-12

Wangerin, Walter. ***The Book of the Dun Cow***. New York: HarperCollins, 1978. 241 p. Chauntecleer the rooster participates in a cataclysmic fight between the forces of good and evil as personified by the mysterious Wyrm. Grades: 6-12

Waugh, Sylvia. "Mennyms Series"
***The Mennyms***. New York: Greenwillow, 1994. 212 p. Avon, 1996 (pb).
The Mennyms, a family of life-size rag dolls created by a lonely, talented seamstress, come to life and pretend to be human. The owner of the house where they live announces he is coming for a visit, and they are afraid that their secret will be found out. Grades: 5 and up

***Mennyms in the Wilderness***. New York: Greenwillow, 1995. 254 p. Camelot, 1996 (pb). The Mennyms continue to face the threat that their existence will soon be discovered by the outside world. Grades: 5 and up

***Mennyms Under Siege***. New York: Greenwillow, 1996. 219 p. Avon, 1997 (pb). Pilbeam, the teenage Mennym, goes on an outing to the theater at which she encounters Anthea Fryer, one of the Mennyms' neighbors. The resulting attention again threatens the Menymns' secret. Grades: 5 and up

***Mennyms Alone***. New York: Greenwillow, 1996. 192 p. Sir Magnus, the head of the Mennym family, has a premonition that on a particular day the world as they know it will end and they will return to their former lifeless state. Grades: 5 and up

***Mennyms Alive***. New York: Greenwillow, 1996, 1997. 224 p. Sir Magnus' premonition comes true in a way, and the Mennymns now find themselves not in their familiar house at Number 5 Broklehurst Grove, but in the hands of an antiques dealer who suspects that they are more than they seem. Grades: 5 and up

White, E. B. ***Charlotte's Web***. Illustrated by Garth Williams. New York: HarperCollins, 1952. 184 p. 1997 (pb). The classic tale of Wilbur the pig and his friendship with Charlotte the spider. Grades: 4-6

_____. ***Stuart Little***. Illustrated by Garth Williams. New York, HarperCollins, 1945. 131 p. 1990 (pb). Mr. Little's second son is different from the rest of his human family: He is a mouse. This book has a slightly disconcerting open-ended ending, in which Stuart goes in search of the family bird who has flown away. Grades: 4-6

_____. ***The Trumpet of the Swan***. Illustrated by Edward Frascino. New York: HarperCollins, 1970. 210 p. 1987 (pb). Louis, a voiceless trumpeter swan, is determined to learn to play a stolen trumpet. Grades: 4-6

White, T. H. ***The Once and Future King***. New York: Putnam, 1958, 1980. 677 p. Ace Books, 1996 (pb). A retelling of the legendary adventures of King Arthur and the Knights of the Round Table. Grades: 8 and up

_____. ***The Sword in the Stone***. Illustrated by Robert Lawson. New York: G. P. Putnam's Sons, 1939. 311 p. Laurel Leaf, 1978 (pb). A retelling of the story of King Arthur's life before he became king. Grades: 5-8

Winthrop, Elizabeth. "Castle Books"
***The Castle in the Attic***. Illustrated by Trina Schart Hyman. New York: Holiday House, 1985. 179 p. Bantam, 1998 (pb). William is launched on a personal quest after he is given a toy castle and a silver knight. Grades: 3-7
***The Battle for the Castle***. New York: Holiday House, 1993. 211 p. Dell, 1994 (pb). William returns to the medieval land of Sir Simon, which is being threatened by a plague of ravenous monster rats with which he and his friend Jason must do battle. Grades: 3-7.

Wiseman, David. ***Jeremy Visick***. Boston: Houghton Mifflin, 1981, 170 p. 1990 (pb). Matthew Clemens feels himself mysteriously drawn to a tombstone of a man and three sons who were killed in a mining accident. The third son's body was never recovered. His name was Jeremy Visick. Matthew finds himself in the past and has a harrowing experience with Jeremy trying to get out of the mine after the explosion has killed Jeremy's dad and brothers. He realizes that his mission was to get Jeremy's body and have it properly buried. Grades: 5-7

_____. ***Thimbles: A Novel***. Boston: Houghton Mifflin, 1982. 134 p. A girl is magically transported through time to join a 1819 demonstration by Manchester mill workers seeking the right to vote. The demonstration ends tragically. Grades: 5-7

Wisler, G. Clifton. "Scott Childers Trilogy"
***The Antrian Messenger***. New York: Dutton, 1986. 117 p. The ordinary life of Scott Childers, a high school freshman, changes drastically when he discovers that he is an alien, a refugee from the Antrian star system that has exploded. This explains his strange dreams, his precognition, and his scientific understandings. Grades: 5-7
***The Seer***. New York: Lodestar Books, 1989. 134 p. Penguin, 1991. Even though he is not from earth, 14-year-old Scott tries to live as a normal teenager while investigating his powers of teleportation, matter conversion, and precognition. Grades: 5-7
***The Mind Trap***. York: Lodestar Books, 1990. 118 p. When Scott is imprisoned in a research institute, his identity as a telepathic alien may be exposed. Grades: 5-7

Wrede, Patricia C. ***Book of Enchantments***. San Diego: Harcourt Brace Jovanovich, 1996. 234 p. Point, 1998 (pb). This collection of short stories includes the hilarious "Utensile Strength." Grades: 4-8

_____. "Enchanted Forest Chronicles"
***Dealing With Dragons***. San Diego: Harcourt Brace & Co., 1990. 212 p. Scholastic, 1992 (pb). Bored by palace life, Princess Cimorene goes off to be princess to the dragon Kazul. She doesn't want to be rescued by any of the princes who come along; in the meantime, she helps Kazul thwart the wizards of the Enchanted Forest in a scheme to rig the ritual in which the dragons choose their next king. Grades: 6-9
***Searching for Dragons***. San Diego: Harcourt Brace Jovanovich, 1991. 242 p. Scholastic, 1992 (pb). King Mandanbar and Princess Cimorene save the Enchanted Forest from the wicked wizards and rescue Kazul the dragon. Grades: 6-9

*Calling on Dragons*. San Diego: Harcourt Brace Jovanovich, 1993. 244 p. Scholastic, 1994 (pb). When the evil wizards begin to soak up the magic of the Enchanted Forest, it is up to Queen Cimorene and her friends Morwen, Telemain, and Kazul to stop them. Grades: 6-9

*Talking to Dragons*. San Diego: Harcourt Brace Jovanovich, 1985, 1993. 255 p. Point, 1995 (pb). Without knowing what his destiny is, Daystar, the 16-year-old son of Queen Cimorene, must restore his father to the throne of the Enchanted Forest. Grades: 6-9

Wright, Betty Ren. *Christina's Ghost*. New York: Holiday House, 1985. 105 p. Scholastic, 1995 (pb). A seemingly dull summer turns into an adventure when Christina encounters some ghosts. Grades: 4-6

_____. *The Dollhouse Murders*. New York: Holiday House, 1983. 149 p. Scholastic, 1995 (pb). Amy and her retarded sister are led into a mystery when their dollhouse fills with a ghostly light and the dolls move from where they left them. The girls discover that some grisly murders took place years ago in the real house of which the dollhouse is a copy, and that the dolls are re-enacting the events. Grades: 3-7

_____. *The Ghost of Popcorn Hill*. Illustrated by Karen Ritz. New York: Holiday House, 1993. 81 p. Scholastic, 1994 (pb). A new dog and two lonely ghosts come into Martin's and Peter's lives at the same time. Grades: 3-6

_____. *Ghosts Beneath Our Feet*. New York: Holiday House, 1984. 137 p. Scholastic, 1995 (pb). Katie and her stepbrother become closer as they dig into the past to solve the mystery of the ghosts beneath their feet. Grades: 3-7

_____. *The Ghosts of Mercy Manor*. New York: Scholastic, 1993. 172 p. Scholastic, 1994 (pb). After coming to live with the Mercy family, 12-year-old Gwen is determined to discover the mystery behind the sad-looking girl ghost who is haunting the house. Grades: 4-7

_____. *Haunted Summer*. New York: Scholastic Inc., 1996. 99 p. Nine-year-old Abby, her older brother, and her baby-sitter are haunted by a ghost who is trying to find a stolen music box. Grades: 3-6

Wrightson, Patricia. *Balyet*. New York: Margaret K. McElderry Books, 1989. 132 p. Fourteen year-old Jo falls under the spell of a ghost girl in the Australian hills. Grades: 6-9.

_____. "Wirrun Trilogy"
*The Ice Is Coming*. New York: Atheneum, 1977. 196 p. Ballantine, 1986 (pb). 222 p. The ancient forces of fire and ice fight a merciless battle with the oldest Nargun and his people. Grades: 6-9

*The Dark Bright Water*. New York: Atheneum, 1978, 1979. 223 p. A young Australian Aborigine is urged by tribal elders to investigate strange events occurring in the interior of their vast continent. Grades: 6-9

*Journey Behind the Wind*. New York: Atheneum, 1981. 156 p. Wirrun is the only one who can save his people from a red-eyed alien thing who steals men's spirits for his master. Grades: 6-9

_____. *The Nargun and the Stars*. New York: Atheneum, 1974, 1986. 184 p. Penguin/Puffin, 1988 (pb). An ancient stone creature threatens the lives of a family on a sheep farm in Australia. Grades: 5-8

Yep, Laurence. "Dragon Quartet"
*Dragon of the Lost Sea*. New York: HarperCollins, 1982. 213 p. 1994 (pb). The dragon princess Shimmer tries to regain her honor by capturing a witch. Grades: 5-9

*Dragon Steel*. New York: HarperCollins, 1985. 276 p. 1993 (pb). Thorn and the dragon princess Shimmer rise up against the Dragon King's treachery to free the dragons from slavery. Grades: 5-9

*Dragon Cauldron*. New York: HarperCollins, 1991. 312 p. 1994 (pb). When a broken magic cauldron is needed to repair the dragon's home, the dragon princess Shimmer, a monkey wizard, a reformed witch, and two humans go on a quest to mend it. Grades: 5-9

*Dragon War*. New York: HarperCollins, 1992. 313 p. 1994 (pb). To restore the underwater home of the dragons and to rescue their friend Thorn, the princess Shimmer and her companions fight a war against the evil Boneless King. Grades: 5-9

Yolen, Jane. "Pit Dragons Series"
*Dragon's Blood*. San Diego: Harcourt Brace, 1996 (hb and pb). 243 p. With the hopes of winning his freedom from the dragon nursery where he works, Jakkin secretly trains one of the fighting pit dragons. Grades: 6 and up

***Heart's Blood***. New York: Delacorte Press, 1984. 238 p. Harcourt Brace, 1996 (pb). The now free dragon trainer Jakkin is asked to spy on the rebel forces that have taken over the planet. Grades: 6 and up

***A Sending of Dragons***. New York: Delacorte Press, 1987. 189 p. Harcourt Brace, 1997 (pb). Jakkin and Akki gain unusual powers with the sacrifice and help of a dragon and her offspring after they have been sent to die in the wilderness of the planet Austa IV. Grades: 6 and up

_____. ***Sleeping Ugly***. Illustrated by Diane Stanley. New York: Coward, McCann & Geoghegan, 1981. 64 p. Putnam, 1997 (pb). 64 p. A unusual and twisted adaptation of the classic Sleeping Beauty fairy tale. Grades: 1-4

_____. ***Wizard's Hall***. San Diego: Harcourt Brace Jovanovich, 1991. 133 p. Scholastic, 1993 (pb). Because he believes and trusts in himself, a young inexperienced apprentice wizard is able to save the wizard's training hall. Grades: 3-7

# Titles Listed by Grade Level

## PRESCHOOL

Barrett, Ron and Judi. *Animals Should Definitely Not Wear Clothing.*
Bonne, Rose. *I Know an Old Lady.*
Brett, Jan. *Town Mouse, Country Mouse.*
Burningham, John. *Mr. Gumpy's Motor Car.*
_____. *Mr. Gumpy's Outing.*
Calhoun, Mary. *The Witch of Hissing Hill.*
DeRegniers, Beatrice. *May I Bring A Friend?*
Freeman, Don. *Corduroy.*
_____. *A Pocket for Corduroy.*
Hissey, Jane. "Old Bear Series"
Kellogg, Steven. *Chicken Little.*
_____. *Jack and the Beanstalk.*
Kent, Jack. *The Fat Cat.*
Lillegard, Dee. *Sitting in My Box.*
Opie, Iona. *My Very First Mother Goose.*
Scieska, Jon. *The Stinky Cheese Man and Other Fairly Stupid Tales.*
Sendak, Maurice. *Where the Wild Things Are.*
Seymour, Peter. *What's in the Cave?*

## KINDERGARTEN

Ahlberg, Janet and Alan. *Funnybones.*
Allen, Pamela. *Who Sank the Boat?*
Aliki. *Keep Your Mouth Closed, Dear.*
Ardizonne, Aingelda. *The Night Ride.*
Bang, Molly. *Tye May and the Magic Paint Brush.*
_____. *Wiley and the Hairy Man.*
Barrett, Ron and Judi. *Animals Should Definitely Not Wear Cothing.*
Barrett, Ron and Judi. *Cloudy With a Chance of Meatballs.*
Bonne, Rose. *I Know an Old Lady.*
Bowden, Joan Chase. *The Bean Boy.*
Brett, Jan. *Town Mouse, Country Mouse.*
Bridwell, Norman. *How to Care for Your Monster.*
Bright, Robert. *Georgie to the Rescue.*
Browne, Anthony. *The Tunnel.*
Burningham, John. *Mr. Gumpy's Motor Car.*
_____. *Mr. Gumpy's Outing.*
Calhoun, Mary. *The Witch of Hissing Hill.*
DePaola, Tomie. *Helga's Dowry.*
DeRegniers, Beatrice. *May I Bring A Friend?*
Devlin, Wende and Harry. *Old Black Witch.*
Domanska, Janina. *The Turnip.*
Freeman, Don. *Corduroy.*
_____. *A Pocket for Corduroy.*
Gaeddert, Louann. *Gustav, the Gourmet Giant.*
Galdone, Joanna. *The Tailypo: A Ghost Story.*
Harper, Wilhemina. *The Gunniwolf.*
Heide, Florence Parry and Roxanne Heide. *A Monster is Coming! A Monster is Coming!*
Hissey, Jane. "Old Bear Series"

Hoban, Russell. *Dinner at Alberta's.*
Howe, James. *There's A Monster Under My Bed.*
Ivimey, John W. *Complete Story of the Three Blind Mice.*
Kahl, Virginia. *The Duchess Bakes a Cake.*
Kellogg, Steven. *Chicken Little.*
_____. *Jack and the Beanstalk.*
Kent, Jack. *The Fat Cat.*
Kroll, Steven. *Big Jeremy.*
Lachner, Dorothea. *Meredith The Witch Who Wasn't.*
Lillegard, Dee. *Sitting in My Box.*
Lobel, Arnold. *Fables.*
Morimoto, Junko. *Mouse's Marriage.*
Ness, Evaline. *Mr. Miacca: An English Folktake.*
Opie, Iona. *My Very First Mother Goose.*
Scieska, Jon. *The Stinky Cheese Man and Other Fairly Stupid Tales.*
Sendak, Maurice. *Outside Over There.*
_____. *Where the Wild Things Are.*
Seymour, Peter. *What's in the Cave?*
Shulevitz, Uri. *One Monday Morning.*
Steptoe, John. *The Story of Jumping Mouse: A Native American Legend.*
Stevenson, James. *The Night After Christmas.*
Thayer, Jane. *Gus Was a Friendly Ghost.*
VanAllsburg, Chris. *The Widow's Broom.*
Wahl, Jan. *Humphrey's Bear.*
Wescott, Nadine Bernard. *The Giant Vegetable Garden.*
Wiesner, David. *Hurricane.*
_____. *June 29, 1999.*
_____. *Tuesday.*
Willard, Nancy. *The Tale I Told Sasha.*
Wood, Audrey and Don. *Heckedy Peg.*
_____. *King Bidgood's in the Bathtub.*
Young, Ed. *The Seven Blind Mice.*

## 1ST GRADE

Ahlberg, Janet and Alan. *Funnybones.*
Allen, Pamela. *Who Sank the Boat?*
Aliki. *Keep Your Mouth Closed, Dear.*
Ardizonne, Aingelda. *The Night Ride.*
Bang, Molly. *Tye May and the Magic Paint Brush.*
_____. *Wiley and the Hairy Man.*
Barrett, Ron and Judi. *Animals Should Definitely Not Wear Clothing.*
Barrett, Ron and Judi. *Cloudy With a Chance of Meatballs.*
Bonne, Rose. *I Know an Old Lady.*
Bowden, Joan Chase. *The Bean Boy.*
Brett, Jan. *Town Mouse, Country Mouse.*
Bridwell, Norman. *How to Care for Your Monster.*
Bright, Robert. *Georgie to the Rescue.*

Browne, Anthony. *The Tunnel.*
Burningham, John. *Mr. Gumpy's Motor Car.*
_____. *Mr. Gumpy's Outing.*
Calhoun, Mary. *The Witch of Hissing Hill.*
DePaola, Tomie. *Helga's Dowry.*
DeRegniers, Beatrice. *May I Bring A Friend?*
Devlin, Wende and Harry. *Old Black Witch.*
Domanska, Janina. *The Turnip.*
Freeman, Don. *Corduroy.*
_____. *A Pocket for Corduroy.*
Gaeddert, Louann. *Gustav, the Gourmet Giant.*
Galdone, Joanna. *The Tailypo: A Ghost Story.*
Harper, Wilhemina. *The Gunniwolf.*
Heide, Florence Parry and Roxanne Heide. *A Monster is Coming! A Monster is Coming!*
Hissey, Jane. "Old Bear Series"
Hoban, Russell. *Dinner at Alberta's.*
Howe, James. *There's A Monster Under My Bed.*
Ivimey, John W. *Complete Story of the Three Blind Mice.*
Kahl, Virginia. *The Duchess Bakes a Cake.*
Kellogg, Steven. *Chicken Little.*
_____. *Jack and the Beanstalk.*
Kent, Jack. *The Fat Cat.*
Kroll, Steven. *Big Jeremy.*
Lachner, Dorothea. *Meredith The Witch Who Wasn't.*
Lillegard, Dee. *Sitting in My Box.*
Lobel, Arnold. *Fables.*
Morimoto, Junko. *Mouse's Marriage.*
Ness, Evaline. *Mr. Miacca: An English Folktale.*
Opie, Iona. *My Very First Mother Goose.*
Osborne, Mary Pope. "Magic Treehouse Series".
Scieska, Jon. *The Stinky Cheese Man and Other Fairly Stupid Tales.*
Sendak, Maurice. *Outside Over There.*
_____. *Where the Wild Things Are.*
Seymour, Peter. *What's in the Cave?*
Shulevitz, Uri. *One Monday Morning.*
Steptoe, John. *The Story of Jumping Mouse: A Native American Legend.*
Stevenson, James. *The Night After Christmas.*
Thayer, Jane. *Gus Was a Friendly Ghost.*
VanAllsburg, Chris. *The Garden of Abdul Gasazi.*
_____. *Jumanji.*
_____. *The Widow's Broom.*
Wahl, Jan. *Humphrey's Bear.*
Wescott, Nadine Bernard. *The Giant Vegetable Garden.*
Wiesner, David. *Free Fall.*
_____. *Hurricane.*
_____. *June 29, 1999.*
_____. *Tuesday.*
Willard, Nancy. *The Tale I Told Sasha.*
Wood, Audrey and Don. *Heckedy Peg.*
_____. *King Bidgood's in the Bathtub.*
Yolen, Jane. *Sleeping Ugly.*
Young, Ed. *The Seven Blind Mice.*

**2ND GRADE**
Ahlberg, Janet and Alan. *Funnybones.*
Allen, Pamela. *Who Sank the Boat?*
Aliki. *Keep Your Mouth Closed, Dear.*
Ardizonne, Aingelda. *The Night Ride.*
Bang, Molly. *Tye May and the Magic Paint Brush.*
_____. *Wiley and the Hairy Man.*
Barrett, Ron and Judi. *Animals Should Definitely Not Wear Cothing.*
Barrett, Ron and Judi. *Cloudy With a Chance of Meatballs.*
Bonne, Rose. *I Know an Old Lady.*
Bowden, Joan Chase. *The Bean Boy.*
Brett, Jan. *Town Mouse, Country Mouse.*
Bridwell, Norman. *How to Care for Your Monster.*
Bright, Robert. *Georgie to the Rescue.*
Browne, Anthony. *The Tunnel.*
Burningham, John. *Mr. Gumpy's Motor Car.*
_____. *Mr. Gumpy's Outing.*
Calhoun, Mary. *The Witch of Hissing Hill.*
Cleary, Beverly. "Ralph S. Mouse Books".
DePaola, Tomie. *Helga's Dowry.*
DeRegniers, Beatrice. *May I Bring A Friend?*
Devlin, Wende and Harry. *Old Black Witch.*
Domanska, Janina. *The Turnip.*
Freeman, Don. *Corduroy.*
_____. *A Pocket for Corduroy.*
Gaeddert, Louann. *Gustav, the Gourmet Giant.*
Galdone, Joanna. *The Tailypo: A Ghost Story.*
Greer, Gery and Bob Ruddick. *Jason and the Aliens Down the Street.*
_____. *Let Me Off This Spaceship!*
Gorog, Judith. *In a Messy Messy Room and Other Strange Stories.*
Gurney, James. *Dinotopia Pop-up Book.*
Harper, Wilhemina. *The Gunniwolf.*
Heide, Florence Parry and Roxanne Heide. *A Monster is Coming! A Monster is Coming!*
Heide, Florence Parry. "Treehorn Books".
Hissey, Jane. "Old Bear Series"
Hoban, Russell. *Dinner at Alberta's.*
Howe, James. *There's A Monster Under My Bed.*
Ivimey, John W. *Complete Story of the Three Blind Mice.*
Kahl, Virginia. *The Duchess Bakes a Cake.*
Kellogg, Steven. *Chicken Little.*
_____. *Jack and the Beanstalk.*
Kent, Jack. *The Fat Cat.*
King-Smith, Dick. *Three Terrible Trins.*
Kroll, Steven. *Big Jeremy.*
Lachner, Dorothea. *Meredith The Witch Who Wasn't.*

Lillegard, Dee. *Sitting in My Box.*
Lobel, Arnold. *Fables.*
Milne, A. A. *The House at Pooh Corner.*
_____. *Winnie the Pooh.*
Morimoto, Junko. *Mouse's Marriage.*
Ness, Evaline. *Mr. Miacca: An English Folktale.*
Opie, Iona. *My Very First Mother Goose.*
Osborne, Mary Pope. "Magic Treehouse Series".
Scieska, Jon. *The Stinky Cheese Man and Other Fairly Stupid Tales.*
_____. *Squids Will Be Squids.*
_____. "Time Warp Trio Series".
Seidler, Tor. *The Wainscott Weasel.*
Sendak, Maurice. *Outside Over There.*
_____. *Where the Wild Things Are.*
Seymour, Peter. *What's in the Cave?*
Shulevitz, Uri. *One Monday Morning.*
Smith, Dodie. *The Hundred and One Dalmatians.*
Steptoe, John. *The Story of Jumping Mouse: A Native American Legend.*
Stevenson, James. *The Night After Christmas.*
Thayer, Jane. *Gus Was a Friendly Ghost.*
VanAllsburg, Chris. *The Garden of Abdul Gasazi.*
_____. *Jumanji.*
_____. *The Polar Express.*
_____. *The Widow's Broom.*
_____. *The Wreck of the Zephyr.*
Van de Wetering, Janwillem. *Hugh Pine.*
Wahl, Jan. *Humphrey's Bear.*
Wescott, Nadine Bernard. *The Giant Vegetable Garden.*
Wiesner, David. *Free Fall.*
_____. *Hurricane.*
_____. *June 29, 1999.*
_____. *Tuesday.*
Willard, Nancy. *The Tale I Told Sasha.*
Wood, Audrey and Don. *Heckedy Peg.*
_____. *King Bidgood's in the Bathtub.*
Yolen, Jane. *Sleeping Ugly.*
Young, Ed. *The Seven Blind Mice.*

### 3RD GRADE
Ahlberg, Janet and Alan. *Funnybones.*
Allen, Pamela. *Who Sank the Boat?*
Aliki. *Keep Your Mouth Closed, Dear.*
Anderson, Lloyd. *Gypsy Rizka.*
Applegate, K. A. "Animorphs Series".
Ardizonne, Aingelda. *The Night Ride.*
Asch, Frank. *Journey to Terezor.*
Avi. *Poppy*
_____. *Poppy and Rye.*
Babbitt, Natalie. *Goody Hall.*
_____. *Kneeknock Rise.*
_____. *The Search for Delicious.*

Bang, Molly. *Tye May and the Magic Paint Brush.*
_____. *Wiley and the Hairy Man.*
Barrett, Ron and Judi. *Cloudy With a Chance of Meatballs.*
Baum, L. Frank. *The Life and Adventures of Santa Claus.*
_____. *Little Wizard Stories of Oz.*
_____. "Oz Series".
_____. *The Surprising Adventures of the Magical Monarch of Mo and his People.*
Bowden, Joan Chase. *The Bean Boy.*
Brett, Jan. *Town Mouse, Country Mouse.*
Bridwell, Norman. *How to Care for Your Monster.*
Bright, Robert. *Georgie to the Rescue.*
Brittain, Bill. *All the Money in the World.*
_____. *Professor Popkin's Prodigious Polish: A Tale of Coven Tree.*
_____. *The Wish Giver: Three Tales of Coven Tree.*
Browne, Anthony. *The Tunnel.*
Burningham, John. *Mr. Gumpy's Motor Car.*
_____. *Mr. Gumpy's Outing.*
Calhoun, Mary. *The Witch of Hissing Hill.*
Carris, Joan Davenport. *Witch Cat.*
Clapp, Patricia. *Jane-Emily.*
Cleary, Beverly. "Ralph S. Mouse Books".
Coville, Bruce. *Jennifer Murdley's Toad: A Magic Shop Book.*
_____. *Jeremy Thatcher, Dragon Hatcher: A Magic Shop Book.*
_____. *The Monster's Ring.*
Dahl, Roald. *Charlie and the Chocolate Factory.*
_____. *Charlie and the Great Glass Elevator.*
_____. *James and the Giant Peach.*
DePaola, Tomie. *Helga's Dowry.*
DeRegniers, Beatrice. *May I Bring A Friend?*
Devlin, Wende and Harry. *Old Black Witch.*
Domanska, Janina. *The Turnip.*
Eager, Edward. *The Time Garden.*
Feiffer, Jules. *A Barrel of Laughs, A Vale of Tears.*
Fleischman, Sid. *The 13th Floor: A Ghost Story.*
Gaeddert, Louann. *Gustav, the Gourmet Giant.*
Galdone, Joanna. *The Tailypo: A Ghost Story.*
Gorog, Judith. *In a Messy Messy Room and Other Strange Stories.*
Greer, Gery and Bob Ruddick. *Jason and the Aliens Down the Street.*
_____. *Let Me Off This Spaceship!*
Gurney, James. *Dinotopia Pop-up Book.*
Harper, Wilhemina. *The Gunniwolf.*
Hass. E. A. *Incognito Mosquito, Private Insective.*
Heide, Florence Parry and Roxanne Heide. *A Monster is Coming! A Monster is Coming!*
Heide, Florence Parry. "Treehorn Books".
Hoban, Russell. *Dinner at Alberta's.*

_____. *The Mouse and His Child.*
Howe, Deborah and James. "Bunnicula Books".
Howe, James. *There's A Monster Under My Bed.*
Hunter, Mollie. *The Mermaid Summer.*
Ivimey, John W. *Complete Story of the Three Blind Mice.*
Jones, Terry. *Fantastic Stories.*
_____. *Fairy Tales.*
Kahl, Virginia. *The Duchess Bakes a Cake.*
Kaye, M. M. *The Ordinary Princess.*
Kellogg, Steven. *Chicken Little.*
_____. *Jack and the Beanstalk.*
Kent, Jack. *The Fat Cat.*
King-Smith, Dick. *Harriet's Hare.*
_____. *Paddy's Pot of Gold.*
_____. *Three Terrible Trins.*
Koller, Jackie French. *The Dragonling.*
Kroll, Steven. *Big Jeremy.*
Lachner, Dorothea. *Meredith The Witch Who Wasn't.*
Levine, Gail Carson. "Princess Tales Series".
Lillegard, Dee. *Sitting in My Box.*
Lobel, Arnold. *Fables.*
Lofting, Hugh. *The Story of Doctor Doolittle.*
MacDonald, George. *The Light Princess.*
Massie, Diane Redfield. *Chameleon Was a Spy.*
Milne, A. A. *The House at Pooh Corner.*
_____. *Winnie the Pooh.*
Morimoto, Junko. *Mouse's Marriage.*
Napoli, Donna Jo. *Jimmy: The Pickpocket of the Palace.*
_____. *The Prince of the Pond: Otherwise Known as De Fawg Pin.*
Naylor, Phillis Reynolds. *Grand Escape.*
Ness, Evaline. *Mr. Miacca: An English Folktale.*
Opie, Iona. *My Very First Mother Goose.*
Osborne, Mary Pope. "Magic Treehouse Series".
Prelutsky, Jack. *Nightmares: Poems to Trouble Your Sleep.*
Reid Banks, Lynne. *The Adventures of King Midas.*
_____. *The Fairy Rebel.*
Scieska, Jon. *The Stinky Cheese Man and Other Fairly Stupid Tales.*
_____. *Squids Will Be Squids.*
_____. "Time Warp Trio Series".
Seidler, Tor. *Mean Margaret.*
_____. *The Wainscott Weasel.*
Selden, George. "Chester Cricket Books".
Sendak, Maurice. *Outside Over There.*
_____. *Where the Wild Things Are.*
Shulevitz, Uri. *One Monday Morning.*
Smith, Dodie. *The Hundred and One Dalmatians.*
Steptoe, John. *The Story of Jumping Mouse: A Native American Legend.*

Stewart, Mary. *The Little Broomstick.*
Stevenson, James. *The Night After Christmas.*
Thayer, Jane. *Gus Was a Friendly Ghost.*
Travers, P. L. *Mary Poppins.*
VanAllsburg, Chris. *The Garden of Abdul Gasazi.*
_____. *Jumanji.*
_____. *The Polar Express.*
_____. *The Widow's Broom.*
_____. *The Wreck of the Zephyr.*
_____. *The Wretched Stone.*
Van de Wetering, Janwillem. *Hugh Pine.*
Wahl, Jan. *Humphrey's Bear.*
Wescott, Nadine Bernard. *The Giant Vegetable Garden.*
Wiesner, David. *Free Fall.*
_____. *Hurricane.*
_____. *June 29, 1999.*
_____. *Tuesday.*
Willard, Nancy. *The Tale I Told Sasha.*
Winthrop, Elizabeth. "Castle Books".
Wood, Audrey and Don. *Heckedy Peg.*
_____. *King Bidgood's in the Bathtub.*
Wright, Betty Ren. *The Dollhouse Murders.*
_____. *The Ghost of Popcorn Hill.*
_____. *Ghosts Beneath Our Feet.*
_____. *Haunted Summer.*
Yolen, Jane. *Sleeping Ugly.*
_____. *Wizard's Hall.*
Young, Ed. *The Seven Blind Mice.*

## 4TH GRADE

Alcock, Vivien. *The Sylvia Game.*
Alexander, Lloyd. *The Arkadians.*
_____. *Gypsy Rizka.*
_____. *The Marvelous Misadventures of Sebastian.*
Applegate, K. A. "Animorphs Series".
Asch, Frank. *Journey to Terezor.*
Avi. *City of Light, City of Dark.*
_____. *Poppy*
_____. *Poppy and Rye.*
Babbitt, Natalie. *Goody Hall.*
_____. *Kneeknock Rise.*
_____. *The Search for Delicious.*
_____. *Tuck Everlasting.*
Barrie, J. M. *Peter Pan.*
Baum, L. Frank. *The Life and Adventures of Santa Claus.*
_____. *Little Wizard Stories of Oz.*
_____. "Oz Series".
_____. *The Surprising Adventures of the Magical Monarch of Mo and his People.*
Bellairs, John. "Johnny Dixon Mysteries".
_____. "House With a Clock in its Walls Trilogy".
_____. *The Dark Secret of Weatherend.*

Boston, L. M. "Green Knowe Books".
Brittain, Bill. *All the Money in the World.*
_____. *Professor Popkin's Prodigious Polish: A Tale of Coven Tree.*
_____. *The Wish Giver: Three Tales of Coven Tree.*
Butterworth, Oliver. *The Trouble With Jenny's Ear.*
Carris, Joan Davenport. *Witch Cat.*
Catling, Patrick Skene. *The Chocolate Touch.*
Clapp, Patricia. *Jane-Emily.*
Clarke, Pauline. *The Return of the Twelves.*
Cleary, Beverly. "Ralph S. Mouse Books".
Collodi, Carlo. *The Adventures of Pinocchio.*
Cooper, Susan. "Boggart Books".
Coville, Bruce. *Jennifer Murdley's Toad: A Magic Shop Book.*
_____. *Jeremy Thatcher, Dragon Hatcher: A Magic Shop Book.*
_____. *The Monster's Ring.*
Dahl, Roald. *The BFG.*
_____. *Charlie and the Chocolate Factory.*
_____. *Charlie and the Great Glass Elevator.*
_____. *James and the Giant Peach.*
_____. *The Witches.*
Duffey, Betsy. *Alien for Rent.*
Eager, Edward. *Seven Day Magic.*
_____. *The Time Garden.*
Farmer, Nancy. *The Warm Place.*
Feiffer, Jules. *A Barrel of Laughs, A Vale of Tears.*
Fleischman, Sid. *The Ghost in the Noonday Sun.*
_____. *The 13th Floor: A Ghost Story.*
Fleming, Ian. *Chitty Chitty Bang Bang, the Magical Car.*
Fry, Rosalie K. *The Secret of Roan Inish.*
Garden, Nancy. *My Sister, the Vampire.*
Gormley, Beatrice. "Andrea Books".
Gorog, Judith. *In a Messy Messy Room and Other Strange Stories.*
Grahame, Kenneth. *The Reluctant Dragon.*
_____. *The Wind in the Willows.*
Greer, Gery and Bob Ruddick. *Jason and the Aliens Down the Street.*
_____. *Let Me Off This Spaceship!*
Gurney, James. "Dinotopia Books".
_____. *Dinotopia Pop-up Book.*
Hahn, Mary Downing. *Wait Till Helen Comes: A Ghost Story.*
Hass. E. A. *Incognito Mosquito, Private Insective.*
Heide, Florence Parry. "Treehorn Books".
Hoban, Russell. *The Mouse and His Child.*
Howe, Deborah and James. "Bunnicula Books".
Hunter, Mollie. *The Mermaid Summer.*
Jones, Terry. *Fantastic Stories.*

_____. *Fairy Tales.*
Kaye, M. M. *The Ordinary Princess.*
Kendall, Carol. *The Gammage Cup.*
Key, Alexander. *Escape to Witch Mountain.*
King-Smith, Dick. *Babe: The Gallant Pig.*
_____. *Harriet's Hare.*
_____. *Paddy's Pot of Gold.*
_____. *Three Terrible Trins.*
Klause, Annette Curtis. *Alien Secrets.*
Koller, Jackie French. *The Dragonling.*
Krensky, Stephen. "Dragon Books".
_____. *The Perils of Putney.*
Levine, Gail Carson. "Princess Tales Series".
Lewis, C. S. "Chronicles of Narnia".
Lofting, Hugh. *The Story of Doctor Doolittle.*
_____. *The Voyages of Doctor Doolittle.*
MacDonald, George. *The Light Princess.*
Massie, Diane Redfield. *Chameleon Was a Spy.*
Milne, A. A. *The House at Pooh Corner.*
_____. *Winnie the Pooh.*
Napoli, Donna Jo. *Jimmy: The Pickpocket of the Palace.*
_____. *The Prince of the Pond: Otherwise Known as De Fawg Pin.*
Naylor, Phillis Reynolds. *Grand Escape.*
_____. "Witch Books".
Norton, Mary. *Bed-Knob and Broomstick.*
_____. *The Borrowers.*
Opie, Iona. *My Very First Mother Goose.*
Osborne, Mary Pope. "Magic Treehouse Series".
Pinkwater, Daniel Manus. *Fat Men From Space.*
Prelutsky, Jack. *Nightmares: Poems to Trouble Your Sleep.*
Reid Banks, Lynne. *The Adventures of King Midas.*
_____. *The Fairy Rebel.*
_____. "Indian in the Cupboard Series".
Roberts, Willo Davis. *The Girl With the Silver Eyes*
Sauer, Julia L. *Fog Magic.*
Scieska, Jon. *The Stinky Cheese Man and Other Fairly Stupid Tales.*
_____. *Squids Will Be Squids.*
_____. "Time Warp Trio Series".
Seidler, Tor. *Mean Margaret.*
_____. *A Rat's Tale.*
_____. *The Tar Pit.*
_____. *The Wainscott Weasel.*
Selden, George. "Chester Cricket Books".
Shannon, Mark. *Sir Gawain and the Green Knight.*
Silverstein, Shel. *Where the Sidewalk Ends.*
Sleator, William. *The Boy Who Reversed Himself.*
_____. *Dangerous Wishes.*

Smith, Dodie. *The Hundred and One Dalmatians.*
Snyder, Zilpha Keatley. *The Witches of Worm.*
Springer, Nancy. *I Am Mordred: A Tale from Camelot.*
Stewart, Mary. *The Little Broomstick.*
Stolz, Mary. *Quentin Corn.*
Travers, P. L. *Mary Poppins.*
Vande Velde, Vivian. *Curses, Inc.*
_____. *A Hidden Magic.*
_____. *A Well-Timed Enchantment.*
VanAllsburg, Chris. *The Garden of Abdul Gasazi.*
_____. *Jumanji.*
_____. *The Polar Express.*
_____. *The Widow's Broom.*
_____. *The Wreck of the Zephyr.*
_____. *The Wretched Stone.*
Van de Wetering, Janwillem. *Hugh Pine.*
White, E. B. *Charlotte's Web.*
_____. *Stuart Little.*
_____. *The Trumpet of the Swan.*
Winthrop, Elizabeth. "Castle Books".
Wrede, Patricia C. *Book of Enchantments.*
Wright, Betty Ren. *Christina's Ghost.*
_____. *The Dollhouse Murders.*
_____. *The Ghost of Popcorn Hill.*
_____. *Ghosts Beneath Our Feet.*
_____. *The Ghosts of Mercy Manor.*
_____. *Haunted Summer.*
Yolen, Jane. *Sleeping Ugly.*
_____. *Wizard's Hall.*

## 5TH GRADE

Aiken, Joan. "Wolves Chronicles"
Alcock, Vivien. *The Sylvia Game.*
Alexander, Lloyd. *The Arkadians.*
_____. "Chronicles of Prydain".
_____. *The First Two Lives of Lukas Kasha.*
_____. *Gypsy Rizka.*
_____. *The Marvelous Misadventures of Sebastian.*
_____. *The Remarkable Journey of Prince Jen.*
_____. "Vesper Holly Series".
Anderson, Margaret Jean. "Time Trilogy".
Applegate, K. A. "Animorphs Series".
Asch, Frank. *Journey to Terezor.*
Avi. *City of Light, City of Dark.*
_____. *Poppy*
_____. *Poppy and Rye.*
Babbitt, Natalie. *Goody Hall.*
_____. *Kneeknock Rise.*
_____. *The Search for Delicious.*
_____. *Tuck Everlasting.*
Barrie, J. M. *Peter Pan.*
Baum, L. Frank. *The Life and Adventures of Santa Claus.*
_____. *Little Wizard Stories of Oz.*
_____. "Oz Series".
_____. *The Surprising Adventures of the Magical Monarch of Mo and his People.*
Bellairs, John. "Johnny Dixon Mysteries".
_____. "House With a Clock in its Walls Trilogy".
_____. *The Dark Secret of Weatherend.*
Boston, L. M. "Green Knowe Books".
Brittain, Bill. *All the Money in the World.*
_____. *Professor Popkin's Prodigious Polish: A Tale of Coven Tree.*
_____. *The Wish Giver: Three Tales of Coven Tree.*
Brooke, William J. *Untold Tales*
Butterworth, Oliver. *The Trouble With Jenny's Ear.*
Carris, Joan Davenport. *Witch Cat.*
Carroll, Lewis. *Alice's Adventures in Wonderland.*
_____. *Through the Looking-Glass and What Alice Found There.*
Catling, Patrick Skene. *The Chocolate Touch.*
Charnas, Suzy McKee. *The Bronze King.*
Chetwin, Grace. *On All Hallows' Eve.*
_____. *Out of the Dark World.*
_____. "Tales of Gom Series".
Clapp, Patricia. *Jane-Emily.*
Clarke, Pauline. *The Return of the Twelves.*
Collodi, Carlo. *The Adventures of Pinocchio.*
Conly, Jane Leslie (AND Robert C. O'Brien). "Rats of NIMH Series".
Cooper, Susan. "Boggart Books".
_____. "Dark is Rising Sequence".
Coville, Bruce. *Jennifer Murdley's Toad: A Magic Shop Book.*
_____. *Jeremy Thatcher, Dragon Hatcher: A Magic Shop Book.*
_____. *The Monster's Ring.*
Dahl, Roald. *The BFG.*
_____. *Charlie and the Chocolate Factory.*
_____. *Charlie and the Great Glass Elevator.*
_____. *James and the Giant Peach.*
_____. *The Witches.*
Duane, Diane. "Wizard Quartet".
Duffey, Betsy. *Alien for Rent.*
Eager, Edward. *Seven Day Magic.*
_____. *The Time Garden.*
Enzensberger, Hans Magnus. *The Number Devil.*
Farmer, Nancy. *The Warm Place.*
Feiffer, Jules. *A Barrel of Laughs, A Vale of Tears.*
Fleischman, Sid. *The Ghost in the Noonday Sun.*
_____. *The 13th Floor: A Ghost Story.*
Fleming, Ian. *Chitty Chitty Bang Bang, the*

*Magical Car.*
Fry, Rosalie K. *The Secret of Roan Inish.*
Garden, Nancy. *My Sister, the Vampire.*
Garner, Alan. "Tales of Alderley".
Gormley, Beatrice. "Andrea Books".
Gorog, Judith. *In a Messy Messy Room and Other Strange Stories.*
Grahame, Kenneth. *The Reluctant Dragon.*
_____. *The Wind in the Willows.*
Greer, Gery and Bob Ruddick. *Jason and the Aliens Down the Street.*
_____. *Let Me Off This Spaceship!*
Gurney, James. "Dinotopia Books".
_____. *Dinotopia Pop-up Book.*
Hahn, Mary Downing. *Time for Andrew: A Ghost Story.*
_____. *The Time of the Witch.*
_____. *Wait Till Helen Comes: A Ghost Story.*
Hass. E. A. *Incognito Mosquito, Private Insective.*
Hoban, Russell. *The Mouse and His Child.*
Howe, Deborah and James. "Bunnicula Books".
Hughes, Monica. *Invitation to the Game.*
Hunter, Mollie. *The Mermaid Summer.*
_____. *The Wicked One: A Story of Suspense.*
Ibbotson, Eva. *The Secret of Platform 13.*
Jacques, Brian. *The Great Redwall Feast.*
_____. "Redwall Series".
Jones, Diana Wynne. "Chrestomanci Series".
Jones, Terry. *Fantastic Stories.*
_____. *Fairy Tales.*
_____. *Nicobobinus.*
Juster, Norton. *The Phantom Tollbooth.*
Kaye, M. M. *The Ordinary Princess.*
Kendall, Carol. *The Gammage Cup.*
Kennedy, Richard. *Amy's Eyes.*
Key, Alexander. *Escape to Witch Mountain.*
_____. *The Forgotten Door.*
King-Smith, Dick. *Babe: The Gallant Pig.*
_____. *Harriet's Hare.*
_____. *Paddy's Pot of Gold.*
_____. *Three Terrible Trins.*
Klause, Annette Curtis. *Alien Secrets.*
Koller, Jackie French. *The Dragonling.*
Krensky, Stephen. "Dragon Books".
_____. *The Perils of Putney.*
Levine, Gail Carson. *Ella Enchanted.*
_____. "Princess Tales Series".
Lewis, C. S. "Chronicles of Narnia".
Lindbergh, Anne. *Travel Far, Pay No Fare.*
Lisle, Janet Taylor. *The Lampfish of Twill.*
Lively, Penelope. *The Wild Hunt of the Ghost Hounds.*
Lofting, Hugh. *The Story of Doctor Doolittle.*
_____. *The Voyages of Doctor Doolittle.*

Lunn, Janet Louise. *The Root Cellar.*
MacDonald, George. *The Light Princess.*
_____. *The Princess and the Goblin.*
Mahy, Margaret. *The Haunting.*
Masefield, John. *The Midnight Folk.*
Massie, Diane Redfield. *Chameleon Was a Spy.*
Mayne, William. *Antar and the Eagles.*
McGowen, Tom. "The Magician Trilogy".
McGraw, Eloise Jarvis. *The Moorchild.*
McKinley, Robin. *Beauty.*
Napoli, Donna Jo. *Jimmy: The Pickpocket of the Palace.*
_____. *The Prince of the Pond: Otherwise Known as De Fawg Pin.*
Naylor, Phillis Reynolds. *Grand Escape.*
_____. "Witch Books".
Nesbit, E. *Five Children and It.*
_____. *Melisande.*
Norton, Andre. *Red Hart Magic.*
Norton, Mary. *Bed-Knob and Broomstick.*
_____. *The Borrowers.*
Opie, Iona. *My Very First Mother Goose.*
Oppel, Kenneth. *Silverwing.*
Pearce, Philippa. *Tom's Midnight Garden.*
_____. *The Way to Sattin Shore.*
Peck, Richard. *Lost in Cyberspace.*
Pierce, Tamora. "Song of the Lioness Series".
Pinkwater, Daniel Manus. *Alan Mendelsohn, the Boy From Mars.*
_____. *Fat Men From Space.*
Prelutsky, Jack. *Nightmares: Poems to Trouble Your Sleep.*
Pullman, Phillip. *Count Karlstein.*
Pyle, Howard. *The Merry Adventures of Robinhood.*
_____. *The Story of King Arthur and His Knights.*
Reid Banks, Lynne. *The Adventures of King Midas.*
_____. *The Fairy Rebel.*
_____. "Indian in the Cupboard Series".
Roberts, Willo Davis. *The Girl With the Silver Eyes*
Rodgers, Mary. *Freaky Friday.*
_____. *A Billion for Boris.*
_____. *Summer Switch.*
Rowling, J. K. "Harry Potter Books".
Sauer, Julia L. *Fog Magic.*
Scieszka, Jon. *Squids Will Be Squids.*
_____. "Time Warp Trio Series".
Seidler, Tor. *Mean Margaret.*
_____. *A Rat's Tale.*
_____. *The Tar Pit.*
_____. *The Wainscott Weasel.*

Selden, George. "Chester Cricket Books".
_____. *The Genie of Sutton Place.*
Senn, Steve. *A Circle in the Sea.*
Service, Pamela F. *Winter of Magic's Return.*
_____. *Tomorrow's Magic.*
Shannon, Mark. *Sir Gawain and the Green Knight.*
Silverstein, Shel. *Where the Sidewalk Ends.*
Sleator, William. *The Boy Who Reversed Himself.*
_____. *Dangerous Wishes.*
_____. *The Duplicate.*
_____. *Strange Attractors.*
Smith, Dodie. *The Hundred and One Dalmatians.*
Snyder, Zilpha Keatley. *Black and Blue Magic.*
_____. "Green-sky Books".
_____. *The Witches of Worm.*
Stewart, Mary. *The Little Broomstick.*
_____. *A Walk in Wolf Wood: A Tale of Fantasy and Magic.*
Stolz, Mary. *Quentin Corn.*
Tannen, Mary. "The Finn Books".
Tolkien, J. R. R. *Roverandom.*
Travers, P. L. *Mary Poppins.*
Turner, Megan Whalen. *The Thief.*
Vande Velde, Vivian. *Curses, Inc.*
_____. *A Hidden Magic.*
_____. *Tales from the Brothers Grimm and the Sisters Weird.*
_____. *User Unfriendly.*
_____. *A Well-Timed Enchantment.*
VanAllsburg, Chris. *The Garden of Abdul Gasazi.*
_____. *Jumanji.*
_____. *The Mysteries of Harris Burdick.*
_____. *The Polar Express.*
_____. *The Wreck of the Zephyr.*
_____. *The Wretched Stone.*
Waugh, Sylvia. "Mennyms Series".
White, E. B. *Charlotte's Web.*
_____. *Stuart Little.*
_____. *The Trumpet of the Swan.*
White, T. H. *The Sword in the Stone.*
Winthrop, Elizabeth. "Castle Books".
Wiseman, David. *Jeremy Visick.*
_____. *Thimbles: A Novel.*
Wisler, G. Clifton. "Scott Childers Trilogy".
Wrede, Patricia C. *Book of Enchantments.*
Wright, Betty Ren. *Christina's Ghost.*
_____. *The Dollhouse Murders.*
_____. *The Ghost of Popcorn Hill.*
_____. *Ghosts Beneath Our Feet.*
_____. *The Ghosts of Mercy Manor.*
_____. *Haunted Summer.*
Wrightson, Patricia. *The Nargun and the Stars.*
Yep, Laurence. "Dragon Quartet".

Yolen, Jane. *Wizard's Hall.*

## 6TH GRADE

Adams, Richard. *Watership Down.*
Aiken, Joan. "Wolves Chronicles"
_____. *The Shadow Guests.*
Alcock, Vivien. *The Haunting of Cassie Palmer.*
_____. *The Sylvia Game.*
Alexander, Lloyd. *The Arkadians.*
_____. "The Chronicles of Prydain".
_____. *The First Two Lives of Lukas Kasha.*
_____. *Gypsy Rizka.*
_____. *The Iron Ring.*
_____. *The Marvelous Misadventures of Sebastian.*
_____. *The Remarkable Journey of Prince Jen.*
_____. "Vesper Holly Series".
_____. "Westmark Trilogy".
Anderson, Margaret Jean. "Time Trilogy".
Applegate, K. A. "Animorphs Series".
Asch, Frank. *Journey to Terezor.*
Avi. *City of Light, City of Dark.*
_____. *Poppy*
_____. *Poppy and Rye.*
Babbitt, Natalie. *Goody Hall.*
_____. *The Search for Delicious.*
_____. *Tuck Everlasting.*
Barrie, J. M. *Peter Pan.*
Baum, L. Frank. *The Life and Adventures of Santa Claus.*
_____. *Little Wizard Stories of Oz.*
_____. "Oz Series".
_____. *The Surprising Adventures of the Magical Monarch of Mo and his People.*
Bellairs, John. "Johnny Dixon Mysteries".
_____. "House With a Clock in its Walls Trilogy".
_____. *The Dark Secret of Weatherend.*
Bethancourt, T. Ernesto. *The Dog Days of Arthur Cane.*
Boston, L. M. "Green Knowe Books".
Briggs, Katharine Mary. *Hobberdy Dick.*
_____. *Kate Crackernuts.*
Brittain, Bill. *All the Money in the World.*
_____. *Professor Popkin's Prodigious Polish: A Tale of Coven Tree.*
_____. *The Wish Giver: Three Tales of Coven Tree.*
Brooke, William J. *Untold Tales.*
Butterworth, Oliver. *The Trouble With Jenny's Ear.*
Carris, Joan Davenport. *Witch Cat.*
Carroll, Lewis. *Alice's Adventures in Wonderland.*
_____. *Through the Looking-Glass and What Alice Found There.*
Cassedy, Sylvia. *Behind the Attic Wall.*

Catling, Patrick Skene. *The Chocolate Touch.*
Charnas, Suzy McKee. *The Bronze King.*
Chetwin, Grace. *On All Hallows' Eve.*
_____. *Out of the Dark World.*
_____. "Tales of Gom Series".
Clapp, Patricia. *Jane-Emily.*
Clarke, Pauline. *The Return of the Twelves.*
Collodi, Carlo. *The Adventures of Pinocchio.*
Conly, Jane Leslie (AND Robert C. O'Brien). "Rats of NIMH Series".
Cooper, Susan. "Boggart Books".
_____. "Dark is Rising Sequence".
_____. *Seaward.*
Coville, Bruce. *Jennifer Murdley's Toad: A Magic Shop Book.*
_____. *Jeremy Thatcher, Dragon Hatcher: A Magic Shop Book.*
_____. *The Monster's Ring.*
Dahl, Roald. *The BFG.*
_____. *Charlie and the Chocolate Factory.*
_____. *Charlie and the Great Glass Elevator.*
_____. *The Witches.*
Dalkey, Kara. *Little Sister.*
_____. *The Heavenward Path.*
DeFelice, Cynthia. *The Ghost of Fossil Glen.*
Dickinson, Peter. "Changes Trilogy".
_____. *Eva.*
Duane, Diane. "Wizard Quartet".
Duffey, Betsy. *Alien for Rent.*
Eager, Edward. *Seven Day Magic.*
_____. *The Time Garden.*
Enzensberger, Hans Magnus. *The Number Devil.*
Farmer, Nancy. *The Ear, the Eye and the Arm.*
_____. *The Warm Place.*
Feiffer, Jules. *A Barrel of Laughs, A Vale of Tears.*
Fleischman, Sid. *The Ghost in the Noonday Sun.*
_____. *The 13th Floor: A Ghost Story.*
Fleming, Ian. *Chitty Chitty Bang Bang, the Magical Car.*
Fletcher, Susan. *Shadow Spinner.*
Fry, Rosalie K. *The Secret of Roan Inish.*
Garden, Nancy. *My Sister, the Vampire.*
Garner, Alan. *Elidor.*
_____. *The Owl Service.*
_____. "Tales of Alderley".
Gilden, Mel. *The Pumpkins of Time.*
Goodwin, Marie D. *Where the Towers Pierce the Sky.*
Gormley, Beatrice. "Andrea Books".
Grahame, Kenneth. *The Reluctant Dragon.*
_____. *The Wind in the Willows.*
Greer, Gery and Bob Ruddick. *Jason and the Aliens Down the Street.*
Gurney, James. "Dinotopia Books".

_____. *Dinotopia Pop-up Book.*
Haddix, Margaret Peterson. *Among the Hidden.*
Hahn, Mary Downing. *Time for Andrew: A Ghost Story.*
_____. *The Time of the Witch.*
_____. *Wait Till Helen Comes: A Ghost Story.*
Hilgartner, Beth. *A Necklace of Fallen Stars.*
Horowitz, Anthony. "Pentagram Chronicles".
Hughes, Monica. *The Dream Catcher.*
_____. *Invitation to the Game.*
_____. "Isis Planet Books".
Hunter, Mollie. *The Mermaid Summer.*
_____. *The Wicked One: A Story of Suspense.*
Ibbotson, Eva. *The Secret of Platform 13.*
Jacques, Brian. *The Great Redwall Feast.*
_____. "Redwall Series".
Jones, Diana Wynne. *Archer's Goon.*
_____. *Castle in the Air.*
_____. "Chrestomanci Series".
_____. "Dalemark Quartet".
Jones, Terry. *Fantastic Stories.*
_____. *Fairy Tales.*
_____. *Nicobobinus.*
Juster, Norton. *The Phantom Tollbooth.*
Kaye, M. M. *The Ordinary Princess.*
Kendall, Carol. *The Gammage Cup.*
Kennedy, Richard. *Amy's Eyes.*
Key, Alexander. *Escape to Witch Mountain.*
_____. *The Forgotten Door.*
King-Smith, Dick. *Babe: The Gallant Pig.*
_____. *Harriet's Hare.*
_____. *Paddy's Pot of Gold.*
_____. *Three Terrible Trins.*
Klause, Annette Curtis. *Alien Secrets.*
Krensky, Stephen. "Dragon Books".
_____. *The Perils of Putney.*
LeGuin, Ursula K. "Earthsea Series".
L'Engle, Madeleine. "Time Quartet".
Levine, Gail Carson. *Ella Enchanted.*
_____. "Princess Tales Series".
Lewis, C. S. "Chronicles of Narnia".
Lindbergh, Anne. *Travel Far, Pay No Fare.*
Lisle, Janet Taylor. *The Lampfish of Twill.*
Lively, Penelope. *The Wild Hunt of the Ghost Hounds.*
Lofting, Hugh. *The Story of Doctor Doolittle.*
_____. *The Voyages of Doctor Doolittle.*
Lunn, Janet Louise. *The Root Cellar.*
MacDonald, George. *The Light Princess.*
_____. *The Princess and the Goblin.*
Mahy, Margaret. *The Changeover: A Supernatural Romance.*
_____. *The Haunting.*
Masefield, John. *The Midnight Folk.*

Massie, Diane Redfield. *Chameleon Was a Spy.*
Mayne, William. *Antar and the Eagles.*
McGowen, Tom. "The Magician Trilogy".
McGraw, Eloise Jarvis. *The Moorchild.*
McKenzie, Ellen Kindt. *The Golden Band of Eddris.*
McKillip, Patricia A. *The Forgotten Beasts of Eld.*
_____. "Star-Bearer Trilogy".
McKinley, Robin. *Beauty.*
_____. *The Blue Sword.*
_____. *The Hero and the Crown.*
Napoli, Donna Jo. *Jimmy: The Pickpocket of the Palace.*
_____. *The Prince of the Pond: Otherwise Known as De Fawg Pin.*
Naylor, Phillis Reynolds. *Grand Escape.*
_____. "Witch Books".
Nesbit, E. *Five Children and It.*
_____. *Melisande.*
Norton, Andre. *Red Hart Magic.*
Norton, Mary. *Bed-Knob and Broomstick.*
_____. *The Borrowers.*
Oppel, Kenneth. *Silverwing.*
O'Shea, Pat. *Hounds of the Morrigan.*
Paton Walsh, Jill. *A Chance Child.*
Paulsen, Gary. *Transall Saga.*
Pattou, Edith. *Hero's Song.*
_____. *Fire Arrow: The Second Song of Eirren.*
Pearce, Philippa. *Tom's Midnight Garden.*
_____. *The Way to Sattin Shore.*
Peck, Richard. *The Ghost Belonged to Me.*
_____. "Blossom Culp Books".
_____. *The Great Interactive Dream Machine.*
_____. *Lost in Cyberspace.*
Pierce, Meredith Ann. "Darkangel Trilogy".
Pierce, Tamora. "Song of the Lioness Series".
Pinkwater, Daniel Manus. *Alan Mendelsohn, the Boy From Mars.*
_____. *Fat Men From Space.*
Prelutsky, Jack. *Nightmares: Poems to Trouble Your Sleep.*
Pullman, Phillip. *Count Karlstein.*
_____. "His Dark Materials Trilogy".
Pyle, Howard. *The Merry Adventures of Robinhood.*
_____. *The Story of King Arthur and His Knights.*
Reid Banks, Lynne. *The Adventures of King Midas.*
_____. *The Fairy Rebel.*
_____. "Indian in the Cupboard Series".
Roberts, Willo Davis. *The Girl With the Silver Eyes*
Rodgers, Mary. *Freaky Friday.*
_____. *A Billion for Boris.*
_____. *Summer Switch.*
Rowling, J. K. "Harry Potter Books".
Sauer, Julia L. *Fog Magic.*
Seidler, Tor. *Mean Margaret.*
_____. *A Rat's Tale.*
_____. *The Tar Pit.*
_____. *The Wainscott Weasel.*
Selden, George. "Chester Cricket Books".
_____. *The Genie of Sutton Place.*
Senn, Steve. *A Circle in the Sea.*
Service, Pamela F. *Winter of Magic's Return.*
_____. *Tomorrow's Magic.*
Shannon, Mark. *Sir Gawain and the Green Knight.*
Silverstein, Shel. *Where the Sidewalk Ends.*
Sleator, William. *The Boy Who Reversed Himself.*
_____. *Dangerous Wishes.*
_____. *The Duplicate.*
_____. *Strange Attractors.*
Smith, Dodie. *The Hundred and One Dalmatians.*
Smith, Sherwood. "Wren Trilogy".
Snyder, Zilpha Keatley. *Black and Blue Magic.*
_____. "Green-sky Books".
_____. *The Witches of Worm.*
Springer, Nancy. *I Am Mordred: A Tale from Camelot.*
Stewart, Mary. *A Walk in Wolf Wood: A Tale of Fantasy and Magic.*
Stolz, Mary. *Quentin Corn.*
Tannen, Mary. "The Finn Books".
Tolkien, J. R. R. *The Hobbit.*
_____. *Roverandom.*
Travers, P. L. *Mary Poppins.*
Turner, Megan Whalen. *The Thief.*
Vande Velde, Vivian. *Companions of the Night.*
_____. *Curses, Inc.*
_____. *Dragon's Bait.*
_____. *A Hidden Magic.*
_____. *Never Trust a Dead Man.*
_____. *Tales from the Brothers Grimm and the Sisters Weird.*
_____. *User Unfriendly.*
_____. *A Well-Timed Enchantment.*
VanAllsburg, Chris. *The Mysteries of Harris Burdick.*
_____. *The Polar Express.*
Vick. H. H. "Walker Books".
Wangerin, Walter. *The Book of the Dun Cow.*
Waugh, Sylvia. "Mennyms Series".
White, E. B. *Charlotte's Web.*
_____. *Stuart Little.*
_____. *The Trumpet of the Swan.*
White, T. H. *The Sword in the Stone.*

Winthrop, Elizabeth. "Castle Books".
Wiseman, David. *Jeremy Visick.*
_____. *Thimbles: A Novel.*
Wisler, G. Clifton. "Scott Childers Trilogy".
Wrede, Patricia C. *Book of Enchantments.*
_____. "Enchanted Forest Chronicles".
Wright, Betty Ren. *Christina's Ghost.*
_____. *The Dollhouse Murders.*
_____. *The Ghost of Popcorn Hill.*
_____. *Ghosts Beneath Our Feet.*
_____. *The Ghosts of Mercy Manor.*
_____. *Haunted Summer.*
Wrightson, Patricia. *Balyet*
_____. "Wirrun Trilogy".
_____. *The Nargun and the Stars.*
Yep, Laurence. "Dragon Quartet".
Yolen, Jane. "Pit Dragons Series".
_____. *Wizard's Hall.*

## 7TH GRADE

Adams, Richard. *Watership Down.*
Aiken, Joan. "Wolves Chronicles"
_____. *The Shadow Guests*
Alcock, Vivien. *The Haunting of Cassie Palmer.*
_____. *The Sylvia Game.*
Alexander, Lloyd. *The Arkadians.*
_____. "The Chronicles of Prydain".
_____. *The First Two Lives of Lukas Kasha.*
_____. *Gypsy Rizka.*
_____. *The Iron Ring.*
_____. *The Marvelous Misadventures of Sebastian.*
_____. *The Remarkable Journey of Prince Jen.*
_____. "Vesper Holly Series".
_____. "Westmark Trilogy".
Anderson, Margaret Jean. "Time Trilogy".
Avi. *City of Light, City of Dark.*
Babbit, Natalie. *Tuck Everlasting.*
Baum, L. Frank. *The Life and Adventures of Santa Claus.*
_____. *Little Wizard Stories of Oz.*
Bethancourt, T. Ernesto. *The Dog Days of Arthur Cane.*
Bond, Nancy. *Another Shore.*
_____. *A String in the Harp.*
Boston, L. M. "Green Knowe Books".
Briggs, Katharine Mary. *Hobberdy Dick.*
_____. *Kate Crackernuts.*
Brittain, Bill. *The Wish Giver: Three Tales of Coven Tree.*
Brooke, William J. *Untold Tales.*
Butterworth, Oliver. *The Trouble With Jenny's Ear.*
Cadnum, Michael. *In a Dark Wood.*

Carmody, Isobelle. *The Gathering.*
Carroll, Lewis. *Alice's Adventures in Wonderland.*
_____. *Through the Looking-Glass and What Alice Found There.*
Cassedy, Sylvia. *Behind the Attic Wall.*
Charnas, Suzy McKee. *The Bronze King.*
_____. *The Kingdom of Kevin Malone.*
Chetwin, Grace. *On All Hallows' Eve.*
_____. *Out of the Dark World.*
_____. "Tales of Gom Series".
Christopher, John. *Empty World.*
_____. *The Lotus Caves.*
_____. "Tripod Series".
Clarke, Pauline. *The Return of the Twelves.*
Collodi, Carlo. *The Adventures of Pinocchio.*
Conly, Jane Leslie (AND Robert C. O'Brien). "Rats of NIMH Series".
Cooper, Susan. "Boggart Books".
_____. "Dark is Rising Sequence".
_____. *Seaward.*
Coville, Bruce. *Jennifer Murdley's Toad: A Magic Shop Book.*
_____. *Jeremy Thatcher, Dragon Hatcher: A Magic Shop Book.*
_____. *The Monster's Ring.*
Dalkey, Kara. *Little Sister.*
_____. *The Heavenward Path.*
DeFelice, Cynthia. *The Ghost of Fossil Glen.*
Dickinson, Peter. "Changes Trilogy".
_____. *Eva.*
Duane, Diane. "Wizard Quartet".
Eager, Edward. *The Time Garden.*
Engdahl, Sylvia Louise. "Elana Books".
_____. "Star Trilogy".
Enzensberger, Hans Magnus. *The Number Devil.*
Farmer, Nancy. *The Ear, the Eye and the Arm.*
Feiffer, Jules. *A Barrel of Laughs, A Vale of Tears.*
Fleischman, Sid. *The 13th Floor: A Ghost Story.*
Fletcher, Susan. *Shadow Spinner.*
Fry, Rosalie K. *The Secret of Roan Inish.*
Garden, Nancy. *My Sister, the Vampire.*
Garner, Alan. *Elidor.*
_____. *The Owl Service.*
_____. "Tales of Alderley".
Gilden, Mel. *The Pumpkins of Time.*
Goodwin, Marie D. *Where the Towers Pierce the Sky.*
Grahame, Kenneth. *The Wind in the Willows.*
Gurney, James. "Dinotopia Books".
Haddix, Margaret Peterson. *Among the Hidden.*
Hahn, Mary Downing. *Time for Andrew: A Ghost Story.*
_____. *The Time of the Witch.*
_____. *Wait Till Helen Comes: A Ghost Story.*

Hamilton, Virginia. "Justice Cycle".
Hilgartner, Beth. A Necklace of Fallen Stars.
_____. "Zan Scarsdale Books".
Hite, Sid. Answer my Prayer.
Horowitz, Anthony. "Pentagram Chronicles".
Hughes, Monica. The Dream Catcher.
_____. Invitation to the Game.
_____. "Isis Planet Books".
Hunter, Mollie. The Mermaid Summer.
_____. The Wicked One: A Story of Suspense.
Ibbotson, Eva. The Secret of Platform 13.
Jacques, Brian. The Great Redwall Feast.
_____. "Redwall Series".
Jones, Diana Wynne. Archer's Goon.
_____. Castle in the Air.
_____. "Chrestomanci Series".
_____. "Dalemark Quartet".
_____. Howl's Moving Castle.
Jones, Terry. Nicobobinus.
Jordan, Sherryl. Winter of Fire
Juster, Norton. The Phantom Tollbooth.
Kendall, Carol. The Gammage Cup.
Kennedy, Richard. Amy's Eyes.
Key, Alexander. Escape to Witch Mountain.
_____. The Forgotten Door.
King-Smith, Dick. Three Terrible Trins.
Klause, Annette Curtis. Alien Secrets.
_____. The Silver Kiss.
LeGuin, Ursula K. "Earthsea Series".
L'Engle, Madeleine. "Time Quartet".
Levine, Gail Carson. Ella Enchanted.
Lewis, C. S. "Chronicles of Narnia".
Lindbergh, Anne. Travel Far, Pay No Fare.
Lisle, Janet Taylor. The Lampfish of Twill.
Lively, Penelope. The Wild Hunt of the Ghost Hounds.
Lofting, Hugh. The Voyages of Doctor Doolittle.
Lowry, Lois. The Giver.
Lunn, Janet Louise. The Root Cellar.
MacDonald, George. The Princess and the Goblin.
Mahy, Margaret. The Changeover: A Supernatural Romance.
_____. The Haunting.
Masefield, John. The Midnight Folk.
Matas, Carol and Perry Nodelman. Two Minds.
Mayne, William. Antar and the Eagles.
McGowen, Tom. "The Magician Trilogy".
McGraw, Eloise Jarvis. The Moorchild.
McKenzie, Ellen Kindt. The Golden Band of Eddris.
McKillip, Patricia A. The Forgotten Beasts of Eld.
_____. "Star-Bearer Trilogy".
McKinley, Robin. Beauty.
_____. The Blue Sword.

_____. The Hero and the Crown.
_____. The Outlaws of Sherwood.
Napoli, Donna Jo. The Magic Circle.
_____. Zel.
Naylor, Phillis Reynolds. Grand Escape.
_____. "Witch Books".
Nesbit, E. Five Children and It.
_____. Melisande.
Nix, Garth. Sabriel.
_____. Shades Children.
Norton, Andre. Red Hart Magic.
Norton, Mary. The Borrowers.
O'Brien, Robert. Z for Zachariah.
Oppel, Kenneth. Silverwing.
O'Shea, Pat. Hounds of the Morrigan.
Paton Walsh, Jill. A Chance Child.
Paulsen, Gary. Transall Saga.
Pattou, Edith. Hero's Song.
_____. Fire Arrow: The Second Song of Eirren.
Pearce, Philippa. Tom's Midnight Garden.
_____. The Way to Sattin Shore.
Peck, Richard. The Ghost Belonged to Me.
_____. "Blossom Culp Books".
_____. The Great Interactive Dream Machine.
_____. Lost in Cyberspace.
Pierce, Meredith Ann. "Darkangel Trilogy".
_____. "Firebringer Trilogy".
Pierce, Tamora. "Song of the Lioness Series".
Pinkwater, Daniel Manus. Alan Mendelsohn, the Boy From Mars.
Prelutsky, Jack. Nightmares: Poems to Trouble Your Sleep.
Pullman, Phillip. Count Karlstein.
_____. "His Dark Materials Trilogy".
Pyle, Howard. The Merry Adventures of Robinhood.
_____. The Story of King Arthur and His Knights.
Rodgers, Mary. Freaky Friday.
_____. A Billion for Boris.
_____. Summer Switch.
Rowling, J. K. "Harry Potter Books".
Selden, George. The Genie of Sutton Place.
Senn, Steve. A Circle in the Sea.
Service, Pamela F. Winter of Magic's Return.
_____. Tomorrow's Magic.
Sherman, Josepha. Child of Faerie, Child of Earth.
_____. Windleaf.
Shannon, Mark. Sir Gawain and the Green Knight.
Silverstein, Shel. Where the Sidewalk Ends.
Sleator, William. The Boy Who Reversed Himself.
_____. The Duplicate.

_____. *House of Stairs.*
_____. *Strange Attractors.*
Smith, Dodie. *The Hundred and One Dalmatians.*
Smith, Sherwood. "Crown and Court Duet"
_____. "Wren Trilogy".
Snyder, Zilpha Keatley. *Black and Blue Magic.*
_____. "Green-sky Books".
_____. *The Witches of Worm.*
Springer, Nancy. *I Am Mordred: A Tale from Camelot.*
Stewart, Mary. *A Walk in Wolf Wood: A Tale of Fantasy and Magic.*
Sutcliff, Rosemary. *The Chronicles of Robin Hood.*
_____. "King Arthur Trilogy".
_____. *Tristan and Iseult.*
Tannen, Mary. "The Finn Books".
Tolkien, J. R. R. *The Hobbit.*
_____. *Roverandom.*
Turner, Megan Whalen. *The Thief.*
Vande Velde, Vivian. *Companions of the Night.*
_____. *Curses, Inc.*
_____. *Dragon's Bait.*
_____. *A Hidden Magic.*
_____. *Never Trust a Dead Man.*
_____. *Tales from the Brothers Grimm and the Sisters Weird.*
_____. *User Unfriendly.*
_____. *A Well-Timed Enchantment.*
VanAllsburg, Chris. *The Mysteries of Harris Burdick.*
_____. *The Polar Express.*
Vick. H. H. "Walker Books".
Wangerin, Walter. *The Book of the Dun Cow.*
Waugh, Sylvia. "Mennyms Series".
White, T. H. *The Sword in the Stone.*
Winthrop, Elizabeth. "Castle Books".
Wiseman, David. *Jeremy Visick.*
_____. *Thimbles: A Novel.*
Wisler, G. Clifton. "Scott Childers Trilogy".
Wrede, Patricia C. *Book of Enchantments.*
_____. "Enchanted Forest Chronicles".
Wright, Betty Ren. *The Dollhouse Murders.*
_____. *Ghosts Beneath Our Feet.*
_____. *The Ghosts of Mercy Manor.*
Wrightson, Patricia. *Balyet.*
_____. "Wirrun Trilogy".
_____. *The Nargun and the Stars.*
Yep, Laurence. "Dragon Quartet".
Yolen, Jane. "Pit Dragons Series".
_____. *Wizard's Hall.*

## 8TH GRADE
Adams, Richard. *Watership Down.*
Aiken, Joan. *The Shadow Guests*

Alcock, Vivien. *The Haunting of Cassie Palmer.*
Alexander, Lloyd. *The Arkadians.*
_____. "The Chronicles of Prydain".
_____. *The First Two Lives of Lukas Kasha.*
_____. *The Iron Ring.*
_____. *The Remarkable Journey of Prince Jen.*
_____. "Vesper Holly Series".
_____. "Westmark Trilogy".
Anderson, Margaret Jean. "Time Trilogy".
Avi. *City of Light, City of Dark.*
Baum, L. Frank. *The Life and Adventures of Santa Claus.*
_____. *Little Wizard Stories of Oz.*
Bethancourt, T. Ernesto. *The Dog Days of Arthur Cane.*
_____. *Tune in Yesterday.*
_____. *The Tomorrow Connection.*
Bond, Nancy. *Another Shore.*
_____. *A String in the Harp.*
Briggs, Katharine Mary. *Hobberdy Dick.*
_____. *Kate Crackernuts.*
Brooke, William J. *Untold Tales.*
Cadnum, Michael. *In a Dark Wood.*
Carmody, Isobelle. *The Gathering.*
Carroll, Lewis. *Alice's Adventures in Wonderland.*
_____. *Through the Looking-Glass and What Alice Found There.*
Cassedy, Sylvia. *Behind the Attic Wall.*
Charnas, Suzy McKee. *The Bronze King.*
_____. *The Kingdom of Kevin Malone.*
Chetwin, Grace. *On All Hallows' Eve.*
_____. *Out of the Dark World.*
_____. "Tales of Gom Series".
Christopher, John. *Empty World.*
_____. *The Lotus Caves.*
_____. "Tripod Series".
Collodi, Carlo. *The Adventures of Pinocchio.*
Conly, Jane Leslie (AND Robert C. O'Brien). "Rats of NIMH Series".
Cooper, Susan. "Dark is Rising Sequence".
_____. *Seaward.*
Dalkey, Kara. *Little Sister.*
_____. *The Heavenward Path.*
DeFelice, Cynthia. *The Ghost of Fossil Glen.*
Dickinson, Peter. "Changes Trilogy".
_____. *Eva.*
Duane, Diane. "Wizard Quartet".
Engdahl, Sylvia Louise. "Elana Books".
Enzensberger, Hans Magnus. *The Number Devil.*
Farmer, Nancy. *The Ear, the Eye and the Arm.*
Fleischman, Sid. *The 13th Floor: A Ghost Story.*
Fletcher, Susan. *Shadow Spinner.*
Fry, Rosalie K. *The Secret of Roan Inish.*
Garden, Nancy. *My Sister, the Vampire.*

Garner, Alan. *Elidor.*
_____. *The Owl Service.*
_____. *Red Shift.*
_____. "Tales of Alderley"
Gilden, Mel. *The Pumpkins of Time.*
Goodwin, Marie D. *Where the Towers Pierce the Sky.*
Grahame, Kenneth. *The Wind in the Willows.*
Gurney, James. "Dinotopia Books".
Haddix, Margaret Peterson. *Among the Hidden.*
Hamilton, Virginia. "Justice Cycle".
Hilgartner, Beth. *A Necklace of Fallen Stars.*
_____. "Zan Scarsdale Books".
Hite, Sid. *Answer my Prayer.*
Horowitz, Anthony. "Pentagram Chronicles".
Hughes, Monica. *The Dream Catcher.*
_____. *Invitation to the Game.*
_____. "Isis Planet Books".
Hunter, Mollie. *The Wicked One: A Story of Suspense.*
Ibbotson, Eva. *The Secret of Platform 13.*
Jacques, Brian. *The Great Redwall Feast.*
_____. "Redwall Series".
Jones, Diana Wynne. *Archer's Goon.*
_____. *Castle in the Air.*
_____. "Chrestomanci Series".
_____. "Dalemark Quartet".
_____. *Howl's Moving Castle.*
Jordan, Sherryl. *Winter of Fire*
Klause, Annette Curtis. *The Silver Kiss.*
LeGuin, Ursula K. "Earthsea Series".
L'Engle, Madeleine. "Time Quartet".
Lindbergh, Anne. *Travel Far, Pay No Fare.*
Lisle, Janet Taylor. *The Lampfish of Twill.*
Lively, Penelope. *The Wild Hunt of the Ghost Hounds.*
Lowry, Lois. *The Giver.*
Mahy, Margaret. *The Changeover: A Supernatural Romance.*
_____. *The Haunting.*
Matas, Carol and Perry Nodelman. *Two Minds.*
Mayne, William. *Antar and the Eagles.*
McKenzie, Ellen Kindt. *The Golden Band of Eddris.*
McKillip, Patricia A. *The Forgotten Beasts of Eld.*
_____. "Star-Bearer Trilogy".
McKinley, Robin. *Beauty.*
_____. *The Blue Sword.*
_____. *The Hero and the Crown.*
_____. *The Outlaws of Sherwood.*
_____. *Rose Daughter.*
Napoli, Donna Jo. *The Magic Circle.*
_____. *Zel.*
Naylor, Phillis Reynolds. "Witch Books".

Nix, Garth. *Sabriel.*
_____. *Shades Children.*
O'Brien, Robert. *Z for Zachariah.*
Oppel, Kenneth. *Silverwing.*
O'Shea, Pat. *Hounds of the Morrigan.*
Paton Walsh, Jill. *A Chance Child.*
Paulsen, Gary. *Transall Saga.*
Pattou, Edith. *Hero's Song.*
_____. *Fire Arrow: The Second Song of Eirren.*
Pearce, Philippa. *Tom's Midnight Garden.*
_____. *The Way to Sattin Shore.*
Peck, Richard. *The Ghost Belonged to Me.*
_____. "Blossom Culp Books".
_____. *The Great Interactive Dream Machine.*
_____. *Lost in Cyberspace.*
Pierce, Meredith Ann. "Darkangel Trilogy".
_____. "Firebringer Trilogy".
Pierce, Tamora. "Song of the Lioness Series".
Pinkwater, Daniel Manus. *Alan Mendelsohn, the Boy From Mars.*
Prelutsky, Jack. *Nightmares: Poems to Trouble Your Sleep.*
Pullman, Phillip. *Count Karlstein.*
_____. "His Dark Materials Trilogy".
Pyle, Howard. *The Merry Adventures of Robinhood.*
_____. *The Story of King Arthur and His Knights.*
Rowling, J. K. "Harry Potter Books".
Service, Pamela F. *Winter of Magic's Return.*
_____. *Tomorrow's Magic.*
Sherman, Josepha. *Child of Faerie, Child of Earth.*
_____. *Windleaf.*
Silverstein, Shel. *Where the Sidewalk Ends.*
Sleator, William. *The Boy Who Reversed Himself.*
_____. *The Duplicate.*
_____. *House of Stairs.*
_____. *Strange Attractors.*
Smith, Dodie. *The Hundred and One Dalmatians.*
Smith, Sherwood. "Crown and Court Duet"
_____. "Wren Trilogy".
Snyder, Zilpha Keatley. "Green-sky Books".
_____. *The Witches of Worm.*
Springer, Nancy. *I Am Mordred: A Tale from Camelot.*
Stewart, Mary. *A Walk in Wolf Wood: A Tale of Fantasy and Magic.*
Sutcliff, Rosemary. *The Chronicles of Robin Hood.*
_____. "King Arthur Trilogy".
_____. *Tristan and Iseult.*
Tolkien, J. R. R. *The Hobbit.*
_____. "The Lord of the Rings Series".
_____. *Roverandom.*

Turner, Megan Whalen. *The Thief.*
Vande Velde, Vivian. *Companions of the Night.*
_____. *Curses, Inc.*
_____. *Dragon's Bait.*
_____. *A Hidden Magic.*
_____. *Never Trust a Dead Man.*
_____. *Tales from the Brothers Grimm and the Sisters Weird.*
_____. *User Unfriendly.*
VanAllsburg, Chris. *The Mysteries of Harris Burdick.*
_____. *The Polar Express.*
Vick. H. H. "Walker Books".
Wangerin, Walter. *The Book of the Dun Cow.*
Waugh, Sylvia. "Mennyms Series".
White, T. H. *The Once and Future King.*
_____. *The Sword in the Stone.*
Wrede, Patricia C. *Book of Enchantments.*
_____. "Enchanted Forest Chronicles".
Wrightson, Patricia. *Balyet*
_____. "Wirrun Trilogy".
_____. *The Nargun and the Stars.*
Yep, Laurence. "Dragon Quartet".
Yolen, Jane. "Pit Dragons Series".

## 9TH GRADE
Adams, Richard. *Watership Down.*
Aiken, Joan. *The Shadow Guests*
Alexander, Lloyd. *The Arkadians.*
_____. *The Iron Ring.*
_____. *The Remarkable Journey of Prince Jen.*
_____. "Vesper Holly Series".
_____. "Westmark Trilogy".
Avi. *City of Light, City of Dark.*
Bethancourt, T. Ernesto. *The Dog Days of Arthur Cane.*
_____. *Tune in Yesterday.*
_____. *The Tomorrow Connection.*
Bond, Nancy. *Another Shore.*
_____. *A String in the Harp.*
Briggs, Katharine Mary. *Kate Crackernuts.*
Brooke, William J. *Untold Tales.*
Cadnum, Michael. *In a Dark Wood.*
Carmody, Isobelle. *The Gathering.*
Charnas, Suzy McKee. *The Kingdom of Kevin Malone.*
Chetwin, Grace. *On All Hallows' Eve.*
_____. *Out of the Dark World.*
_____. "Tales of Gom Series".
Christopher, John. *Empty World.*
_____. *The Lotus Caves.*
_____. "Tripod Series".
Cooper, Susan. "Dark is Rising Sequence".
_____. *Seaward.*

Dalkey, Kara. *Little Sister.*
_____. *The Heavenward Path.*
Dickinson, Peter. "Changes Trilogy".
_____. *Eva.*
Engdahl, Sylvia Louise. "Elana Books".
_____. "Star Trilogy".
Farmer, Nancy. *The Ear, the Eye and the Arm.*
Fleischman, Sid. *The 13th Floor: A Ghost Story.*
Fletcher, Susan. *Shadow Spinner.*
Garner, Alan. *The Owl Service.*
_____. *Red Shift.*
Gilden, Mel. *The Pumpkins of Time.*
Goodwin, Marie D. *Where the Towers Pierce the Sky.*
Haddix, Margaret Peterson. *Among the Hidden.*
Hamilton, Virginia. "Justice Cycle"
Hilgartner, Beth. "Zan Scarsdale Books".
Hite, Sid. *Answer my Prayer.*
Hughes, Monica.. *Invitation to the Game.*
Jacques, Brian. *The Great Redwall Feast.*
_____. "Redwall Series".
Jones, Diana Wynne. *Archer's Goon.*
_____. *Castle in the Air.*
_____. "Chrestomanci Series".
_____. "Dalemark Quartet".
_____. *Howl's Moving Castle.*
Jordan, Sherryl. *Winter of Fire*
Klause, Annette Curtis. *The Silver Kiss.*
LeGuin, Ursula K. "Earthsea Series".
L'Engle, Madeleine. "Time Quartet".
Lisle, Janet Taylor. *The Lampfish of Twill.*
Lowry, Lois. *The Giver.*
Mahy, Margaret. *The Changeover: A Supernatural Romance.*
Matas, Carol and Perry Nodelman. *Two Minds.*
Mayne, William. *Antar and the Eagles.*
McKenzie, Ellen Kindt. *The Golden Band of Eddris.*
McKillip, Patricia A. *The Forgotten Beasts of Eld.*
_____. "Star-Bearer Trilogy".
McKinley, Robin. *Beauty.*
_____. *The Blue Sword.*
_____. *The Hero and the Crown.*
_____. *The Outlaws of Sherwood.*
_____. *Rose Daughter.*
Napoli, Donna Jo. *The Magic Circle.*
_____. *Zel.*
Nix, Garth. *Sabriel.*
_____. *Shades Children.*
O'Brien, Robert. *Z for Zachariah.*
O'Shea, Pat. *Hounds of the Morrigan.*
Paton Walsh, Jill. *A Chance Child.*
Pattou, Edith. *Hero's Song.*
_____. *Fire Arrow: The Second Song of Eirren.*

Peck, Richard. *The Ghost Belonged to Me.*
_____. "Blossom Culp Books".
_____. *The Great Interactive Dream Machine.*
_____. *Lost in Cyberspace.*
Pierce, Meredith Ann. "Darkangel Trilogy".
_____. "Firebringer Trilogy".
Pierce, Tamora. "Song of the Lioness Series".
Pinkwater, Daniel Manus. *Alan Mendelsohn, the Boy From Mars.*
Prelutsky, Jack. *Nightmares: Poems to Trouble Your Sleep.*
Pullman, Phillip. "His Dark Materials Trilogy".
Pyle, Howard. *The Merry Adventures of Robinhood.*
_____. *The Story of King Arthur and His Knights.*
Rowling, J. K. "Harry Potter Books".
Sherman, Josepha. *Child of Faerie, Child of Earth.*
_____. *Windleaf.*
Silverstein, Shel. *Where the Sidewalk Ends.*
Sleator, William. *The Duplicate.*
_____. *House of Stairs.*
_____. *Strange Attractors.*
Smith, Dodie. *The Hundred and One Dalmatians.*
Smith, Sherwood. "Crown and Court Duet"
_____. "Wren Trilogy".
Sutcliff, Rosemary. *The Chronicles of Robin Hood.*
_____. "King Arthur Trilogy".
_____. *Tristan and Iseult.*
Tolkien, J. R. R. *The Hobbit.*
_____. "The Lord of the Rings Series".
Turner, Megan Whalen. *The Thief.*
Vande Velde, Vivian. *Companions of the Night.*
_____. *Curses, Inc.*
_____. *Dragon's Bait.*
_____. *Never Trust a Dead Man.*
_____. *Tales from the Brothers Grimm and the Sisters Weird.*
_____. *User Unfriendly.*
VanAllsburg, Chris. *The Mysteries of Harris Burdick.*
_____. *The Polar Express.*
Vick. H. H. "Walker Books".
Wangerin, Walter. *The Book of the Dun Cow.*
Waugh, Sylvia. "Mennyms Series".
White, T. H. *The Once and Future King.*
Wrede, Patricia C. "Enchanted Forest Chronicles".
Wrightson, Patricia. *Balyet*
_____. "Wirrun Trilogy".
Yep, Laurence. "Dragon Quartet".
Yolen, Jane. "Pit Dragons Series".

## 10TH GRADE

Adams, Richard. *Watership Down.*
Alexander, Lloyd. *The Iron Ring.*
_____. *The Remarkable Journey of Prince Jen.*
_____. "Westmark Trilogy".
Avi. *City of Light, City of Dark.*
Bethancourt, T. Ernesto. *Tune in Yesterday.*
_____. *The Tomorrow Connection.*
Bond, Nancy. *Another Shore.*
_____. *A String in the Harp.*
Brooke, William J. *Untold Tales.*
Cadnum, Michael. *In a Dark Wood.*
Carmody, Isobelle. *The Gathering.*
Charnas, Suzy McKee. *The Kingdom of Kevin Malone.*
Chetwin, Grace. *On All Hallows' Eve.*
_____. *Out of the Dark World.*
_____. "Tales of Gom Series".
Christopher, John. *Empty World.*
_____. *The Lotus Caves.*
_____. "Tripod Series".
Cooper, Susan. "Dark is Rising Sequence".
Dalkey, Kara. *Little Sister.*
_____. *The Heavenward Path.*
Engdahl, Sylvia Louise. "Elana Books".
_____. "Star Trilogy".
Fleischman, Sid. *The 13th Floor: A Ghost Story.*
Garner, Alan. *Red Shift.*
Gilden, Mel. *The Pumpkins of Time.*
Hamilton, Virginia. "Justice Cycle"
Hilgartner, Beth. "Zan Scarsdale Books".
Hite, Sid. *Answer my Prayer.*
Jones, Diana Wynne. *Castle in the Air.*
_____. *Howl's Moving Castle.*
Klause, Annette Curtis. *The Silver Kiss.*
LeGuin, Ursula K. "Earthsea Series".
L'Engle, Madeleine. "Time Quartet".
Lisle, Janet Taylor. *The Lampfish of Twill.*
Mahy, Margaret. *The Changeover: A Supernatural Romance.*
Matas, Carol and Perry Nodelman. *Two Minds.*
Marsden, John. *Tomorrow, When the War Began.*
McKenzie, Ellen Kindt. *The Golden Band of Eddris.*
McKinley, Robin. *The Blue Sword.*
_____. *The Hero and the Crown.*
_____. *The Outlaws of Sherwood.*
_____. *Rose Daughter.*
Napoli, Donna Jo. *The Magic Circle.*
_____. *Zel.*
Nix, Garth. *Sabriel.*
_____. *Shades Children.*
O'Brien, Robert. *Z for Zachariah.*
Pattou, Edith. *Hero's Song.*
_____. *Fire Arrow: The Second Song of Eirren.*
Peck, Richard. *The Great Interactive Dream*

Machine.
_____. Lost in Cyberspace.
Pierce, Meredith Ann. "Darkangel Trilogy".
_____. "Firebringer Trilogy".
Pierce, Tamora. "Song of the Lioness Series".
Prelutsky, Jack. Nightmares: Poems to Trouble Your Sleep.
Pullman, Phillip. "His Dark Materials Trilogy".
Pyle, Howard. The Merry Adventures of Robinhood.
_____. The Story of King Arthur and His Knights.
Rowling, J. K. "Harry Potter Books".
Sherman, Josepha. Child of Faerie, Child of Earth.
_____. Windleaf.
Silverstein, Shel. Where the Sidewalk Ends.
Sleator, William. The Duplicate.
_____. House of Stairs.
_____. Strange Attractors.
Smith, Dodie. The Hundred and One Dalmatians.
Smith, Sherwood. "Crown and Court Duet"
_____. "Wren Trilogy".
Springer, Nancy. I Am Mordred: A Tale from Camelot.
Sutcliff, Rosemary. The Chronicles of Robin Hood.
_____. "King Arthur Trilogy".
_____. Tristan and Iseult.
Tolkien, J. R. R. The Hobbit.
_____. "The Lord of the Rings Series".
Vande Velde, Vivian. Companions of the Night.
_____. Never Trust a Dead Man.
_____. Tales from the Brothers Grimm and the Sisters Weird.
_____. User Unfriendly.
VanAllsburg, Chris. The Mysteries of Harris Burdick.
_____. The Polar Express.
Vick. H. H. "Walker Books".
Wangerin, Walter. The Book of the Dun Cow.
Waugh, Sylvia. "Mennyms Series".
White, T. H. The Once and Future King.
Yolen, Jane. "Pit Dragons Series".

## 11TH GRADE

Adams, Richard. Watership Down.
Alexander, Lloyd. "Westmark Trilogy".
Avi. City of Light, City of Dark.
Bond, Nancy. Another Shore.
_____. A String in the Harp.
Brooke, William J. Untold Tales.
Carmody, Isobelle. The Gathering.
Charnas, Suzy McKee. The Kingdom of Kevin Malone.

Chetwin, Grace. On All Hallows' Eve.
_____. Out of the Dark World.
_____. "Tales of Gom Series".
Christopher, John. Empty World.
_____. The Lotus Caves.
_____. "Tripod Series".
Cooper, Susan. "Dark is Rising Sequence".
Engdahl, Sylvia Louise. "Elana Books".
_____. "Star Trilogy".
Fleischman, Sid. The 13th Floor: A Ghost Story.
Garner, Alan. Red Shift.
Gilden, Mel. The Pumpkins of Time.
Hamilton, Virginia. "Justice Cycle"
Hilgartner, Beth. "Zan Scarsdale Books".
Jones, Diana Wynne. Castle in the Air.
_____. Howl's Moving Castle.
Klause, Annette Curtis. The Silver Kiss.
LeGuin, Ursula K. "Earthsea Series".
Lisle, Janet Taylor. The Lampfish of Twill.
Marsden, John. Tomorrow, When the War Began.
McKinley, Robin. The Blue Sword.
_____. The Hero and the Crown.
_____. The Outlaws of Sherwood.
_____. Rose Daughter.
Napoli, Donna Jo. The Magic Circle.
_____. Zel.
O'Brien, Robert. Z for Zachariah.
Peck, Richard. The Great Interactive Dream Machine.
_____. Lost in Cyberspace.
Prelutsky, Jack. Nightmares: Poems to Trouble Your Sleep.
Pullman, Phillip. "His Dark Materials Trilogy".
Pyle, Howard. The Merry Adventures of Robinhood.
_____. The Story of King Arthur and His Knights.
Rowling, J. K. "Harry Potter Books".
Sherman, Josepha. Child of Faerie, Child of Earth.
_____. Windleaf.
Silverstein, Shel. Where the Sidewalk Ends.
Sleator, William. The Duplicate.
_____. House of Stairs.
_____. Strange Attractors.
Smith, Dodie. The Hundred and One Dalmatians.
Smith, Sherwood. "Crown and Court Duet"
_____. "Wren Trilogy".
Sutcliff, Rosemary. The Chronicles of Robin Hood.
_____. "King Arthur Trilogy".
_____. Tristan and Iseult.
Tolkien, J. R. R. The Hobbit.
_____. "The Lord of the Rings Series".
Vande Velde, Vivian. Tales from the Brothers

*Grimm and the Sisters Weird.*
_____. *User Unfriendly.*
VanAllsburg, Chris. *The Mysteries of Harris Burdick.*
_____. *The Polar Express.*
Vick. H. H. "Walker Books".
Wangerin, Walter. *The Book of the Dun Cow.*
Waugh, Sylvia. "Mennyms Series".
White, T. H. *The Once and Future King.*
Yolen, Jane. "Pit Dragons Series".

### 12TH GRADE

Adams, Richard. *Watership Down.*
Alexander, Lloyd. "Westmark Trilogy".
Avi. *City of Light, City of Dark.*
Bond, Nancy. *Another Shore.*
_____. *A String in the Harp.*
Brooke, William J. *Untold Tales.*
Carmody, Isobelle. *The Gathering.*
Charnas, Suzy McKee. *The Kingdom of Kevin Malone.*
Chetwin, Grace. *On All Hallows' Eve.*
_____. *Out of the Dark World.*
_____. "Tales of Gom Series".
Christopher, John. *Empty World.*
_____. *The Lotus Caves.*
_____. "Tripod Series".
Cooper, Susan. "Dark is Rising Sequence".
Engdahl, Sylvia Louise. "Elana Books".
_____. "Star Trilogy".
Fleischman, Sid. *The 13th Floor: A Ghost Story.*
Garner, Alan. *Red Shift.*
Gilden, Mel. *The Pumpkins of Time.*
Hamilton, Virginia. "Justice Cycle".
Hilgartner, Beth. "Zan Scarsdale Books".
Jones, Diana Wynne. *Castle in the Air.*
_____. *Howl's Moving Castle.*
Klause, Annette Curtis. *The Silver Kiss.*
LeGuin, Ursula K. "Earthsea Series".
Lisle, Janet Taylor. *The Lampfish of Twill.*
Marsden, John. *Tomorrow, When the War Began.*
McKinley, Robin. *The Blue Sword.*
_____. *The Hero and the Crown.*
_____. *The Outlaws of Sherwood.*
_____. *Rose Daughter.*

Napoli, Donna Jo. *The Magic Circle.*
_____. *Zel.*
O'Brien, Robert. *Z for Zachariah.*
Peck, Richard. *The Great Interactive Dream Machine.*
_____. *Lost in Cyberspace.*
Prelutsky, Jack. *Nightmares: Poems to Trouble Your Sleep.*
Pullman, Phillip. "His Dark Materials Trilogy".
Pyle, Howard. *The Merry Adventures of Robinhood.*
_____. *The Story of King Arthur and His Knights.*
Rowling, J. K. "Harry Potter Books".
Sherman, Josepha. *Child of Faerie, Child of Earth.*
_____. *Windleaf.*
Silverstein, Shel. *Where the Sidewalk Ends.*
Sleator, William. *The Duplicate.*
_____. *House of Stairs.*
Smith, Dodie. *The Hundred and One Dalmatians.*
Smith, Sherwood. "Crown and Court Duet"
_____. "Wren Trilogy".
Sutcliff, Rosemary. *The Chronicles of Robin Hood.*
_____. "King Arthur Trilogy".
_____. *Tristan and Iseult.*
Tolkien, J. R. R. *The Hobbit.*
_____. "The Lord of the Rings Series".
Vande Velde, Vivian. *Tales from the Brothers Grimm and the Sisters Weird.*
_____. *User Unfriendly.*
VanAllsburg, Chris. *The Mysteries of Harris Burdick.*
_____. *The Polar Express.*
Vick. H. H. "Walker Books".
Wangerin, Walter. *The Book of the Dun Cow.*
Waugh, Sylvia. "Mennyms Series".
White, T. H. *The Once and Future King.*
Yolen, Jane. "Pit Dragons Series".

# General Index

## A
Anansi the Spider, 6
Animal Tricksters, 6
Arthurian myth, 8

## B
Barriers to Appreciation, 17-20
    Effort Required to Read, 17
    Escapism, 19
    Fear, 20
    Sexism, 18
    Violence, 18-19
Booktalks, 64
Brer Rabbit, 6

## C
Characters, 26-27
CHILDLIT Listserv, 122
Computer Culture, 11-12
Contemporary Fantasy, 8-12
Coyote, 6
Creative Dramatization, 63-64
Cumulative Tales, 6
Curriculum, 37-61
    History, 43-46
    Humanities, 47-48
    Language Arts, 50-51
    Mathematics, 49
    Science, 39
    Social Studies, 42
Crockett, Davy, 6

## E
Eccentric Characters, 8
Enchanted Realism, 10-12
Epic Fantasy. *See High Fantasy*
Epics, 8
External Barriers, 18-20

## F
Fables, 7, 8, 90
Fairy Tales, 3
Fantasy
    Barriers to Appreciation, 17-20
    Categorizing, 4-5, 9
    Definition of, 4-5
    Children's Response to, 16
    Elements of
        Eccentric Characters, 8
        Noodleheads, 6
        Talking Animals, 8
        Time Travel, 8
        Toys That Come to Life, 8
        Traditional Elements, 9
        Unrealistic Situations, 8
        Worlds Apart From the One We Know, 8
    Popularity of, 15
    Types of, 5
        Contemporary, 8-12
        High Fantasy, 9-10
        Science Fiction, 4-5
        Supernatural Tales, 4
        Talking Animals, 8
        Traditional, 5-8
        Folk Tales, 6-7
FOLKLORE Listserv, 122
Folk Tales, 6-7
    Origin of,
        Britain, 7
        France, 7
        Germany, 7
        Scandinavia, 7
        United States, 6-7

## H
Hans Christian Andersen Award, 128
Hero Journey, 28-31
    Inward Journey, 30
    Outward Journey, 28-30
High Fantasy, 9-10
Horror, 15

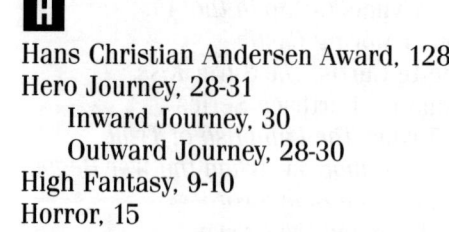

## I

Internal Barriers, 17-18
Internet, 121-122
Internet Resources, 121-122

## J

Joseph Campbell Foundation, 121

## K

KIDLIT-L Listserv, 122

## L

Legends, 8
LISTSERV Discussion Groups, 122
    CHILDLIT, 122
    FOLKLORE, 122
    KIDLIT-L, 122
    PUBYAC, 122

## M

Magical Realism, *See Enchanted Realism*
Main Idea, See Theme
Modern Fantasy, *See Contemporary Fantasy*
Mother Goose Rhymes, 6
Myth, 8
Mythopoeic Society, 121

## N

New York Times Book Review, 3
Noodleheads, 6

## P

Plot, 27-31
Point of View, 25-26
Pourquoi Tales, 6
PUBYAC Listserv, 122

## R

Realistic Tales, 6

## S

Science Fiction, 4-5

# Names Index

## A
Adams, Richard, 39
Aesop, 7, 90
Ahlberg, Janet and Allan, 110
Alcock, Vivien, 46
Alexander, Lloyd, 3, 10, 26, 28, 30, 42, 43, 47, 49, 50, 123
Aliki, 94
Allen, Pamela, 106
Andersen, Hans Christian, 3, 6, 84
Applegate, K. A., 16, 88
Ardizonne, Aingelda, 119
Asbj⁻rnsen, Peter, 7
Asch, Frank, 48, 55

## B
Babbitt, Natalie, 29, 31, 48, 50, 123-124
Bang, Molly, 47, 113
Banks, Lynne Reid, 71
Barrett, Judi and Ron, 94
Baum, L. Frank, 10, 28, 75-82, 121, 124-125
Bethancourt, T. Ernesto, 48
Bettleheim, Bruno, 16
Bond, Nancy, 44
Bonne, Rose, 94
Bowden, Joan Chase, 49, 94
Brett, Jan, 39, 95
Bridwell, Norman, 114
Bright, Robert, 110
Brown, Marc, 12, 110
Brown, Marcia, 91
Browne, Anthony, 12
Burnett, Frances Hodgson, 17
Burningham, John, 106
Butterworth, Oliver, 40

## C
Calhoun, Mary, 110
Campbell, Joseph, 28, 29, 30, 121
Carroll, Lewis, 10, 121
Cassedy, Sylvia, 72
Charlip, Remy, 94
Christopher, John, 11, 40
Chukovsky, Kornei, 20
Cleary, Beverly, 11
Cooper, Susan, 3, 9, 11, 12, 18, 24, 29, 31, 41, 43, 50, 66, 86, 121, 125

## D
Dahl, Roald, 39, 121, 125-126
Daugherty, James, 91
De Regniers, Beatrice, 107
DePaola, Tomie, 107
Devlin, Wende and Harry, 108
Dickinson, Peter, 41
Domanska, Janina, 94
Dr. Seuss, 121
Duane, Diane, 12, 18, 26, 40, 121, 126

## E
Egoff, Sheila, 4, 5, 9, 10
Emberly, Ed, 108
Engdahl, Sylvia Louise, 121

## F
Farmer, Nancy, 41
Favat, F. Andre, 16, 17
Feiffer, Jules, 33
Freeman, Don, 115

## G
Gaeddert, Louann, 118
Galdone, Paul, 91, 114
Garner, Alan, 127
Gorog, Judith, 111
Grimm Brothers, 6, 7

## H
Hamilton, Virginia, 7
Harper, Wilhemina, 113
Hayes, Sara, 113
Hearne, Betsy, 7
Heide, Florence Parry and Roxanne Heide, 113
Hissey, Jane, 115
Hoban, Russell, 11, 94
Howe, James, 113

## I
Ivimey, John W., 39, 95

## J
Jacobs, Joseph, 7
Jacques, Brian, 10, 16, 89, 121, 127
Jansson, Tove, 121
Jones, Diane Wynne, 10, 48, 121, 127-128
Jones, Terry, 84
Juster, Norton, 29, 49, 57

## K

Kahl, Virginia, 107
Kellogg, Steven, 93, 118
Kennedy, Richard, 51
Kent, Jack, 49, 94
King-Smith, Dick, 43, 45
Kroll, Steven, 118

## L

LeGuin, Ursula K., 18, 19, 20, 128-129
L'Engle, Madeleine, 5, 32, 33, 40, 68, 87, 129
Levine, Gail Carson, 25, 69, 84
Lewis, C. S., 10, 87, 121, 129
Lillegard, Dee, 106
Lobel, Arnold, 7-8, 90
Lopshire, Robert, 118
Lynn, Ruth Nadelman, 4

## M

Mahy, Margaret, 11
Marshall, James, 91
Mayne, William, 40
McGraw, Eloise, 25
McKee Charnas, Suzy, 4
McKillip, Patricia, 18
McKinley, Robin, 7, 18, 70, 121
Milne, A. A., 85
Moe, Jørgen E., 7
Morimoto, Junko, 95

## N

Napoli, Donna Jo, 9
Nesbit, Edith, 17
Ness, Evaline, 94
Nichols, Judy, 106
Norton, Andre, 44
Norton, Mary, 51

## O

Opie, Iona, 18
Osborne, Mary Pope, 42, 44, 46, 52

## P

Packard, Edward, 25
Pearce, Phillippa, 11, 27
Peck, Richard, 12, 41, 45
Perrault, Charles, 3, 7
Prelutsky, Jack, 113-114, 118
Pullman, Phillip, 24-25, 121

## R

Rowling, J. K., 89

## S

Sauer, Julia, 29
Scieszka, Jon, 8, 9, 43
Selden, George, 11
Sendak, Maurice, 12, 29
Senn, Steve, 40
Seymour, Peter, 113
Shannon, Mark, 83
Sherman, Josepha, 46, 59
Shulevitz, Uri, 107
Silverstein, Shel, 94
Sleator, William, 43, 46
Smith, Dodie, 86
Smith, Lane, 8, 9
Smith, Sherwood, 18
Steptoe, John, 95
Stevenson, Deborah, 18
Stevenson, James, 119
Supree, Burton, 94
Sutherland, Zena, 4, 5

## T

Thayer, Jane, 110
Tolkien, J. R. R., 10, 27, 29, 30, 31, 33, 121, 129-130
Trousdale, Ann, 19

## U

Uncle Remus, 7

## V

VanAllsburg, Chris, 16, 51, 85
Van de Wetering, Janwillem, 39
Vande Velde, Vivian, 9, 18, 33, 44, 88
Vick, H. H., 43

## W

Wahl, Jan, 115
Weisner, Davis, 94
Wells, Rosemary, 18
Westcott, Nadine Bernard, 94
White, E. B., 40, 48, 65, 130
White, T. H., 131
Wiesner, David, 37, 39
Wood, Audrey and Don, 107
Wrede, Patricia C., 10, 18, 32-33, 72, 83, 131-132
Wrightson, Patricia, 42, 43

## Y

Yolen, Jane, 18, 132
Young, Ed, 91, 95

## Z

Zemach, Margot, 92

# Titles Index

NOTE: Page Numbers in **bold print** are in the Annotated Book List.

## A

The Adventures of King Midas, **162**
The Adventures of Pinocchio, **145**
Afternoon on the Amazon, 42, **160**
"Ah Ha!," 110
Alan Mendelsohn, the Boy From Mars, **162**
Alanna: The First Adventure, **161-162**
Alice's Adventures in Wonderland, 4, 10, 123, 130, **143**
Alien for Rent, **147**
Alien Secrets, **154**
And All Between, **166**
All the Money in the World, **143**
The Amber Spyglass, **162**
Among the Hidden, **150**
Amy's Eyes, 51, **154**
"Andrea Books", **149**
Andy and the Lion, 91
Animals Should Definitely Not Wear Cothing, **133**
"Animorphs Series", 16, 88, **140**
Another Shore, 44, **142**
Answer my Prayer, **151**
"The Ant and the Grasshopper," 7
Antar and the Eagles, 40, **157**
The Antrian Messenger, **169**
Archer's Goon, **153**
The Arkadians, **138**

## B

Babe: The Gallant Pig, **154**
Balyet, **170**
A Barrel of Laughs, A Vale of Tears, 33, **148**
The Battle for the Castle, **169**
The Bean Boy, 49, 94, **133**
Beauty, 7, 69, **158**
Bed-Knob and Broomstick, **159**
The Begger Queen, **139**
Behind the Attic Wall, 71, **143**
The Bellmaker, **152**
Below the Root, **166**
Beowulf, 8
Beyond the Tomorrow Mountains, **148**
The BFG, **146**
Big Jeremy, 118, **135**
A Billion for Boris, **163**
Birth of the Firebringer, **161**
Black and Blue Magic, **166**

The Black Cauldron, **138**
Black Hearts in Battersea, **137**
Blossom Culp and the Sleep of Death, 45, **161**
"Blossom Culp Books", **161**
The Blue Sword, **158**
The Boggart, 12, 41, 86, **145**
The Boggart and the Monster, 85, **145-146**
"Boggart Books", **145-146**
"Boo!," 110
The Book of the Dun Cow, **168**
Book of Enchantments, 84, **169**
The Book of Three, 28, 30, 42, 43, 49, 123, **138**
The Borrowers, 51, **159**
"The Boy Who Cried Wolf," 7
The Boy Who Reversed Himself, **165**
The Bronze King, **144**
Bunnicula, a Rabbit Tale of Mystery, **151**
"Bunnicula Books", **151**

## C

Calling on Dragons, **170**
Cart and Cwidder, 48, 128, **153**
"Castle Books", **169**
Castle in the Air, **153**
The Castle in the Attic, **169**
The Castle of Llyr, **138**
The Celery Stalks at Midnight, **151**
Chameleon Was a Spy, **157**
A Chance Child, **160**
The Changeover: A Supernatural Romance, 11, **157**
"Changes Trilogy", **147**
Charlie and the Chocolate Factory, 126, **146**
Charlie and the Great Glass Elevator, 126, **146**
Charlotte's Web, 5, 11, 65, 130, **169**
Charmed Life, 128, **153**
"Chester Cricket Books", **164**
Chicken Little, 93, **135**
Child of Faerie, Child of Earth, 45, 59 **165**
The Children of Green Knowe, **142**
"Cinderella," 6
Chitty Chitty Bang Bang, the Magical Car, **148**
The Chocolate Touch, **143**
"Chrestomanci Series", 128, **153**
Christina's Ghost, **170**
"Chronicles of Narnia", 10, 87, 129, **156**
"Chronicles of Prydain", 123, **138**
The Chronicles of Robin Hood, **166**
A Circle in the Sea, 40, **164**
City of Light, City of Dark: A Comic Book Novel, **140**

*The City of Gold and Lead,* **144**
*Cloudy With a Chance of Meatballs,* 94, **133**
"Cock A Doodle Doo! My Dame Has Lost Her Shoe," 93
"The Cock's on the Rooftop," 93
*Cold Shoulder Road,* **137-138**
*Colors in the Dreamweaver's Loom,* **150**
*Companions of the Night,* **167**
*Complete Story of the Three Blind Mice,* 39, 95, **135**
*Corduroy,* 115, **134**
*Count Karlstein,* **162**
*Court Duel,* **165**
*The Cricket in Times Square,* 11, **164**
"Crown and Court Duet", **165**
*Crown Duel,* **165**
*The Crown of Dalemark,* **153**
*The Crystal Stair,* **144**
*The Cuckoo Tree,* **137**
*Curses Inc.,* 88, **167**
*The Curse of the Blue Figurine,* **141**

### D

"Dalemark Quartet", 128, **153**
*Dangerous Games,* **138**
*Dangerous Wishes,* 43, **165**
*The Darkangel,* **161**
"Darkangel Trilogy", **161**
*The Dark Bright Water,* 42, **170**
*The Dark is Rising,* 29, 43, 66, 125, **146**
"Dark is Rising Sequence" 11-12, 126, **146**
*Dark Moon,* **161**
*The Dark Secret of Weatherend,* **142**
*Dealing with Dragons,* 132, **169**
*Deep Wizardry,* 40, **147**
*The Devil's Children,* **147**
*The Devil's Doorbell,* **151**
*Dido and Pa,* **137**
*Dinner at Alberta's,* 94, **134**
*Dinosaurs Before Dark,* 42, 52, **160**
*Dinotopia: A Land Apart From Time,* **150**
"Dinotopia Books", **150**
*Dinotopia Pop-up Book,* **150**
*Dinotopia: The World Beneath,* **150**
*The Dog Days of Arthur Cane,* **142**
*Dogsbody,* 128, **138**
*The Dollhouse Murders,* **170**
*The Doors of the Universe,* **148**
*Dorothy and the Wizard of Oz,* 75, **141**
*The Drackenberg Adventure,* **139**
*The Dragonling,* **154-155**

"Dragon Books", **155**
*Dragon Cauldron,* **170**
*The Dragon Circle,* **155**
*Dragon of the Lost Sea,* **170**
"Dragon Quartet", **170**
*Dragon Steel,* **170**
*Dragon War,* **170**
*Dragon's Bait,* 44, **168**
*Dragon's Blood,* **170**
*The Dreadful Future of Blossom Culp,* **161**
*The Dream Catcher,* **151**
*Drowned Ammet,* **153**
*The Duchess Bakes a Cake,* 107, **135**
*The Duplicate,* **165**
*Dustland,* **150**

### E

*The Ear, the Eye and the Arm,* 41, **148**
"Earthsea Series", 129, **155**
"Elana Books", **147-148**
*The El Dorado Adventure,* **139**
*Elidor,* **149**
*Ella Enchanted,* 25, 69, **155**
"The Elves and the Shoemaker," 6
*The Emerald City of Oz,* 75, **141**
*Empty World,* 40, **144**
"Enchanted Forest Chronicles", 132, **169-170**
*An Enemy at Green Knowe,* **142**
*The Enormous Vegetable Garden,* 94
*Escape to Witch Mountain,* **154**
*Enchantress from the Stars,* **147-148**
*Eva,* **147**

### F

*Fables,* 8, 90, **135**
*The Fairy Rebel,* **162**
*The Fairy's Mistake,* **156**
*Fairy Tales,* **153**
*Fantastic Stories,* 84, **153**
*The Farthest Shore,* **155**
*The Far Side of Evil,* **148**
*The Fat Cat,* 49, 94, **135**
*Fat Men From Space,* **162**
*Father Goose, His Book,* 124
*The Feast of the Trickster,* **150**
*The Fellowship of the Ring,* **167**
*The Figure in the Shadows,* **142**
"The Finn Books", **167**
*Fire Arrow: The Second Song of Eirren,* **160**
"Firebringer Trilogy", **161**

*The First Two Lives of Lukas Kasha,* **138**
*Five Children and It,* **159**
*Fog Magic,* 29, **163**
*The Forgotten Beasts of Eld,* **158**
*The Forgotten Door,* **154**
*The Forty-Ninth Magician,* 124
*Freaky Friday,* **163**
*Free Fall,* 37, **136**
*Funnybones,* 110, **133**

### G

*The Cammage Cup,* **154**
*The Garden of Abdul Gasazi,* **136**
*The Gathering (Carmody),* **143**
*The Gathering (Hamilton),* **150**
*A Gathering of Gargoyles,* **161**
*The Ghastly Glasses,* **149**
*The Genie of Sutton Place,* **164**
*Georgie to the Rescue,* 110, **134**
*The Ghost Belonged to Me,* **161**
*The Ghost in the Noonday Sun,* **148**
*The Ghost of Fossil Glen,* **147**
*The Ghost of Popcorn Hill,* **170**
*A Ghostly Business,* **155**
*Ghosts Beneath Our Feet,* **170**
*Ghosts I Have Been,* **161**
*The Ghosts of Mercy Manor,* **170**
"Giant Jim," 118
*The Giant Vegetable Garden,* **136**
*The Girl With the Silver Eyes,* **163**
*The Giver,* **157**
*Glinda of Oz,* 124
*The Golden Band of Eddris,* **158**
*The Golden Compass,* **162**
*The Good, the Bad and the Goofy,* **164**
*Goody Hall,* 124, **141**
*Gom on Windy Mountain: From Tales of Gom,* **144**
*Grand Escape,* **159**
"The Grand Old Duke of York," 107
*The Great Interactive Dream Machine,* 12, **161**
*The Great Redwall Feast,* **152**
"Green Knowe Books", **142**
"Green-sky Books", **166**
*Greenwitch,* **146**
*Gremlins,* 126
*The Grey King,* 11, **146**
*The Guardian of Isis,* **151**
*The Gunniwolf,* 113, **134**
*Gus Was A Friendly Ghost,* 110, **136**
*Gustav, the Gourmet Giant,* 118, **134**
*Gypsy Rizka,* **138**

### H

*Harpist in the Wind,* **158**
*Harriet's Hare,* **154**
*Harry Cat's Pet Puppy,* **164**
*Harry Potter and the Chamber of Secrets,* 89, **163**
*Harry Potter and the Prisoner of Azkaban,* **163**
*Harry Potter and the Sorcerer's Stone,* 89, **163**
"Harry Potter Books", **163**
*Haunted Summer,* **170**
*The Haunting,* **157**
*The Haunting of Cassie Palmer,* **138**
*The Headless Horseman Rides Tonight: More Poems to Trouble Your Sleep,* 114
*Heart's Blood,* **171**
*Heartsease,* 41, **147**
*The Heavenward Path,* **147**
*Heckedy Peg,* **137**
*Heir of Sea and Fire,* **158**
*Helga's Dowry,* 107, **134**
*Henny Penny,* 6, 93
*The Hero and the Crown,* **158**
*Hero's Song,* **160**
"Hickety Pickety My Black Hen," 93
*A Hidden Magic,* **168**
*The High King,* **138**
*High Wizardry,* 12, **147**
"His Dark Materials Trilogy", **162**
*Hobberdy Dick,* **143**
*The Hobbit,* 19, 27, 29, 30, 130, **167**
*The Horse and His Boy,* **156**
*Hounds of the Morrigan,* **160**
*The House at Pooh Corner,* 11, 84, **158**
*House of Stairs,* 45, **165**
"The House that Jack Built," 6
*The House With a Clock in its Walls,* **142**
*The "House With a Clock in its Walls Trilogy",* **142**
"How the Elephant Got It's Trunk," 6
*How to Care for Your Monster,* 114, **133**
*How to Make Flibbers, Etc.,* 118
*Howl's Moving Castle,* **153**
*Hugh Pine,* 39, **168**
*Humphrey's Bear,* 115, **136**
*The Hundred and One Dalmatians,* 86, **165**
*Hurricane,* **136**

## I

*I Am Mordred: A Tale from Camelot*, **166**
*The Ice is Coming*, **170**
*I Know an Old Lady*, 94, **133**
*The Illyrian Adventure*, 50, **139**
*In a Dark Wood*, **143**
*In a Messy Messy Room and Other Strange Stories*, 111, **149**
*In the Circle of Time*, **140**
*In the Hand of the Goddess*, **162**
*In the Keep of Time*, **139-140**
*Incognito Mosquito, Private Insective*, **150**
*The Indian in the Cupboard*, 71, **163**
"Indian in the Cupboard Series", **163**
*The Invasion*, **140**
*Invitation to the Game*, **151**
*The Iron Ring*, 26, **138-139**
*The Isis Pedlar*, **151**
"Isis Planet Books", **151**
*Is Underground*, **137**

## J

*Jack and the Beanstalk*, 6, 118, **135**
"Jack Sprat," 94
*James and the Giant Peach*, 39, 126, **146**
*Jane-Emily*, **144-145**
*Jason and the Aliens Down the Street*, **149**
*The Jedera Adventure*, 47, **139**
*Jennifer Murdley's Toad: A Magic Shop Book*, **146**
*Jeremy Thatcher, Dragon Hatcher: A Magic Shop Book*, **146**
*Jeremy Visick*, **169**
*Jimmy: The Pickpocket of the Palace*, **158**
"John Henry," 7
"John Watts," 95
"Johnny Appleseed," 7
"Johnny Dixon Mysteries", **141-142**
*Journey Behind the Wind*, **170**
*Journey Between Worlds*, **148**
*Journey to Terezor*, 48, 55, **140**
*Jumanji*, **136**
*June 29, 1999*, 39, 94, **136**
*Justice and Her Brothers*, **150**
"Justice Cycle", **150**

## K

*Kate Crackernuts*, **143**
*Keep Your Mouth Closed, Dear*, 93, **133**
*Keeper of the Isis Light*, **151**
*The Kestrel*, **139**

*The Key to the Indian*, **163**
"King Arthur Trilogy", **166**
*King Bidgood's in the Bathtub*, 107, **137**
*The Kingdom of Kevin Malone*, 4, **144**
*Klippity Klop*, 108
*Kneeknock Rise*, 124, **141**
*The Knight at Dawn*, 44, **160**
*Knights of the Kitchen Table*, **163**

## L

*The Lampfish of Twill*, **156**
*The Land of Oz*, 75, 81-82, 124, **141**
*The Last Battle*, **156**
"Lazy Jack," 6
*Let Me Off This Spaceship!*, **149**
*The Letter, the Witch and the Ring*, **142**
*The Life and Adventures of Santa Claus*, **141**
*The Light Beyond the Forest: The Quest for the Holy Grail*, **166**
*The Light Princess*, **157**
*Lioness Rampant*, **162**
*The Lion, the Witch and the Wardrobe*, 87, 129, **156**
*The Little Broomstick*, **166**
"The Little Old Lady Who Swallowed a Fly," 7
"The Little Red Hen," 93
"Little Red Riding Hood," 91
*Little Sister*, **147**
"Little Tommy Tucker," 94
*Little Wizard Stories of Oz*, **141**
*The Lives of Christopher Chant*, 10, **153**
*The Long Patrol*, **152**
*Lon Po Po: A Red Riding Hood Story from China*, 91
"The Lord of the Rings Series", 40, 130, **167**
*Lost in Cyberspace*, 15, 53, **161**
*The Lost Legend of Finn*, **167**
*The Lotus Caves*, **144**

## M

*The Magic Circle*, 9, **158**
*The Magician's Apprentice*, **157**
*The Magician's Challenge*, **157**
*The Magician's Company*, **157**
*The Magician's Nephew*, **156**
*The Magicians of Caprona*, **153**
"The Magician Trilogy", **157**
"Magic Treehouse Series", **160**
*Mail Order Wings*, **149**
*Many Waters*, **155**
*Mariel of Redwall*, **152**
*Marlfox*, **153**
*Martin the Warrior*, **152**

*The Marvelous Misadventures of Sebastian*, **139**
*Mary Poppins*, **167**
*Mattimeo*, **152**
*May I Bring A Friend?*, 110, **134**
*Mean Margaret*, **164**
*Melisande*, **159**
*The Mennyms*, **168**
*Mennyms Alive*, **168-169**
*Mennyms Alone*, **168**
*Mennyms in the Wilderness*, **168**
"Mennyms Series", **168-169**
*Mennyms Under Siege*, **168**
*Meredith The Witch Who Wasn't*, **135**
*The Mermaid Summer*, **151**
*The Merry Adventures of Robinhood*, **162**
*The Midnight Folk*, **157**
*The Mind Trap*, **169**
*The Mists of Time*, **140**
*A Monster is Coming! A Monster is Coming!*, 113, **134**
*The Monster's Ring*, **146**
*The Moon of Gomrath*, 127, **149**
*The Moorchild*, 25, **158**
*Mossflower*, **152**
*The Mouse and His Child*, 11, **151**
*Morte d'Arthur*, **143**
*Mother, Mother I Feel Sick*, 94
*The Mouse and the Motorcycle*, **145**
*Mouse's Marriage*, 95, **135**
*Mr. Gumpy's Motor Car*, 12, **134**
*Mr. Gumpy's Outing*, 106, **134**
*Mr. Miacca: An English Folktake*, 94, **135**
*Mrs. Frisby and the Rats of NIMH*, **159**
*Mummies in the Morning*, **160**
*The Mummy, the Will and the Crypt*, **141**
*The Mysteries of Harris Burdick*, 51, 85, **136**
*The Mystery of the Cupboard*, **163**
*My Sister, the Vampire*, **149**
*My Very First Mother Goose*, 18, **135**

## N

*The Nargun and the Stars*, 43, **170**
*A Necklace of Fallen Stars*, 150
*Never Trust a Dead Man*, 168
*Nicobobinus*, **153-154**
*The Night After Christmas*, 119, **166**
*Night of the Ninjas*, 60, **160**
*The Night of the Scorpion*, **151**
*Nightbirds on Nantucket*, **137**
*Nightmares: Poems to Trouble Your Sleep*, 114, **162**
*The Night Ride*, 119, **133**

*The Not-So-Jolly Roger*, **164**
*Now We Are Six*, 85
*The Number Devil*, **148**

## O

*The Odyssey*, 8
*Old Bear*, 115, **134**
"Old Bear Series", **134**
*Old Black Witch*, 110-111, **134**
"Old King Cole," 107
*On All Hallows' Eve*, **144**
*One Monday Morning*, 107, **135-136**
*The Once and Future King*, 131, **169**
*The Ordinary Princess*, **154**
*Outcast of Redwall*, **152**
*The Outlaws of Sherwood*, **158**
*Out of the Dark World*, **144**
*Outside Over There*, **135**
*Over Sea Under Stone*, 125, **146**
*The Owl Service*, **149**
"Oz Series", **141**
*Ozma of Oz*, 75, **141**

## P

*Paddy's Pot of Gold*, 43, **154**
"Paul Bunyan," 7
*The Pearl of the Soul of the World*, **161**
*Pearls of Lutra*, **152**
"Pecos Bill." 7
"Pentagram Chronicles", **151**
*The Perils of Putney*, **155**
*Peter Pan*, **141**
*The Phantom Tollbooth*, 29, 49, 57, **154**
*The Philadelphia Adventure*, **139**
*Pirates Past Noon*, **160**
"Pit Dragons Series", **170-171**
*A Pocket for Corduroy*, 115, **134**
*The Polar Express*, 16, **136**
*The Pool of Fire*, **144**
*Poppy*, **140**
*Poppy and Rye*, **140-141**
*Prince Caspain*, **156**
*The Prince of the Pond: Otherwise Known as De Fawg Pin*, **159**
*The Princess and the Goblin*, **157**
"Princess Tales Series", **156**
*The Princess Test*, 83, **156**
*Professor Popkin's Prodigious Polish: A Tale of Coven Tree*, **143**
*The Pumpkins of Time*, **149**
"Pussy Cat, Pussy Cat," 91

**Q**

*Quentin Corn,* **166**

**R**

*Racannon's World,* 129
*Racso and the Rats of NIMH,* **145**
*Ralph S. Mouse,* 11, **145**
"Ralph S. Mouse Books", **145**
"Rats of NIMH Series", 145, **159**
*A Rat's Tale,* **164**
*Red Hart Magic,* 44, **159**
*Red Shift,* 127, **149**
*Redwall,* 127, **152**
"Redwall Series", 107, **152-153**
*The Reluctant Dragon,* **149**
*The Remarkable Journey of Prince Jen,* 43, **139**
*The Return of the Indian,* **163**
*The Return of the King,* **167**
*The Return of the Twelves,* **145**
*The Riddle and the Rune: From Tales of Gom in the Legends of Ulm,* **144**
*The Riddle-Master of Hed,* **158**
*Rip Van Winkle,* 7
*The River at Green Knowe,* **142**
*The Road to Camlann,* **166**
*The Road to Oz,* 75, **141**
*The Root Cellar,* **157**
*Rose Daughter,* 7, **158**
*Roverandom,* **167**
"Row, Row, Row Your Boat," 106
*R-T, Margaret, and the Rats of NIMH,* **145**
*Runaway Ralph,* **145**

**S**

*Sabriel,* **159**
*Salamandastron,* **152**
"Scott Childers Trilogy", **169**
*The Search for Delicious,* 29, 48, **141**
*Searching For Dragons,* 32, 73, **169**
*Seaward,* **146**
*The Secret Garden,* 17
*The Secret of Platform 13,* **152**
*The Secret of Roan Inish,* **148**
*The Secret of the Indian,* **163**
*The Seer,* **169**
*A Sending of Dragons,* **171**
*Seven Blind Mice,* 95, 137, **137**
*Seven Day Magic,* **147**
*Shades Children,* **159**

*The Shadow Guests,* **138**
*Shadow Magic,* **144**
*Shadow Spinner,* **148**
*The Shrinking of Treehorn,* **150**
*The Silver Chair,* **156**
*The Silver Kiss,* **154**
*Silver on the Tree,* 24, 50, **146**
*Silverwing,* **160**
"Sing a Song of Sixpence," 107
*Sir Gawain and the Green Knight,* 83, **165**
*Sitting in My Box,* 106, **135**
"Six Little Mice," 95
*Sleeping Ugly,* **171**
"Song of the Lioness Series", **161-162**
*The Son of Summer Stars,* **161**
*So You Want to Be a Wizard,* 26, **147**
*The Spellcoats,* **153**
*Spooky Riddles,* 110
*Squids Will Be Squids,* 8, **163**
"Star-Bearer Trilogy", **158**
*The Starstone,* **144**
"Star Trilogy", **148**
*The Stinky Cheese Man and Other Fairly Stupid Tales,* 9, **135**
*The Stolen Lake,* 137
*The Stones of Green Knowe,* **142**
*The Story of Doctor Doolittle: Being the History of His Peculiar Life at Home and Astonishing Adventures in Foreign Parts,* **156**
*The Story of Jumping Mouse: A Native American Legend,* 95, **136**
*The Story of King Arthur and His Knights,* **162**
*A Stranger at Green Knowe,* **142**
*Strange Attractors,* **165**
*A String in the Harp,* **142**
*Stuart Little,* 130, **169**
*The Subtle Knife,* 24, **162**
*Summer Reading is Killing Me,* **164**
*Summer Switch,* **163**
*Sunset of the Sabertooth,* **160**
*The Surprising Adventures of the Magical Monarch of Mo and his People,* **141**
*A Swiftly Tilting Planet,* **155**
*The Sword and the Circle: King Arthur and the Knights of the Round Table,* **166**
*The Sword in the Stone,* **169**
*The Sylvia Game,* 47, **138**

## T

Tag Against Time, **169**
The Tailypo: A Ghost Story, 114, **134**
The Tale I Told Sasha, 136
Tales from the Brothers Grimm and the Sisters Weird, 9, **168**
"Tales of Alderley", **149**
"Tales of Gom Series", **144**
Talking to Dragons, **170**
Taran Wanderer, **138**
The Tar Pit, **164**
Tehanu: The Last Book of Earthsea, **155**
"There Was An Old Woman," **110**
There's A Monster Under My Bed, 113, **135**
The Thief, **167**
Thimbles: A Novel, **169**
The 13th Floor: A Ghost Story, **148**
This Star Shall Abide, **148**
"The Three Bears," 6, 91
The Three Bears Rhyme Book, 115
Three Terrible Trins, 46, **154**
"The Three Billy Goats Gruff," 91
"Three Little Ghostesses," 110
"The Three Little Kittens," 91
"The Three Little Pigs," 6, 91
Through the Looking-Glass and What Alice Found There, 10, **143**
Time Cat, 123
Time for Andrew: A Ghost Story, **150**
The Time Garden, **147**
The Time of the Witch, **150**
"Time Trilogy", **140**
"Time Quartet", **155**
"Time Warp Trio Series", **164-165**
The Tin Woodman of Oz, 75, **141**
The Tombs of Atuan, **155**
The Tomorrow Connection, **142**
Tomorrow's Magic, **165**
Tomorrow, When the War Began, **157**
Tom's Midnight Garden, 11, 27, **161**
"The Tortoise and the Hare," 90
Town Mouse, Country Mouse, 39, 95, **133**
Transall Saga, **160**
Travel Far, Pay No Fare, **156**
"Treehorn Books", **150**
Treehorn's Treasure, **150**
Treehorn's Wish, **150**
"Tripod Series", **144**
Tristan and Iseult, **166**

The Trolley to Yesterday, **141-142**
The Trouble With Jenny's Ear, 40, **143**
The Trumpet of the Swan, 40, 48, **169**
Tucker's Countryside, **164**
Tuck Everlasting, 31-32, 50, 123, **141**
Tuesday, **136**
Tune in Yesterday, 48, **142**
The Tunnel, 12, **134**
The Turnip, 94, **134**
Tut Tut, **164**
Two Minds, **157**
The Two Towers, **167**
2095, **164**
Tye May and the Magic Paint Brush, 47, **133**

## U

Until the Celebration, **166**
Untold Tales, **143**
User Unfriendly, **168**

## V

"Vesper Holly Series", **139**
Voyage of the Dawn Treader, **156**
The Voyages of Doctor Doolittle, **156**

## W

The Wainscott Weasel, **164**
Wait Till Helen Comes: A Ghost Story, **150**
"Walker Books", **168**
Walker of Time, 43, **168**
Walker's Journey Home, **168**
A Walk in Wolf Wood: A Tale of Fantasy and Magic, **166**
The Warm Place, **148**
Watership Down, 39, **137**
The Way to Sattin Shore, **161**
The Weathermonger, **147**
The Weirdstone of Brisingamen, 127, **149**
A Well-Timed Enchantment, **168**
Westmark, **139**
"Westmark Trilogy", **139**
What's in the Cave, 113, **135**
When the Tripods Came, **144**
When We Were Very Young, **85**
Where the Sidewalk Ends, **165**
Where the Towers Pierce the Sky, **149**
Where the Wild Things Are, 4, 12, 29, **135**
The White Mountains, **144**
Who Sank the Boat?, 106, **133**
"Why the Sun and Moon Live in the Sky," 6

*The Wicked One: A Story of Suspense*, **152**
*The Widow's Broom*, **136**
*The Wild Hunt of the Ghost Hounds*, **156**
*Wiley and the Hairy Man*, 113, **133**
*A Wind in the Door*, 32, 40, **155**
*The Wind in the Willows*, **149**
*Windleaf*, **165**
*Winnie the Pooh*, 11, 85, **158**
*Winter of Fire*, **154**
*Winter of Magic's Return*, **165**
"Wirrun Trilogy", **170**
*The Wish Giver: Three Tales of Coven Tree*, **143**
"Witch Books", **159**
*Witch Cat*, **143**
*The Witch Herself*, **159**
*The Witch of Hissing Hill*, 110, **134**
*Witch Water*, **159**
*Witch Week*, **153**
*The Witches*, **147**
*The Witches of Worm*, **166**
*The Witching Hour*, **155**
*Witch's Sister*, **159**
*Wizard Abroad*, **147**
*The Wizard Children of Finn*, **167**
*A Wizard of Earthsea*, 129, **155**
*The Wizard of Oz*, 4, 28, 77-80, 124, **141**

"Wizard Quartet", **147**
*Wizard's Hall*, **171**
"Wolves Chronicles", **137-138**
*The Wolves of Willoughby Chase*, **137**
*The Woman Who Rides Like a Man*, **162**
*The World of Narnia: Edmund and the White Witch*, **87**
*The World of Narnia: Lucy Steps Through the Wardrobe*, **87**
*The Wreck of the Zephyr*, **136**
*Wren to the Rescue*, **165**
*Wren's Quest*, **165**
*Wren's War*, **165-166**
"Wren Trilogy", **165**
*The Wretched Stone*, **136**
*A Wrinkle in Time*, 5, 68, 128, **155**

# Y

*Yeh Shen: A Cinderella Story from China*, **91**
*Your Mother Was a Neanderthal*, 43, **164**

# Z

"Zan Scarsdale Books", **150**
*Zel*, **159**
*Z for Zachariah*, **159**

LEE COUNTY LIBRARY SYSTEM
DISCARD
3 3262 00203 4855

1/01

809
W
Wadham
Bringing fantasy alive

LEE COUNTY LIBRARY
107 Hawkins Ave.
Sanford, NC 27330

GAYLORD R